Hell-Bent
FOR LIFE

Dr. John Valentine

John Valentine Publishing

Published in 2009 by

John Valentine Publishing
34 Messenger Terrace
Oakura
New Zealand
johnvalentine@xtra.co.nz

Design and layout
Mike Lander
100 Graphics
txp@xnet.co.nz

All rights reserved. No part of this publication may be reproduced, transmitted, or stored in a retrieval system, in any form or by any means without permission in writing from the author.

Cover concept and design
Jo Massey
Re-strained Art
Jo.massey@xtra.co.nz

ISBN number 978-0-473-14665-8

Disclaimer
This book is an autobiography. Some characters have had their name's changed to protect identities. The rest of the content is factual.

Contents

INTRODUCTION

CHAPTER 1	**The beginning – Early family history and life in Kurow** Family history 1870 - 1925 John Valentine's early years 1925 - 1935	1
CHAPTER 2	**Early adolescence in Kurow** 1935 - 1937	36
CHAPTER 3	**College education at St. Kevin's** 1938 - 1942	45
CHAPTER 4	**Otago Medical School** 1943 - 1950	66
CHAPTER 5	**Southland Hospital** 1951	80
CHAPTER 6	**The Colonial War Memorial Hospital in Fiji** 1951 - 1952	84
CHAPTER 7	**Micronesia** August 1952 - August 1953	104
CHAPTER 8	**The Micronesian Leprosy Survey, Yap and Japan** 1 August 1953 - 28 August 1953	145
CHAPTER 9	**Australia, New Zealand, Canton Island, Hawaii and the U.S.** 28 August 1953 - 27 October 1953	177

CHAPTER 10	**Canada and the Yukon** January 1954 - 18 February 1955	192
CHAPTER 11	**Mexico and Canada** 19 February 1955 - 27 February 1955	225
CHAPTER 12	**London and South Africa** 29 September 1955	267
CHAPTER 13	**Swaziland and Basutoland** December 1955 - 8 January 1956	304
EPILOGUE		350
GLOSSARY		353

Hell-Bent FOR LIFE

1920 – 1955

Introduction

THE MAIN THEME IN THIS STORY IS HOW I ROSE above my humble rural beginnings and ended up travelling widely and broadening my horizons - that of a New Zealand South Island country boy 'made good'

When I was about ten my mother, Dais, heard the rumour that Kurow School students were experimenting with sex, so she sent me off to St. Kevin's College in Oamaru to spare me from inevitable temptation. My school life there was good for the first year but in the second I was selected for full time bullying by the senior students and later, by a Brother who was nick-named 'Big Dig'. He eventually hit me hard enough to knock me out. To survive this bullying I had to learn to use my fists. I probably became the best fighter in the school; certainly nobody challenged me, and I went from the bottom to the top of the heap, and life at St. Kevin's became quite cruisy.
Later, as a young man, I formed my own ideas; I questioned the existence of an omnipotent God in the Heavens, I disagreed with apartheid, I was shocked by the suppression of people – even that of my Auntie and her children by her husband.

I'm thankful for the influences that directed me onto the path I took (and can blame no one but myself for a few less than wise life choices I made along the way) as they have afforded me an interesting and satisfying life.

Looking back, I am encouraged to see that things do change for the better over time; for example the segregationist policies in South Africa and some attempts to address school-room bullying. In other areas I see less indication of a change in practices; the newspapers still report that the Catholic hierarchy allow little latitude for discussion surrounding their inflexible dogma. As far as I know, they remain adamant about the fires of Hell and the myth of Heaven.

Travel and broader life-experience has helped lessen my fear of damnation and confirmed my belief in the damage bullying does to people. It has given me a tolerance of differences; the realisation that people everywhere are very much alike although their circumstance differs is liberating. I now know that it's unfair to get people to 'see things your way' through coercion and fear, whether in the school room, church or consultation room.

I leave it to you, to make your own decision about the value of the observations I have made along the way.

It is worth mentioning that I seriously considered another title for this book;

"Not Enough Bloody Good Sheilas"
1920 – 1955.

When I was leaving my first hospital job I had a good friend who was a senior physician. As we were passing he said "Now Jack," (I was Jack then, as although I was christened John, I was namesaked after an Uncle who had died) "when you move around the world you shouldn't try and seduce girls. You will however occasionally meet girls who are suffering, and it's alright to relieve THEIR suffering!"

I found it wasn't easy to find the suffering ones who required my attentions, as they tended to be either too young, old, fat, thin, worried, menstruating, married, malicious or afflicted with cystitis, urethritis, vaginitis, or headaches. Others suffered from a hearing loss as they were listening so hard for the sound of wedding bells they were oblivious to anything else. I hesitate to tell you this, but some of these ladies didn't like me anyway, so attending to their needs wasn't an issue, and so I moved on.

As a healthy, robust and hormonally driven young man, I was always particularly thrilled when a female companion appeared to alleviate my loneliness. Good company and the pleasures of these womens humour, intellect and flesh often rounded out my experiences. These women also shared their cultural perspectives, welcomed me into their homes and were the bridge to deeper understanding of the places I found myself.

I would ask the reader to keep in mind that the few female companions mentioned in this book were those I engaged with over a 15 year period of my life, so I was not a frequent 'conqueror' of women. These delightful episodes were a rarity and provided respite from my solitary travels. To these lovely ladies, I remain indebted, although in retrospect I feel my travels could have been further enhanced by their number being larger – just not quite enough bloody good 'Sheilas' for my ultimate liking!

This book covers the early years of a life that has been enriched by travel, and I hope the reader enjoys some small bencfit (and pleasure) from reading them.

John Valentine

2009

Dedication

To those nearest and dearest to me; without whose constant and continued help this book would have been in your hands a year ago.

Acknowledgement

I'm thankful to the following people for their assistance:

Dr. Jon Simcock (neurologist) and Dr. Fitzgerald Sanje (cardiologist) for allowing me to bounce a few of my pet theories past them.

Jo Massey, who typed and edited the manuscript. Her mentoring and project management ensured the project's realisation.

Kate Stevens who was my proof reader and assured 'quality control' was maintained throughout.

Bruce Petty who offered suggestions that enhanced the book's 'readability'.

Rob Tucker from Rob Tucker Photography www.robtucker.co.nz who kindly provided the image used as a background on the front cover.

Thanks are also due to Denece Rae from St. Kevin's in Oamaru and Joe Lauren from The Christian Brothers for their part in securing permission to use images from "The 1938 Red Castle Year Book" and "1876 – 1976 The First Hundred Years in New Zealand at Christian Brothers School, Dunedin" respectively.

Thank you all!!

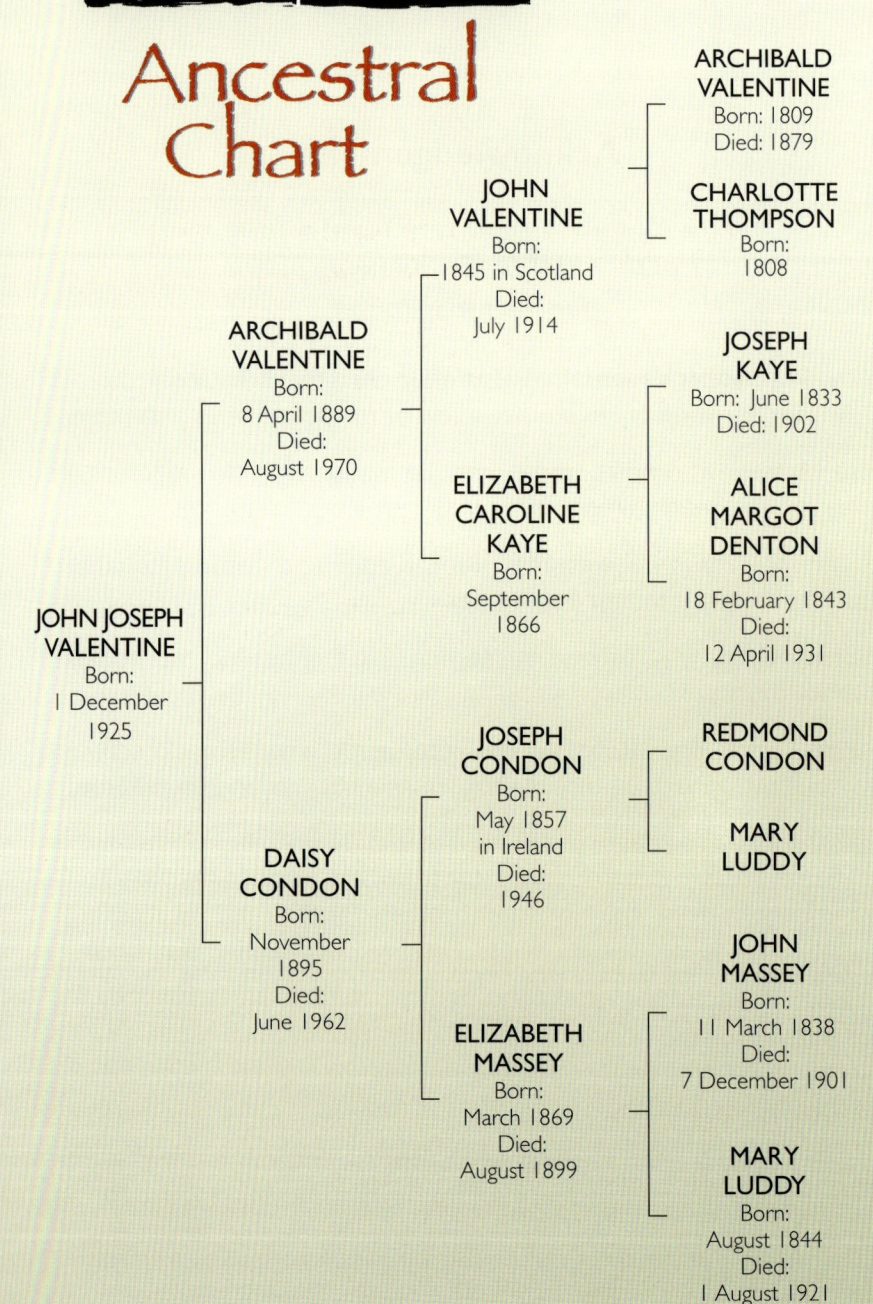

John Joseph Valentine

Ancestral Chart

JOHN JOSEPH VALENTINE
Born: 1 December 1925

- **ARCHIBALD VALENTINE**
  Born: 8 April 1889
  Died: August 1970
  - **JOHN VALENTINE**
    Born: 1845 in Scotland
    Died: July 1914
    - **ARCHIBALD VALENTINE**
      Born: 1809
      Died: 1879
    - **CHARLOTTE THOMPSON**
      Born: 1808
  - **ELIZABETH CAROLINE KAYE**
    Born: September 1866
    - **JOSEPH KAYE**
      Born: June 1833
      Died: 1902
    - **ALICE MARGOT DENTON**
      Born: 18 February 1843
      Died: 12 April 1931

- **DAISY CONDON**
  Born: November 1895
  Died: June 1962
  - **JOSEPH CONDON**
    Born: May 1857 in Ireland
    Died: 1946
    - **REDMOND CONDON**
    - **MARY LUDDY**
  - **ELIZABETH MASSEY**
    Born: March 1869
    Died: August 1899
    - **JOHN MASSEY**
      Born: 11 March 1838
      Died: 7 December 1901
    - **MARY LUDDY**
      Born: August 1844
      Died: 1 August 1921

CHAPTER 1

The Beginning - Early family history and life in Kurow

Family history 1870 - 1925
John Valentine's early years 1925 - 1935

INTRODUCED CHARACTERS:

JOHN VALENTINE, the author (also known as 'Jack' in his earlier years).
ARCHIE 'Arch' VALENTINE, the author's father.
DAISY 'Dais' VALENTINE (née Condon), the author's mother. The author never called his mother 'Mum' or 'Mother' but used her Christian name.
JACK CONDON, the author's uncle (his mother's younger brother).
AQUINAS 'Queenie/Queen' CONDON, the author's auntie (his mother's older sister).
JOE 'Pampa Joe' CONDON, the author's maternal grandfather.
ELIZABETH CONDON (née Massey), the author's maternal grandmother and Joe's wife, who died when only 30 years of age.
MARY 'Granny Massey' MASSEY, the author's great grandmother, who took over care of the 3 Condon children (Dais, Jack and Queenie) after her daughter Elizabeth died.

I WAS BORN ON THE FIRST DAY OF DECEMBER 1925, in the front room of my grandfather's home on Gordon Street, Kurow. This was a small town of only 300 people, located in the remote Waitaki River Valley, in the North Otago region, South Island, New Zealand. At the time, Kurow was the second largest township, after Oamaru, in the North Otago district and was unusual in that it had a doctor. There was no local maternity hospital in those days, so all local births were home deliveries. Labouring mothers would be assisted by a midwife or female family member and on rare occasions a doctor would be in attendance.

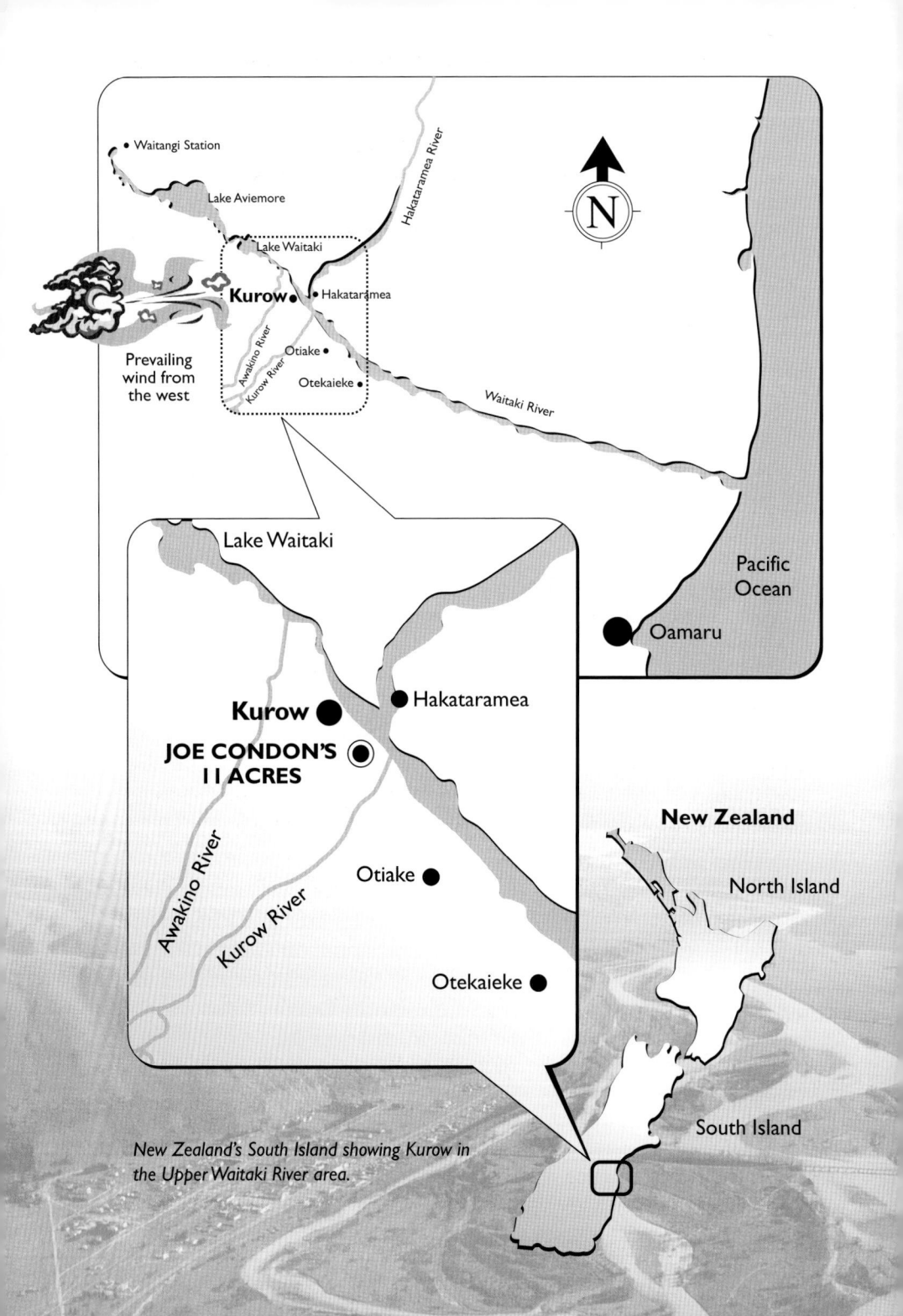

New Zealand's South Island showing Kurow in the Upper Waitaki River area.

At the time of my birth Rene Robinson, a registered nurse and housewife, assisted the doctor. Rene said that I was blue when I emerged, and it took them ages to get me breathing spontaneously and see the reassuring pink skin colour that means life is underway. There was no bottled oxygen back then and suction methods were primitive. I'd have been held upside down and slapped on the buttocks in a 'hit and hope technique' to get me breathing.

Most people know that severe oxygen deprivation at birth will often leave the unfortunate baby with mental retardation and sometimes cerebral palsy. In turn, I have often wondered if oxygen deprivation affected my higher mental functions and memory. My anaesthetist colleagues and contemporaries tell me that after a prolonged general anaesthetic, a patient's memory is sometimes compromised. Perhaps other brain functions can also be affected by lack of oxygen, as my musical appreciation is non-existent. It may well be that I was affected by the anoxia I experienced at birth, and had I not suffered it I may well have turned out to be a different person.

In 2008 research into the effects of low oxygen levels on the new born's brain was continued by Professor Dorothy Oorschot at Otago University. Her research explores the possibility that two treatments (administration of anti-oxidants and the creation of a state of mild hypothermia in the subject), can protect the neonatal brain cells from the damaging effects of oxygen deprivation. There is also new, exciting evidence suggests that even the mature brain can be altered physiologically and new cells may be encouraged to grow. As Professor Oorschot had not been born when I first appeared gasping for air in Kurow, the possibility of remedial help for me was still a long way off, both in time and in distance. My friends say that I am eccentric, though others may have different opinions and describe me in less kind terms. You, the reader will have to make up your own mind as we move along. Perhaps you've already made a quick assessment, and we will see if you change your opinion as you read deeper into my story.

My parents, Arch and Dais, had a good appreciation of music and could hold a tune. I, on the other hand, feel deprived in that

Hell-Bent for Life

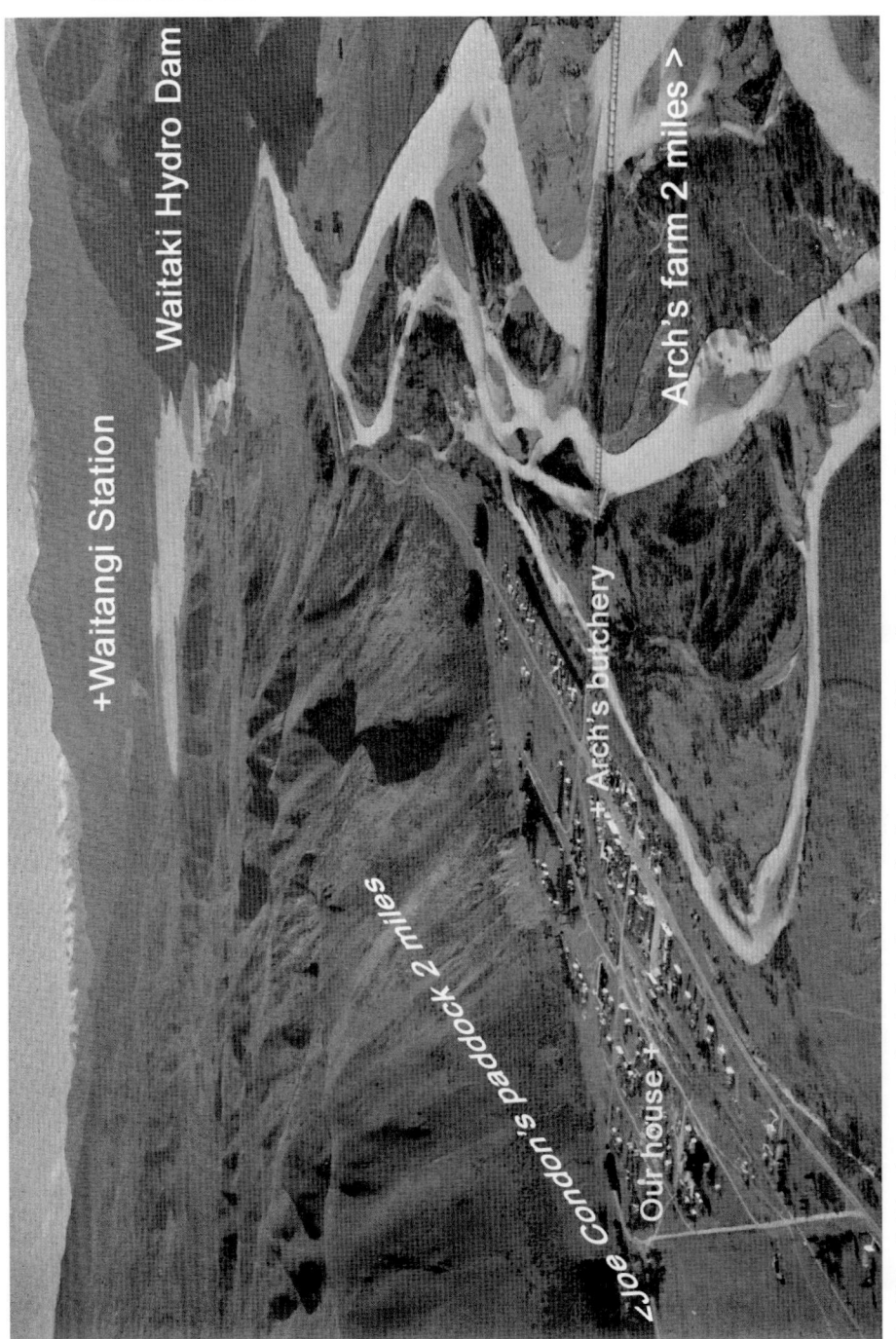

The 135 mile Waitaki river provides the boundary for the Canterbury and Otago Provincial districts. In addition, its waters feed the Waitaki Hydro-Electric station, one of the chain of seven stations in the South Island. In the foreground and on the left is the township of Kurow, 43 miles from Oamaru by road.

I did not inherit this ability. My mother said that as an infant I would sit on the ground and cry when she played the piano. She was a competent pianist, and I was the only one disturbed by her playing.

Things didn't improve with age, and to this day I am unable to derive any pleasure from music of any kind. I can't participate in conversations about music and the bulk of religious material presented to me (for my immediate delectation and ultimate salvation) also fails to interest me. Gregorian chants bore me to distraction and when I learned that if I reached Heaven I was to be entranced by the presence of the 'Beatific Vision of God' in all his glory, while being entertained by the Heavenly Choir, I was left completely unimpressed. The fact that this heavenly state was a crowded place that was to go on for ever made the situation even less appealing. I would have thought that two hours, which is the length of most movies, would have been enough of that type of entertainment.

Most of us know that there are separate areas on the surface of the brain's cerebral hemispheres associated with and responsible for hearing, sensation and movement. When these areas are wiped out by a disease or a stroke the unfortunate patient loses all or part of these functions. I am unaware of any MRI studies that identify specific areas responsible for appreciation of music and religion and my neurological colleagues haven't been able to shed light on this question. If there are higher centres in the cerebrum for musical and religious appreciation, they could have developed later in the foetus's brain evolution and thus been more susceptible to the effects of oxygen deprivation. It is known that intelligence levels and memory function are decreased by any episode of severe anoxia either at birth or later in life and I'm still wondering about this. My memory for names of any sort has always been poor, and is getting worse. Some 'friends' wonder if it is Alzheimer's beginning to take its toll, but I'd prefer to think they have only just noticed my deficiency in these areas.

When I was a junior doctor, anaesthesia was an unrefined art. We gave ethyl chloride and ether via the 'rag and bottle' method.

A cloth was placed over the patient's face and we poured various amounts of the liquids directly onto the cloth. In retrospect I realise that the anaesthetist could be affected and was sometimes mildly anaesthetised too. Once the patient was fully unconscious, it was only when their faces turned blue that we realised the subject had become seriously anoxic. This would not have helped their post-operative cerebral function, and present-day anaesthetists, with more accurate oxygen measuring devices and readily available oxygen, don't let their customers become anoxic. My anaesthetist colleagues say that they don't understand the mechanism by which an anaesthetic agent causes unconsciousness. It is accepted that any unconscious state, other than sleep, can decrease short term memory function so this damage is an accepted risk when using anaesthesia. I've made no effort to differentiate the causes of post-anaesthetic memory loss, but I suspect it is due to the anaesthetic agent, the unnatural state of unconsciousness and the accompanying anoxia.

I am left to ponder what effect arriving in an extremely anoxic state had on the future development of 'Little Jackie Valentine'.

My parents, Dais and Arch Valentine, and the 300 other people who lived in Kurow, didn't realise that they lived in a desert. It was aptly termed a 'man made desert' by the ecologist Leonard Cockayne, who said that its geological condition was caused by the thoughtless practice of excessive burning of the tussock cover, plus the infestation by rabbits brought in from Britain in the 1830s.

When I was a teenager I saw a twenty-foot relief map of the South Island of New Zealand on display at the Dunedin Museum. They coloured the area surrounding the Upper Waitaki River yellow, which was identified by Cockayne's same description, 'a man-made desert'.

The New Zealand Oxford dictionary provides this definition:
> *"DESERT / 1. a dry barren often sand covered area of land. 2. an uninteresting or barren subject, period etc: a cultural desert."*

I may have to disappoint you a little here, dear reader. There was certainly desert, but no sand, date palms, camels or Arabs and especially no dark eyed damsels. There were none of these features, but it was a desert nevertheless. The second part of the definition 'a cultural desert' will be examined later.

In the nineteenth century, the government built a 130km-long rabbit-proof fence, stretching between the Waitaki River and up into the McKenzie country, in an effort to stop the invasion of rabbits. It was to no avail. The 'run-holders' also brought in ferrets, stoats and weasels in a further attempt to control the rabbits, but the bunnies bounced right past them all. The rabbits had left the neat fields of England far behind and found the wide-open spaces of North Otago to their liking. In Britain the rabbits were easily controlled but here they were a plague and a pestilence.

The prevailing wind from the west was as dry as a chip when it arrived in the Waitaki Valley. Whatever moisture it had picked up on its long journey from the Indian Ocean had been dropped as rain or snow when it rose over the mountains in the McKenzie country. This desert was a bare landscape of surface rock where only sparse matagouri shrubs grew. Sheep won't eat matagouri, and it repels even the most ravenous rabbits.

In prehistoric times, the watershed that fed the Waitaki River had been covered with trees. Large ancient burnt logs are preserved and can still be seen lying in the shingle slips on the surrounding hills. Some experts think that the devastation of the vegetation started when Maoris burned the trees to hunt the giant moa. This great flightless bird, extinct for several hundred years, has left skeletal remains over ten feet tall behind, and is regarded as the largest bird that has ever lived.

I don't know why the trees disappeared, but there was almost no forest left when the Europeans arrived one hundred and seventy years ago, and by this time the moas were long gone. Had the forests survived, the Waitaki region would have been a better place to live. Instead, this vast, barren landscape became suitable for marginal grazing only.

Before European colonialisation there were very few Maori in this part of New Zealand. Their staple food, the semi-tropical kumara, did not thrive so far south. They must have been preoccupied with finding and transporting pounamu (New Zealand green stone or jade) to trade with the more populous tribes to the north. This hard stone was valuable for weapons and carving, since the Maori didn't have access to steel until the European explorers arrived.

It's tempting to propose that the Maori lit fires to hunt the moa, and this was the main cause of the forest's destruction but I doubt that this burning caused the permanent destruction of the whole forest. Certainly, there is plenty of evidence to show that Maori feasted on the birds over long periods, but I don't believe that a handful of Polynesians with Stone Age weapons had the ability to completely extinguish the moa population from millions of acres of rugged land. In other parts of the world forests regenerate naturally after significant fires, so why didn't this forest recover? In drought prone Australia, some attribute the massive burn offs to lightning strikes. Could this be the case here or could meteorite showers have devastated the forest? What is known for sure is that the forests are gone, the moas are gone and there are few Maori left in the Upper Waitaki area now.

While all seemed quiet and peaceful in the third decade of the twentieth-century in Kurow, there were some stirrings below the surface of this temperate desert environment. Far from being a 'cultural desert' there were interesting things afoot. A small group of the local elite met regularly at the solo doctor's house, to discuss social issues - some will tell you that they met at the local Presbyterian Parson's house, but this was not the case. This group planned the foundations of the Social Services and Health programme for New Zealand, which was eventually put into legislation when the Labour government came to power for the first time in 1935. The 'Kurow Group' as it was known, included the local Presbyterian Minister, the doctor and the secretary of the Labourers Union at the Waitaki Hydro Scheme. All of these people went on to become ministers in the first Labour Government, after the party's landslide win.

The leader in this discussion group was the head master of the

The Beginning - Early family history and life in Kurow

Kurow School, 'Squat' Davidson (I think his correct name was Andrew Davidson). He didn't want to give up his teaching job to stand for parliament, but if he had accepted the nomination he could well have gone on to become the Prime Minister.

Dr. MacMillan was another member of the group, and even in those early days he had initiated a pre-paid medical scheme for the workers at the Waitaki Hydro works camp. He was always busy and sped up and down the four-mile long shingle highway to the camp at reckless speed to attend to his patients. All the workmen's houses in the camp looked the same, and once, when he was called out at 2 a.m. he knocked at the door of a worker's home, raised the occupants, shot into the bedroom, and on realising his error called a hasty, "Oh sorry, wrong house. Let's try next-door!" as he beat a retreat.

Dr. MacMillan became Minister of Health in the new Labour government, and later, when he retired from Parliament, he set up a general medical practice in Dunedin. He was known for putting his patients through quickly but efficiently, and when my friend, Dr. Kevin O'Connor, was working as the Senior Resident at Dunedin Hospital, some of the hospital doctors wrote to Dr. MacMillan, pointing out five mistakes he had made in the previous year; he wrote back listing ten mistakes the hospital doctors had made in the same period.

After I was born my mother said that she wanted a daughter who was to be named Mary, but she did not become pregnant again. I don't think that my parents used contraception. Although Arch had lost a testicle as a result of being kicked in the groin by a sheep, this should not have caused infertility on his part. I think it more likely that the main reason for Dais's failure to conceive again was her obesity. Her weight was a lifelong problem, and once when I was a teenager, we were discussing her size and she said "You did this to me!" She felt that the weight gained during her pregnancy, which she never lost, was my fault. In those days many people did not accept the relationship between excessive food intake and obesity and blamed their weight problems on being 'big boned'. In photos taken before her marriage, Dais was already clearly overweight, so in spite of her high intelligence her logic was faulty in this area.

My mother was a bright lady, and I think her IQ would have been in the top five percent had IQ testing got as far as Kurow in those times. Dais's lack of intellectual training and discrimination could be seen later in her life, in her acceptance of everything priests would say, whether in the confessional or in casual conversation.

On August 16th 1959, disaster struck the Condon family. Elizabeth, my maternal Grandmother, was hit with a massive cerebral hemorrhage. She collapsed into Joe's arms and died soon after, leaving the family without a mother. Elizabeth was only 30 years old when she died, and she left three young children; Queenie (Aquinas) was seven years old, Dais was four, and their younger brother Jack had only just turned one.

Joe Condon, the newly widowed father, worked on a sheep station twelve miles from Kurow, further up the Waitaki River, and came home every second weekend. He tried to provide care for his children by employing a series of housekeepers, but this resulted in a sequence of disasters. Eventually his mother-in-law, Mary Massey sold her boarding house in Oamaru, and moved to Kurow to look after the family. Everyone loved her and called her "Granny Massey". She did her best, but was at least sixty years old and as time went on transferred more and more of her family responsibilities to Dais. I never found out why this extra responsibility was not taken up by Queenie, the elder daughter, but Dais had to cope as best she could, given that she had no choice in the matter.

As she was needed at home, Daisy had to leave school when she was eleven years old and could not stay to sit her Proficiency Exam, which students sat when they were about twelve years old. In those days Kurow only had a primary school and the proficiency was the end of the schooling for the majority of children with few students continuing on to secondary education in the larger centres.

When Daisy was in her teens, Queenie was accepted for nurse training in New Plymouth. She went off with the promise that

The Beginning - Early family history and life in Kurow

when she was finished she would come back to mind the family and allow my mother to go off for her own training. Queenie did very well in the nursing exams and received the highest marks for New Zealand in her finals. Dais had been accepted for nurse training at Dunedin Hospital, and awaited Queenie's return to take over and look after Jack and Granny Massey. However, when Queenie returned she was no longer a country girl. She was tall, had beautiful legs, and was now smartly and fashionably dressed. Her well-cut suits showed off her slim waist, and she had learned to speak clearly so that she didn't sound like a country hick.

When my mother reminded Queenie of her promise to return to Kurow to relieve her of the house duties she said, "Oh no Dais, you stay at home and look after Jack. I can make enough money

Mary 'Granny' Massey (sitting) with John (Jack) and Daisy at Joe Condon's house in Kurow.

Hell-Bent for Life

A look-alike Pampa Joe Condon. In those days, cameras were not usually owned by working class families. As I did not have a photo of my beloved 'Pampa Joe', when I saw this picture of an unidentified man in a magazine, (in about 1945) I cut it out. The likeness to Pampa Joe was so amazing that I kept it pasted in my photo album. Until finding the image of Joe and his dog in the Waitangi Station book, this was the only likeness I had of him.

for both of us!" This left Queenie free to continue working as a receptionist in their Uncle Ted Massey's up-market Coker's Hotel in Christchurch, while she was saving to travel overseas.

Queenie was finished with Kurow; she was a good woman, as good women go, and as good women go, she left. Christchurch and her future plans had a lot more going for her than Kurow's 300 people and her family's needs. Queenie never sent any money home, even though she later married a South African sugar millionaire, Wilhelm Bohler. I am tempted to describe him as a 'sugar daddy', but you will realise he was far from that as you learn more about Wilhelm and Queenie's life together.

My mother, Dais, had a strong yet pleasing personality, with a pleasant face and ready smile. Most people in the district liked her and regarded her highly. I suspect this was because she was bright, intelligent, kind and a born leader. My mother talked a lot, but she also had a lot to say that was worth hearing.

In today's social climate, Daisy would have gone on to higher tertiary education or run multiple businesses. She had the potential to make her mark, but was restricted by poverty, lack of basic education and family responsibilities. This was a sad situation but not unusual back then. Women, especially in the rural sector, were mainly relegated to the position of being housewives, looking after their family and supporting their husband's careers. This left little chance for them to develop their own potential.

Many working husbands spent a lot of time and money at the local pubs, and it followed that there were many unhappy and frustrated women at home with their children. If the women found the situation intolerable, and left their marriage, there was minimal help from government agencies, and their parents could not always be counted on to help.

Joe Condon, my mother's father, was an attractive character who was well known and liked by everyone in this small community. He was very tall, and prematurely bald, which he explained by saying "You can't have hair and brains at the same time!"

As a child, I was unable to say "Grandpa" so I called him "Pampa" and the whole district got to know him as 'Pampa Joe'. His family had emigrated from Ireland as Government 'assisted' immigrants when he was a child. He had started school in Ireland and continued his education in New Zealand, as the 1877 Education Act made education free and compulsory. Despite this, he was unable to read or write. Pampa Joe had dyslexia, a condition that was prevalent amongst Irish immigrants at the time. Dyslexia describes one of the many ways in which people have abnormal difficulty in their ability to learn to read and spell words. Throughout history many prominent people have had this condition, and being dyslexic does not mean there is a lack of intelligence. The specialised teaching programmes that are now available to help overcome learning disabilities were not available in the junior schools in those days. Most of the teaching was left to student teachers who did their best with little knowledge of the condition and only rudimentary books and equipment. Even though Pampa Joe was illiterate he was still a very bright person, a good conversationalist and very entertaining as well as he had a good memory for jokes and knew how to tell them. As he could not read, Pampa Joe kept up with world affairs and national politics by listening to the radio. The local news was well catered for as the neighbourhood pubs were clearinghouses for local chit-chat and gossip. Here news was carefully masticated, processed and regurgitated for general consumption. Some information that went in crooked came out straight and vice versa. They knew who was liaising with whom within a thirty-mile radius, and a missed menstrual period was especially noted. Not a bird fell from the sky that wasn't known about in these establishments. They were the citadels of local lore with memory banks that held information for generations. If the scientists who were asked to develop radar in WW II had known about the Kurow pubs, they could have saved themselves a lot of trouble and avoided having to experiment with microwave frequencies. They could have just visited these bastions of information and knowledge to obtain their intelligence.

Because Pampa Joe had a wide general knowledge, was erudite and obviously intelligent, his friends never suspected that he could not read. Early in their married life, my grandmother Elizabeth tried to teach Pampa Joe to read, but during the lessons he would break out in a sweat from the strain, so she made no progress. About all he was able to do was sign his name, and this he still did with difficulty.

The Beginning - Early family history and life in Kurow

Arthur Sutton (part owner of Waitangi Station) on the left with Pampa Joe and horses on the right.

Before she died, my grandmother had been negotiating to get them a job managing a sheep station where my grandfather would do the stock work and she would manage the books and the administrative side of the property. My grandmother's premature death, however, terminated that idea and committed grandfather to a lifetime of labouring. Pampa Joe eventually became a foreman at Waitangi Station, but was never paid more than a labourer's wage. In those days three to five pounds was the going rate for a week's work, although musterers were paid three to five pounds a day. Musterers were employed to help bring the sheep down from the high country in the autumn. This enabled the sheep to be pastured on the low paddocks during the severe winter cold, where they were at least partially protected from the snow. The higher pay for musterers was due to their irregular seasonal employment and their need to bring a horse and half a dozen dogs with them.

Fortunately, illiteracy did not stop my grandfather from being a good employee, and he worked at Waitangi Station for forty years. He lived on the station in a large hut and was encouraged

Joe Condon aka Pampa Joe with one of his working dogs.

to ride the twelve miles to Kurow to visit his family every second weekend. He owned a house in Kurow, along with an eleven-acre back paddock that was two miles from the house.

The paddock was usually used for grazing cattle, but one year my mother arranged for contractors to plough the land and sow it with wheat. It produced a good crop, and the grain merchants in Dunedin asked for a sample to be sent, so they could determine a price for it. Dais carefully blew the dust and rubbish out of a handful and sent this as the sample. When the payment cheque came back for the grain that was sold, there was a deduction taken from it with the explanatory note, "Grain not up to sample."

This land had been part of the large Kurow station before the Liberal Party government purchased it at the beginning of the century and divided it into smaller holdings. It was supposed to be a 'working man's property' for the support of a family, and the owner was supposed to live on the land. However, my grandfather never took his family to live in the two-bedroom cottage on the eleven acres. Later he rented out the cottage and my father, Arch, used the land to graze bullocks until they were slaughtered, to be sold in our butcher shop.

I don't know how Pampa Joe was able to afford these properties, and I never heard any mention of mortgages, so the money must have come from a family inheritance. My grandfather's weekly wage of three pounds certainly wouldn't have enabled him to afford two properties.

Pampa Joe was a competent stockman, with a team of good dogs and in normal circumstances would have gone on to own his own farm. The challenge of illiteracy and being a solo parent made his chances of making substantial progress difficult if not impossible. In a sheep-farming community, a stockman's status depended on his owning a team of good dogs. When people complimented my grandfather on the quality of his dogs, they sometimes asked him why he didn't enter them into the local dog trials. He'd ask them "Oh, so I've got a good reputation?" and they'd say "Yes" to which he'd reply "Well then, I'm going to keep it!" This reflected his dry and intelligent good humour, which was never far below the surface.

There is a renowned story about my grandfather and his best dog, the giant "Bounce". Seven men had spent a week of arduous work in the steep hills or 'high tops' as they are known, at Waitangi Station, mustering 20,000 wild merino sheep. As the large mob finally approached the station yards, an undisciplined young dog barked at the wrong time and the whole mob turned and bolted back into the hills. Each musterer sent his 'heading dogs' to try and head the bolters off, stop them and turn them back, but the maddened merinos simply ran over them. After five failed attempts Pampa Joe was asked to send Bounce out after them. Bounce bounded off into the distance, headed the mob and the day was saved, with the mob brought back to the yards. It could have been that the sheep were running out of steam at that stage, but the whole thing added to Pampa Joe and Bounce's reputations.

My Father, Archie, or "Arch," as he was known, had a difficult early life. His mother, Gran Valentine, had left her husband in Waikouaiti because he had thoughtlessly neglected to tell her that he was already married and had another family! Gran Valentine was left to support her family alone so she moved her three sons and a daughter to the Hakataramea (Haka) Valley, near Kurow, and took a job as a housekeeper. It became my father's job to clean and polish the riding boots of the boss's daughters, but he mistakenly polished the tan boots with black polish and the black boots with tan, with the result being the end of his mother's employment there. She then moved her family to a house in the Haka Township on the other side of the Waitaki River from Kurow. It must have been difficult for Gran Valentine to support her family in those years, as Social Security support payments were pretty thin at the beginning of the Twentieth Century. The 'Old Age Pension' had been introduced in 1898 but only those who were on the brink of destitution and of good character were considered to be worthy, as they were the 'deserving poor'.

It was during these difficult years that my father was admitted to a private hospital in Dunedin, and I cannot understand how Granny Valentine was able to meet this expense. He spent months with a suspected tuberculosis hip. However this was later diagnosed as a slipped femoral head, which resulted in a shortening of the leg, a marked limp and eventually a painful arthritis. He suffered pain for the rest of his life, and the limp excluded him from service in WWI. Arch was forever swallowing aspirin for his hip pain and then baking soda for the stomach inflammation caused by the aspirin.

The only work available for Arch was rabbiting, mustering and shearing sheep for the local run holders. I don't know how he was able to walk those steep hills with his hip problems, but he always had good dogs to assist him. He beat his dogs if they didn't measure up to his high standards. My mother once admitted that before they were married, he was in trouble for having killed a dog. Certainly pups didn't last long if they were slow to learn to "shut up" and "sit down" when my father told them to. If a young dog kept running when my father told him to stop, he turned the mature dogs onto him. After the youngster had been cart-wheeled through the air a few times he learnt to pay attention to his master's voice.

Fortunately, my father seemed to like me, which was just as well given the treatment he metered out to his dogs and his tendency to harbour major antagonism towards those who annoyed him. His disrupted early home life and the pain from the chronic hip must have caused him continual discomfort and disturbed his temperament. Without the pain from his hip, and with a normal family background, he might have been a different person. Today he would probably be diagnosed as having a borderline personality disorder. When he was upset he was liable to go into a rage, stamping and cursing and calling on the divinity to witness the unfairness of his situation. Conversely, if he liked someone they could do no wrong. In the Merck Manual (the medical bible) in the psychiatric disorders section we find: "Borderline personalities are unstable in several areas including interpersonal relationships, behaviour, mood and self-image. These persons are extremists for whom the whole world is black or white, hated or loved - never neutral."

Ginger was the best dog and seldom missed a placing in the 'huntaway' category at dog trial competitions. In his old age, Ginger was not tied up and chose to sleep his days away lying in the middle of the main road, in front of Arch's butcher shop. The black tar must have been warm and comforting to his old bones. It also says something for the tolerance and good driving of the locals that Ginger was never run over. Cars weren't as common then and the main road was wide enough to turn a bullock-team, leaving plenty of room for Ginger to relax undisturbed.

Twice a week cattle were brought to the slaughter house. When the remaining cattle needed to be returned to the back paddock they had to travel two miles on the road around three sides of a square. Ginger had no trouble taking them back alone. This was not easy as it was a public road with an occasional car passing, and on some afternoons there were many children walking home from school to distract him.

The gate to the tennis courts always seemed to be left open, and the cattle would sometimes do a right turn into the courts. If they did it took forever to get them out, so to prevent this from happening Ginger would go along their right side and stand in the gateway. Once Ginger had guided the cattle into the back paddock, he wasn't able to close the gate, so he'd come back to base through the paddocks and someone would need to drive around to secure the gate. Archie never managed to teach Ginger how to close and lock it which showed a deficiency in their otherwise exemplary partnership.

Ginger was an invaluable work mate who was a constant companion for my father, and virtually a member of the family. Pups sired by Ginger were highly sought after by farmers and musterers in the district. The three pounds, or even five pounds my mother received for a pup went into my bank savings.

As WWI approached, my uncle Jack Condon, who was under my mother's care, had grown into a personable, tall and good-looking young man. Certainly all of Dais's girlfriends thought that he was the best thing going, even before sliced bread came along. In a rural town of 300 people, there was little competition or even much choice in the marital lottery.

At one time, Jack had been on holiday with relatives in the North Island, and on his way home he stopped at his Uncle Ted's hotel in Christchurch, where Queenie had been working. Coker's Hotel had a resident boxer who was training with a view to going on to contest the New Zealand Championships, and potentially further. Boxing, racing and beer drinking were a dominant part of male life in Christchurch in those days. On arrival, Jack was asked to go a few rounds with their boxer, and he agreed. They found some light shoes for him and assumed he wouldn't have much of a show against their champion. The boxer gave Jack a clip over the left ear, and Jack responded with a solid right cross and knocked him out. When he returned home early from his holiday he explained to my mother, "Oh Dais, I had to cut my holiday short - I wasn't welcome there anymore."

My father and Uncle Jack were best friends, and in 1916, before my parents were married, Jack signed up and went off to the war in France. My father stayed behind as he had failed his army medical because of his hip. Going over to England there were several hundred men on the troopship 'Willochra', and Jack won the Light-Heavy Weight Boxing Championship while aboard. He told my mother that the fighters had to wait until the rolling and pitching of the ship stopped as it was only then that they could get on with the business of trying to knock each other down.

John Joseph Condon (Jack) in army dress before his WW1 tour.

Hell-Bent for Life

Jack went on for further military training in England, and then onto Flanders flooded fields in Belgium. Flanders had held a strategic place in medieval wars, but this was the first time that high explosives had destroyed its drainage system, and this damage allowed the land to revert to its original swampy nature. When Jack's regiment arrived, there was no trace of the original fields, which were now replaced with a muddy morass; when heavily laden men or pack horses slipped off the wet boardwalks leading to the frontlines, many drowned in the mud. Men sank in this morass and called to their friends to shoot them, as they couldn't be helped. There must still be the bodies of soldiers fully clothed and with all their gear, and packhorses with their loads of shells, deep under Flanders fields to this day. Many of our men have "no known graves," and we hear that farmers are still turning up bones as they cultivate their fields.

Flanders had sided with England during the Hundred Years War, and had been fought over by Spain, Austria, Germany and Holland. Each spring the red poppies appear to brighten Flanders fields, reminding us all of the meaningless destruction of life that occurred there over the centuries.

The British General Haig was in charge. He was a Scotsman, being a scion of the Haig & Haig whisky dynasty, which still manages to distil "the good stuff" and distribute it worldwide. Despite his high-priced education he struggled with his army exams, with mathematics being his weakest subject. In Belgium, he directed his soldiers to 'go over the top' onto the flat muddy fields and walk slowly towards the German lines, where the German machine gunners must have thought they had died and gone to heaven; they were presented with such 'easy pickings'. The German gunners kept their fire at waist level, and it was so intense that some of our soldiers were cut in two at the hips. The casualty rate was 40%, with half of those dying. It was not possible to bury all the dead, so the battlefield was a stinking mess, populated with huge rats and blowflies.

Since mathematics wasn't General Haig's strong point, I wonder if he realised that the thousands of dead soldiers left many thousands of grieving relatives, with their lives permanently blighted by the loss of those near and dear to them. The Kiwi troops fiercely resented the senior British officers who kept insisting that the troops continue to go over the top to likely death or serious injury, with little or no prospect of gaining ground. The wounded were carried through the mud to first aid stations, which soon became overwhelmed. Many of them were left outside the medical tents for hours, or even days before they could be attended to. Men called for water and their pleas could not always be answered. The junior officers who led the troops had a distinct uniform and the German gunners soon picked out the officers, who had even shorter fighting lives than their troops.

When Jack's team was ready to go to the front he was asked to stay behind and fight for his regiment in a boxing tournament. He turned this down to go up to the trenches with his mates. They were sent to Passchendaele in Flanders, and awaited Haig's big push. Jack's regiment went over the top on 12 October 1917, the first day of the Battle of Passchendaele. He became one of the 2,735 New Zealanders who were among the 13,000 allied casualties suffered there.

Jack was wounded in the left lower leg in the first five minutes of the battle, and had to wait two hours before he was carried out of the battlefield on a stretcher. At great risk to themselves, the stretcher-bearers slogged through the rain and mud and carried him to the forward casualties clearing station, where he was left for hours in the rain, enduring increasing pain, until his turn came for attention.

After he had been seen at the clearing station, Jack, along with all the other casualties, had a 24 hour wait before being evacuated. The injured were still in their filthy clothes spattered with the mud and shit of Flanders. Some of the lucky ones had wounds infested with maggots; 'lucky' because the enzymes secreted by the maggots dissolved the putrid tissue, and in many cases saved limbs from gangrene and subsequent amputation. Jack, however, had no criticism of the nurses and medical orderlies who did their best under those hellish conditions. If Sir Douglas Haig knew about the horrific military and medical situation, he took no action to remedy it and continued to send soldiers to their fate.

After days on troop trains and the ferry crossing over the Dover Straits, Jack eventually arrived at the Walton-on-Thames Hospital, situated up river from London. Like so many others, his leg injury became gangrenous and was amputated below the knee. The doctors did not have antibiotics, and once gas gangrene set in it was necessary to take off the limb to save the patient's life. There are tragic photos of officers sitting for the photographer, all with one or both legs missing. They must have wondered what sort of life lay before them.

Months of rehabilitation lay ahead for Jack, and it was to be a year before he finally returned to Kurow. Many other casualties were in one of the three psychiatric hospitals set up in England, for New Zealanders who were traumatised by emotional stress caused by the inhuman conditions in the trenches. Half a dozen New Zealand soldiers who had broken down emotionally, and had appeared before English tribunals, had been shot for 'cowardice'. The Australians, on the other hand, would not allow their men to be tried by the British and condemned to execution. The New Zealand authorities sheltered the New Zealand public from most of this traumatic information but did nothing to stop it. I wonder what was said in the dreaded telegram to next of kin of the New Zealand soldiers who had been shot for cowardice? I suspect it was probably the standard, "The Government regrets to inform you that your volunteer son has been killed in action........."

My mother had received the occasional letter from Jack while he was convalescing in England. She knew that he was in hospital at Walton-on-Thames, but the Motorist Atlas of Great Britain shows that there are eighteen other Waltons. Most are in southeast England, so it could be an Anglo-Saxon name.

It must have been agony for Dais to know that her brother was on the other side of the world, needing her physical help and emotional support, and she could do nothing but write to him. There was no way for her to see him until he returned to New Zealand. Today you can get on a plane and wing your way 12,000 miles to the other side of the world, but that wasn't an option for another twenty years. My mother had to rely on the kindness and compassion of the nurses and orderlies at Walton-on-Thames until Jack's return. Thank God for them! I wonder at their ability to be so compassionate to the amputees and others whose lives lay in ruin so far from home.

Jack returned to New Zealand on the hospital ship 'Maheno', where again the staff did their best to make ruined lives tolerable. He had a pair of crutches and a heavy, unsatisfactory leg prosthesis that chafed his stump and could only be worn for an hour or so. Jack experienced the common sensation known as the 'phantom limb' as well as crippling shooting pains in that leg. He was able to tolerate the pain and discomfort during the day time, but his nights were hell, with only aspirin for pain relief. The psychological support given to these men before discharge was minimal and they had to rely on encouragement from a spouse or family members when they returned to their civilian lives.

Sir Douglas Haig is now long gone, and nary a bottle of 'the hard stuff' was sent to assuage the pain of dispossessed and damaged New Zealand veterans. They had only small expectations of assistance, and so were not disappointed when little appeared.

After a tearful reunion with Archie and Dais, Jack went off for two months of vocational 'rehabilitation' where he was given training as a shoe repairman. He hated having to work with smelly boots and shoes, but finished the course and the government rented him a boot repair shop on Kurow's main street. My mother was indignant because this smart young man had been re-trained to be a shoe repairman. His intelligence suited him for one of the many Inspector jobs created by the post-war government. She thought that he had done his bit for the country and the country should have reciprocated, but the country missed the call.

Jack's artificial leg was heavy and badly fitted. The amputation stump was painful through chafing so his walking was laborious. He could only weight bear on his leg for an hour at a time, so was forced to use crutches most of the time. This bright and handsome youth had become a 'lost-limbed beneficiary'. He would play-fight with my father occasionally, but would have to get his hands on my father to wrestle with him, as his mobility was so limited. His athletic days were long gone, and this capable young man had gone from the top of the heap to the bottom and, understandably, he lapsed into apathy and then depression.

At eight o'clock one morning Dais walked into the washhouse and found Jack. He had shot a .22-calibre bullet through the roof of his mouth and was lying unconscious on the floor. As he was still alive he was taken to the Oamaru Hospital, which was a forty-mile trip by ambulance, over a rough road.

My mother's sister, Queenie, was contacted in Christchurch and asked to come home because of Jack's injury. Rather than hurry home, Queenie rang a neighbour (one of the few who had a phone in those days), and asked if Jack was ill enough for her to return to Kurow.

Jack died in the Oamaru Hospital after a few days. His body was returned to Kurow, where there was a question of whether he could be buried by a priest and interred in the Catholic part of the cemetery as his death was a suicide. In those days the Catholics and Protestants had separate sides in the graveyard and a priest was not expected to bury someone who had committed suicide. In the end, he was buried by a priest on the Catholic side of the cemetery in the family plot. My mother and father had to live lives blighted forever by Jack's suicide, but I defend Jack's decision to take his life, which he found intolerable. For Jack, far from seeing light at the end of the tunnel, there was only the prospect of continual pain, disability and depression. Another reason why I don't blame my uncle for killing himself is that he must have known that his pain and depression were dragging his family and friends down. In his own eyes he had lost everything; he went from being an active, handsome country boy who excelled in all activities, to being less physically able than an 80 year old. His artificial leg was almost useless and he had continual pain, which could not be managed. Loss of mobility excluded him from all sports and most social activities. He must have felt that death by suicide was his only escape.

The family had a .22-calibre rifle used to shoot rabbits. My mother had been using it and she was left wondering whether she had left the bullet in the rifle that Jack had used. From then on she talked about Jack as if he was still alive. She would say in conversation, "Jack says" or "Jack has always..." This puzzled me when I was a child, but now I know that denial is one defence against severe emotional pain, and she maintained this defence for the rest of her life. My father, on the other hand, would never talk about Jack, but thirty years later I found that he was carrying Jack's cracked and creased photograph around in his suit pocket.

In this small community, with both of them sharing deep suffering and trauma over Jack's death, they became closer, and married two years later. In a bigger community with diverse interests their situation may have been better and I'm unsure whether their mutual suffering was a good reason for getting married. Despite this, the marriage endured. The underlying stress from the suicide caused tension within the marriage, and some must have rubbed off on me. In those days males were encouraged to be tough and not talk about emotional pain, and my father remained silent while my mother maintained her denial. There was no budget in Kurow for mutual healing after Jack's suicide.

Queenie returned to Kurow for Jack's funeral, and three weeks later she and Dais took a cruise on the 'banana boat' in the South Pacific. This ship did a circuit around Fiji and Samoa, picking up bananas and copra and delivering supplies and the mail. The boat carried passengers and provided good meals and regular dances for entertainment. Queenie was tall and elegant, with all the good clothes, and was a magnet for male attention. My mother, on the other hand, was a bit overweight and had woolly jumpers, and her presentation was not up to Queenie's sartorial standard. Despite this, my mother talked fondly of the trip and obviously enjoyed it.

When I was three years old Arch and Dais took a job managing Lake Ohau Station, which was forty miles up the Waitaki River. Since Gran Valentine's family had grown up and moved out, she also moved in with us for a while. The station house was a mile from the road, and I used to ride my tricycle around the house. I would occasionally come in and call out, "Big car coming up the road!" to give warning of visitors. In those days most adults had only two sets of clothes, their 'working' and 'best'. When I had alerted Dais and Gran Valentine to the imminent arrival of guests, they would run off and change from their usual day wear into their best in preparation for the arrival. After a few false alarms they ceased to take any notice of my playful warnings. On one occasion, however, I called out a warning and they ignored me. A whole carload of doctors arrived from Christchurch for duck shooting, and caught them in their less than best clothes, which caused them great embarrassment.

It was a very isolated life for Dais and Archie and must have been even worse for Gran Valentine. She was a devout Presbyterian, and would not look at a book or newspaper on the Sabbath. But one Sunday, I was sitting on her knee, while she turned the pages of the "Illustrated Weekly News" to entertain me. She would not even glance at the pages in fear of eternal damnation. I pointed to a photo of a large rugby forward and said, "Look at that big bugger!" When Gran's eyes turned to the page she felt that her Sabbath was violated and being a very pious woman this possibly contributed to her moving on to live with one of her other sons.

After a couple of years, my parents moved back to Kurow, and obtained the lease of the Kurow Butchery. This was a challenge, as my father knew nothing about butchery and my mother had no business experience. They were able to keep on the existing staff so they could learn the basics from them.

Cattle, sheep and pigs were killed at the slaughter yard a mile away from town. Cattle were put in a 'crush' to restrict their movement, and a .22-calibre bullet was shot into the back of the animal's head. It then fell unconscious and had its throat cut so it would 'bleed out'. It is necessary for the heart to be beating for most of the blood to be pumped out from the carcass. If this isn't done the meat is full of clotted blood and is unpalatable. The sheep, on the other hand, had their throats cut while they were still alive,

The Kurow Butchery established in 1882 was believed to be the longest running butchers shop in New Zealand (meaning that the building was only ever used as a butchers shop since it was opened). It was demolished in 2004. This photo was taken when it was owned by McGregor, who then sold it to Dais and Arch Valentine. Note snow and slush on the unsealed road, and the ever present dogs.

with their neck stretched over the slaughter man's thigh. I still have a vivid and enduring memory of a sheep's eyes looking at me as the knife sliced through the arteries and soft tissues of the neck. They too were allowed to bleed out while the heart continued to pump.

My father developed a reputation for making good bacon. We kept fifty or sixty pigs at the slaughter yards, ensuring a supply of meat for bacon and pork. The pigs were fed offal from slaughtered sheep and cattle. The offal was supposed to be boiled before it was fed to the pigs but Arch felt this was unnecessary bureaucratic interference so mostly ignored this step, except for the day before the stock inspector was due. If Arch's own pigs weren't enough to supply the shop, he would buy more from the Otekaieke Special School, when they were available. The school had a farm and residential facilities for offenders who were too young to go to prison. The pigs they raised were fed on grain for the last few weeks of their lives and this meant they were leaner and the meat was of higher quality.

Dais did the bookwork for the family business, and started a duplicate record card system of sales to women whose husbands were working on the Waitaki Hydro Scheme, which was four miles up river from Kurow. We had two vans which went up to the camp twice a week. At the end of each month, on the worker's pay day, Dais would go up to the hydro camp in the passenger's seat of one of the vans. The housewives would bring out their card, and my mother would compare it with her records. When both parties were satisfied that the records agreed, payment was made and a new record started for the next month. As far as I know, my mother came up with this system herself, without the benefit of an accounting education. The wives could buy meat before payday, and we sold more meat without complicated bookkeeping.

There were many stories of families at the work camp doing a 'mid-night flit', where they put their meager possessions on a truck during the night and drove off without leaving a forwarding address for their various creditors. These were typically the butcher, the baker and the coal man, (who stood in for the candlestick maker). Electricity had long done away with the need for candles in the early part of the century, but the electricity supplier would have been a creditor also.

At five years of age, I was sent off to the local Kurow School. On the very first morning I went up to the teacher and said, "Miss, I'm hungry." I was expected to go home for lunch so hadn't brought any food. The teacher asked Nancy Harris to give me some of her lunch to carry me over. I haven't seen Nancy for 55 years, and although things change daily, let alone over half a century, Nancy was a kind person then and I expect she's still kind now.

My first teacher was called Miss Hogg. She told my mother that one day I stood up in class and asked her, "Please Miss Hogg, do you know how many tits a sow's got?" Given her surname,

I thought this was something she would know. She could well have said, "I don't know, but I've got two!" As she didn't know, I was able to tell her that different sows had between fourteen and eighteen nipples lined along their abdomens. Medical texts say that an occasional woman has an extra breast on the line from nipple to the groin but this must be excessively rare. I have not seen a case in my long career in medicine or my time taking in the sights of the Pacific Islands and the topless beaches in Europe and Australia. My appreciation of music may have been impaired, but my vision and visual appreciation remains intact. I'm thankful for small mercies.

On Tuesday evenings, I would go to the Junior Foresters Lodge which was held in the social hall at the rear of the local Presbyterian Church. One of the junior girls at the Lodge told me that a Presbyterian Preacher had come to their church and said, "Your Church is the Red woman and the Whore of Babylon." I wasn't up with whoring or Babylon, so had to put that in the back of my mind to be exhumed much later when the real world and further experience came along.

There was some tension between the Presbyterians and the Catholics in those days, but it was modest and became a less serious preoccupation as religion faded in importance. There were also a handful of Anglicans in Kurow, and they had a lovely old church, which had been gifted to them by Mr. Campbell who was the original owner of Otekaieke Station. Campbell was an 'Eton educated' man who sat in parliament and had holdings of almost a million acres. He took long absences from parliament to holiday in Great Britain, and he had a wonderfully interesting life until alcohol became a major problem for him.

The High Presbyterians from Scotland brought with them the rigid traditions of John Knox, who called down "fire and brimstone" on the head of the gentle Mary, Queen of Scots, for remaining loyal to the French Catholic Court. Under Knox's encouragement, the Scots banished Mary to England, and kept her son, the young James, who was brought up as a Presbyterian. He became James the Sixth of Scotland, and later James the First of England, uniting the two crowns.

In Kurow, the Anglicans remained friends with both Presbyterians and Catholics. They had a foot in both camps, reflecting their legacy from Henry the Eighth, who thought of himself as still a Catholic, and did not fully embrace the Protestant cause. If they criticised Henry, both Catholic and Protestant alike could find themselves occupying a suite in the Tower of London. It is remarkable that changes in religion in England, 400 years ago, affected the social tension in Kurow in the twentieth century. Can you imagine alterations in today's emotional and religious life influencing our descendents four hundred years from today? We don't have Henry the Eighth, John Knox or Mary Queen of Scots and I can't visualize our current leaders casting as long a shadow.

While at primary school one of my jobs, before school started, was to go around to half a dozen customers who had difficulty getting to the butcher shop, and take orders for their meat. One of my customers was Mrs. Hammond, a white haired lady whose son was a teacher. I used to write her name down as 'Mrs. Whitehead'.

I would take the orders to the shop, wait for them to be filled and then deliver them to my customers. While I waited, my father would fill the orders that were being taken by the weekly coach to customers 'up country'. We called it a 'coach', rather than bus, as the name was derived from the days when a coach and horses did the big circuit up into the McKenzie Country.

The floor of the butcher's shop was covered with sawdust to absorb any blood dripping from the carcasses awaiting dismemberment. The sawdust was renewed every month or so and gave a nice pine smell to the shop. While I was delayed, I would sometimes amuse myself by kicking the sawdust around. Occasionally, I did this with such enthusiasm that some of the sawdust flew up and stuck to the carcasses. This angered my father and he chased me around the shop when he was annoyed beyond endurance. Being quick on my feet, I could always avoid capture. If

Arch had put my orders together first, and the coach orders later, I wouldn't have been hanging around at a loose end decorating the meat with sawdust.

Each year dog trial competitions were held over the river from Kurow at Hakataramea Township. At one of these annual dog trials, I was competing in the children's heading event with my father's dog Rock, who was a lovely long-haired border collie with a very laid-back temperament. When the start bell rang I told Rock to "head" the sheep. Unfortunately I had neglected to let him off the chain early enough to attend to his own needs and Rock ignored my directions and went around urinating on the dry thistles in front of the audience. I encouraged him to get on with the business of the day by throwing rocks at him but I wasn't an accurate shot and my efforts didn't disturb Rock at all. By this time the crowd was helpless with laughter, which only subsided when eventually Rock got the message and went off to bring the sheep back to the yard. I can't remember if I got them into the pen, but we at least provided some unexpected entertainment for the spectators.

As I was locally famous for this, one of the top dog trialists, Jack Dunstan, gave me a pup from one of his prize bitches. This was prestigious, as he had good dogs, but unfortunately my father backed over the pup with the truck. However, I was given another soon after. The same thing happened again and, can you believe it, one more time after that! My career as a musterer never really got off the ground because of this. My father seemed incapable of learning from his mistakes, probably because he attributed events like this to bad luck or malicious intervention by the deity.

Arch frequently offended people, and Dais was forever running around patching things up in his wake. Looking back I think Arch's inability to control his temper made me determined to work on controlling my own. If a customer told my father that the meat she had bought was tough, he would reply "You just didn't know how to cook it properly." If complaints about this kind of treatment got back to my mother she'd get back to the offended customer and say, "I'm sure he didn't mean that. Here, take these sausages; they've

A truck on the slip road between Waitangi Station and Kurow. Joe Condon made the trip over this road with Bill Sutton driving, in preference to a long horseback ride.

just been made so see how they go."

My father's sausages were popular, and he kept his recipe secret and locked it away in the safe. I can remember him making up his sausage mix, which seemed to have a lot of mace and coriander, stale white bread to bulk it up and a German preparation that solidified the fat so that the sausages didn't shrink too much when they were fried. The sausage skins were made from sheep's small intestines, which made the sausage making a messy and time-consuming process. Later, Arch used artificial skins which were made from gelatin or some other edible product.

Every second weekend Pampa Joe would come home to his house that we lived in. At first he used to ride his horse but later on Bill Sutton, one of the two owners of the station, would give him a lift down to Kurow in his powerful 'tourer' car. Bill would come and pick him up for the dangerous drive back up over the perilous Slip Road. This was a narrow track and its name reflected the unstable nature of its shale and rock surface. It clung to the steep Waitaki Valley hillside, and had a 100-metre drop on one side, which ended at the deepest part of the Waitaki River. Many times when Bill came to pick my grandfather up, he was quite drunk and if people asked Pampa Joe about this, he would say, "I'd rather drive over the Slip Road with Bill Sutton drunk, than most people sober." He probably preferred this perilous fifteen-minute trip to two or three hours in the saddle, and I don't blame him.

One weekend when Pampa Joe was home visiting I complained that bigger boys were threatening me when walking to school. Pampa Joe's response was "What did they put all the stones on the road for?" meaning that I should throw a few at my schoolmates to balance the equation. If my accuracy hadn't improved since the incident at the dog trials with Rock, they wouldn't have been in much danger.

Once I got into a fight with David Neave, who was a similar age to me. We were going at it surrounded by a small audience and his elder brother, Tom, came along. I said, "If I hit him again, you'll hit me" but Tom, to his lasting credit, said "No, I won't interfere." This gave me all the encouragement I needed. David was getting the worst of it and he began limping and said "I've hurt my foot". As I felt confident of winning I responded "When your foot's better come back and we'll start again."

I may have been forgiven for thinking my whole life was going to be a series of interesting and happy play sessions with the odd civilised scuffle, but change was in the air.

CHAPTER 2

Early Adolescence in Kurow

1935 – 1937

INTRODUCED CHARACTERS

FATHER WALL, one of the Catholic priests who came from Oamaru to Kurow, each month, to say Mass on Sunday at the local Catholic Church.
BERT O'REILLY, the author's teacher at Kurow Primary School.
MR. BLYTHE, the Head Master of the school and one of the significant people who motivated the author's love of travel.
KEVIN O'CONNOR, a friend from Kurow and St.Kevin's School days who went to Medical School before the author and became a life-long friend.
MICK, Pampa Joe's brother.

A FRIEND'S DAUGHTER WHO WAS A COUPLE OF years older than me came to stay with us when I was ten. We ended up in the back of our family car, a 1936 Ford, that was in the garage. She took off her clothes from the waist down and with a little organization arranged it so that I was laying on top of her with my flaccid penis on her thighs. I didn't get an erection and don't remember her being too annoyed with me, though over the following years I was certainly regretful about my poor performance. An opportunity like that didn't present itself again and remained a vague, but aspired to dream from that time.

As I further matured I began to have 'wet dreams'. This is when a young man has an erotic dream semen explodes, unexpectedly and without control, from his penis and results in a 'nocturnal emission'. This was a pleasurable experience and I found out quickly enough that it was easy to achieve this happy result with more control by the process of masturbation.

During this period Father Wall came from Oamaru each month to say Mass on Sunday at the Kurow Catholic Church. He stayed with Arch and Dais the night before so that he could hear confessions on the Saturday evenings. He was a tall, good looking but austere man. I never heard him laugh but perhaps he had to smother a giggle at some of the revelations in the confessional box.

I had become pretty enthusiastic about my new found ability to masturbate when I found out that it was a 'mortal sin'. I got up the courage to confess to Father Wall that I had 'done it' six times. His response was "You are killing yourself and you are going to Hell!" He gave me a penance of "three Our Fathers and three Hail Marys" and told me to resolve never to repeat the dose under ANY circumstances. I could hardly believe my good luck at getting off so lightly, and went on my way rejoicing.

I was too embarrassed to ask any other adult about my secret sins so when I fell 'into sin' again I was forced to believe that I was on the slippery slope to perdition, and Hell was waiting for me if I died without having been to confession. Guilt surrounding masturbation was recurrent and a major concern for me. It was to remain a source of fear and anxiety throughout my school days.

On a later occasion, another young lady came to stay with us and we entertained each other by showing our pubic areas to each other. I can't remember that either of us had any pubic hair because we were too young to have grown any. When I dutifully reported this to Father Wall at the next confession, he said, "You're going to Hell; don't take somebody else with you!" As I am remembering and writing this it astounds me that a highly educated adult with the backing of Christ's Catholic Church would threaten a 10 year old boy with eternal damnation. Father Wall's beliefs, whilst sincerely held, were based on nothing more than myth and legend. It is sad that wars have been started defending religious ideas based on comparatively flimsy grounds, and people continue to be slaughtered over these 'matters of principle'.

A few months later, my teacher, Bert O'Reilly, discovered that

Kurow Primary School, Intermediate Class 1936 (John 3rd from left in back row).

I was tone deaf. Bert would have the class stand around the piano while he played popular songs. We were encouraged to make the rafters ring with sweet melodies. After one of these sing-a-longs Bert asked me to stay behind and played the tunes again for me. The only one I recognised was "God save the King" (yes, we had a King in those days!) After that, whenever the class music hour came around, I was given reading to engage my attention while they practised without the distraction of my less than melodious contribution.

While he taught in Kurow, Bert drove a baby Austin motor car. One day it caught on fire while he was driving it across a paddock to his boarding house near the school, and the burned out chassis sat rusting in the paddock for years. As children, we enjoyed hours of fun pretending that we were driving it around and were delighted that Bert had had the bad luck to have his car destroyed. It is likely Bert felt quite differently about the situation, with the disintegrating hulk reminding him of the event. Clearly a case of "One man's loss being another child's gain."

In 1937, Bert left and went on his overseas experience (the 'Big O.E.' as it is referred to in more modern times) and he was kind enough to send me a postcard from Colombo in Sri Lanka. Later, when New Zealand went to war in 1939, he signed up with the New Zealand forces and he reached the rank of colonel. After the war ended he became the head of the Correspondence School in Wellington.

During my last year at primary school the head master, Mr. Blythe, encouraged us to do 'projects'. The first project we did was a History of Kurow. I was told that the old people said that when the Maori were brought down the river by soldiers in the late 1800s, they were a ragged bunch. Their few possessions were in 'spring drays' pulled by horses and accompanied by numerous dogs. A group of Maori had made a camp at Chain Hills, which were located thirty miles from Kurow, up stream on the Waitaki River. They were living there while protesting the loss of their land, but the run holders said that they were stealing their sheep. An army unit came from Oamaru to tell them that "Picnicking on other people's property was naughty and barbequing the mutton was anathema" and they should hot-foot it back to the Kaik, which was their village at the mouth of the Waitaki River.

My history project of the Kurow district took up eight pages of a medium sized school notebook. I read it to Pampa Joe who thought it was pretty good and Arch and Dais were understandably delighted that their sole progeny had learnt to read and write. My script was not illustrated and was never edited or considered for publication for a wider audience. That's something I'd aspire to later in my life.

In the North Island the Maori had lost most of their land through confiscation after their defeat in the 'Land Wars' in the 1860s. Europeans had acquired high powered rifles while the Maori were using muzzle loaders, so the home team was severely disadvantaged in the firepower department. The high powered rifles tipped the balance of power in the Land Wars, and we all know that the victors not only get the spoils, but write the history as well. The Maori lost their land after the Land Wars in the North Island, and by sale in the South Island and were only left minuscule land reserves.

In the South Island land was purchased from the Maori in massive blocks. The enormous Canterbury block, of 20 million acres, had sold for 2,000 pounds in 1848. This block was almost a third of all the land in New Zealand and included North Otago. Twenty million (acres) divided by 2,000 (pounds) yields 10,000 so the Crown was able to get 10,000 acres for each pound spent. I don't know of a better deal in the area of bargain land acquisition, unless America did equally well from the purchase of Alaska from Russia in the 1800s. It was all over my head at the time, but now I can visualise a group of poor and unarmed Maori families being escorted off their ancestral lands by armed troops.

One of my other school projects was about the three Great Rivers of China. I still remember the Yellow River and the Yangtze River but the third one slips my mind. This project was the beginning of my fascination for travel, and curiosity about how other nations manage their countries and their lives. My mother was envious of her sister's travels and I think this also added to my keenness to explore the wider world. I remain grateful to those people who encouraged me to get up, get out, and meet the world half-way. I developed a love of different cultures and my interest in science developed later when I went on to medical school.

Half way through my final year at Kurow Primary School it was widely suspected that a group of senior students were having sex with each other. I was never involved and the names of the suspected participants are forever locked away in my memory. Dais had finely-tuned antennae for any deviation from the social norms and she would not have missed a beat in these areas. It wasn't long before she produced a brochure from St. Kevin's College in Oamaru and it was obvious that I was to be sent to a male convent to be 'saved' from a fate worse than death.

St. Kevin's was run by Irish Christian Brothers who had established themselves in Dunedin in 1876 and then opened a school in Oamaru in 1927. The order had been founded in Ireland in the 19th Century by Edmund Rice and had spread worldwide. The Brothers were a teaching order from the Roman Catholic Church

'Redcastle', the property that St. Kevin's College occupied.

and when they had completed their training they took the vows of poverty, chastity and obedience. The vow of poverty required that they had minimal possessions and I don't know if they even owned their own clothes. The vow of chastity required that they not marry and lead sexually 'pure' lives. The vow of obedience obligated the Brothers to do whatever their superiors, or their Bishop, required of them.

All of the above seemed highly demanding in the 1930s and seems almost more so these days when individual freedom is sacrosanct. As some compensation for their compliance the Order gave them bed and board during their lifetime in this world, and they were assured of a high place in Heaven in the next. As long as they didn't die in a state of 'mortal sin' they would be forever in the sight of God and so be assured happiness for the rest of eternity.

My life was about to undergo a massive change, and I was destined to leave what was really an idyllic life for a child, where I was surrounded with friends, pets and farm animals. Most of my parent's time and energy was spent running their business and I was able to wander at will doing as I liked (within reasonable limits).

When I went to get my Driver's Licence, the garage owner, Ike Neave said "My God, you've been driving for years!" so he sat and wrote the licence out for me without my having been tested.

They were good times, especially after Pampa Joe had retired and come to live with us. Every Saturday night Pampa and I went to the local film show, and I remember walking home after a film, with my mother following 100 metres behind us. She could see two glowing cigarettes in the dark ahead of her, but when she caught up to us there was only one. I had heard her footsteps and had wisely jettisoned my cigarette.

Pampa used to tell the story of an older relative who was dying in Oamaru, and wished to leave a large sum of money to Pampa. He sent someone to get the lawyer to remake his will that night. The lawyer said that he would come in the morning, but the relative died during the night, so Pampa missed out. When Pampa told the story listeners would sometimes say, "Money can't buy happiness!" And Pampa would reply, "I'd be prepared to risk it."

Most days when there was no school Pampa Joe and I walked out to the other block, and occasionally we picked up lost golf balls as we walked through the Kurow Golf Course. Pampa Joe had plenty of anecdotes to fill in the twenty-minutes that it took to get to the back paddock. One he told was about a racehorse he owned named Windsor who had won most of the races he contested. It must have been that they didn't 'put up the weights' in those days. Today, race officials increase the weight carried by horses that have been winning by putting extra weights in their saddle bags. This 'levels' the field so even horses with less form have a reasonable chance of winning.

Once when Joe was working, Joe's brother Mick, and another handler took off through Central Otago for a series of horse race meetings. They dyed Windsor's white fetlocks and decided to enter him in a race under the name "The Vagabond". This was in order to get better 'odds'. The odds determine the amount that a wager on a horse returns to the gambler. Better or higher odds meant a higher payout on any money they bet on a horse, if it came in first, second or third. 'The Vagabond' won his race and went back to his racing career as Windsor. It's fortunate it didn't rain on that occasion, or his fetlocks might have gone back to their original colour.

Although Windsor had kept winning and the handlers were collecting the stakes, they sent back to Joe for more money. Windsor's stakes were being spent on booze. I hope there was enough left to keep Windsor in oats because he deserved to be well fed. Dais said that Windsor's winning record was still being featured in the racing pages of the Otago Daily twenty years later.

From the time Arch had the butchery I was aware that animals were being killed on a weekly basis, but it didn't affect me negatively as I thought that was the way of the world. It all seemed natural and normal to me.

Once I was watching a large pig being killed for bacon. They shot it and cut its throat to bleed it. When it was lowered into a bath of scalding water before being retrieved to have the hair scraped off its carcass, the unexpected happened; as soon as the pig's back hit the water it exploded into life and sprayed hot water over the bystanders. Once we cooled ourselves off and put another bullet into the pig's head to make sure that it was quite dead, we had to repeat the scalding process. Things like this were neither shocking or a source of concern for me and just part of daily life.

Since Dais had decided I needed the protection of a cloistered environment she enrolled me at St. Kevin's, and preparations were made for me to go to Oamaru. We picked up all my gear for the new school at Hallensteins Store, which was the college supplier in Oamaru. Appropriately attired, off I went, bright eyed and bushy tailed to start a new life.

I later heard that my old teacher from the Kurow School, Mr. Blythe, said to his remaining pupils a week later "There was only one student who was any good and he's gone now, and I'm left with YOU!" Many of the boys and girls that I left behind in Kurow had good minds and were bright, but none I know of went on to gain secondary or tertiary qualifications.

Before leaving Kurow, my father gave me two pieces of advice; one good and the other bad. The good advice, (which was more of a threat) was, "If you don't work at school, you can come home and work in the butcher's shop." That was incentive enough for me to stay in school, as I wasn't keen to be a country butcher for the rest of my life. The bad advice was, "If you don't complain of anything at the school I'll give you five pounds at the end of each term." As butchers were paid six pounds a week, this was a magnificent incentive not to complain.

As you will see, I was extremely unhappy at St. Kevin's, but I suspect that had I ignored Arch's advice and complained, the situation would not have improved and I would have lost the promised five pounds as well.

CHAPTER 3

College Education at St. Kevin's
1938 – 1942

INTRODUCED CHARACTERS

MICK O'BRIEN, a fellow student whom the author shared the Dux award with in Junior School.
'BIG DIG' (short for 'Big Digger'), a teaching Brother at St. Kevin's who was the author's nemesis while there.
'PORK CHOP', one of Big Dig's 'pet' students.
JIM MUIR, one of the 6th form bullies who was 'the straw that broke this camel's back'.
BROTHER TOM, the Head Master at St. Kevin's.
Brothers 'ZEB' and PADDY CONNOLLY, class teachers at St. Kevin's.
JOHN HUGHES, one of the author's rugby team mates and a boxing opponent.

OAMARU, WHERE ST.KEVIN'S WAS SITUATED, WAS A small town of only 15,000 people but we thought of it as a large city, when compared to Kurow.

When I arrived at St Kevin's, it only had 100 pupils, and so was a fairly small school. The majority of students were boarders with a few 'day boys'. At that time, all the teachers were Irish Christian Brothers.

The school had been established at Red Castle. The magnificent red brick building, faced with Oamaru Stone, had been built by John Buckley at the beginning of the century. Buckley was the heir of his uncle, a land Baron, who lived in the previous century.

The brothers slept in the original building. Buckley's racing stables, which had been built to the same high standards as the castle, had been converted into school rooms. We slept in a new three story dormitory block that had washing facilities at one end, and we ate our meals in the large dining room on the ground floor.

The domestic work was taken care of by half a dozen women who lived in a cottage down by the tennis courts. The Matron managed the staff and acted as medical advisor to the students. Each afternoon, at 5 p.m. she dispensed aspirin and kind words to those pupils who turned up at the kitchen door on 'sick parade'.

St Kevin's was the antithesis of my lifestyle in Kurow. Suddenly I found myself leading a semi-monastic existence. Unless we had to go into Oamaru to the dentist or for essential shopping, we were restricted to the school grounds. We were woken each morning with the birds and our first stop was to hear mass in the unheated Chapel. We were encouraged to fast overnight and go to Holy Communion during mass. This meant that we hadn't had anything to eat or drink since the previous evening. We looked forward to breakfast despite the bread being kept until it was two to three days old. Maybe this was to discourage ravenous, conspicuous consumption and the sin of gluttony.

Our head master was Brother Tom, and we called him "Uncle Tom." He was a handsome man in his late fifties. Brother Tom was in good shape both physically and personally – I never heard him raise his voice and he always seemed stable and in control. He was an accomplished French speaker and could also teach German, Latin and English. Some said that he had studied at The Sorbonne, but I have no proof of this. He could well have been a tutor at University, his education was of such a high standard.

When my father and mother visited St. Kevin's, Brother Tom would invite Arch into his office and give him a whisky. Arch always said that the bottle seemed to be at the same level whenever he was offered a drink, so it was either not being used or those that used it replaced the whisky with the equivalent amount of water.

I cannot remember Uncle Tom doing anything unkind or unfair to the students, and have often wondered how he put up with some of the less educated brothers who relied on physical punishment to enforce their discipline.

Most of our Christian Brothers had been born in Australia but we had a few from Ireland and New Zealand. Their headquarters was in Ireland, but they were also well represented in Australia, where they ran both schools and orphanages for boys. They recruited young Catholic boys in New Zealand, who then undertook three-years of training to become brothers, at the Christian brothers training College at Strathfield in New South Wales, Australia. The new recruits, who were sometimes only fourteen years old, studied philosophy in the first year, theology in the second and in the final year they received teacher training. This left them light on 'life skills' and poorly educated for secondary teaching; often they were only one page ahead of us in the textbooks. I think most of them were teaching on a wing and a prayer, but there were a couple of exceptions that I will come to soon. In contrast to the three years training given to the teaching brothers, the Catholic priests had six or seven years preparation for the priesthood. Clearly, more importance was put on training the priests to save our souls, than for the brothers to educate our minds.

It was a proud Irish mother whose son became a priest as she was automatically elevated in the Catholic world and had immediate entry into the higher echelons of the Heavenly Host when she eventually went to claim her heavenly reward.

In large Catholic families of Celtic Ireland they picked out a boy for the cloth, and a girl to be a nun. The 'Island of Saints', as Ireland is sometimes known, exported thoroughbred racehorses, nuns and priests all over the world. The priests seemed to get home to Ireland regularly, often visiting Rome on the way. The racehorses and the nuns weren't so lucky. The horses never made it back, and the nuns infrequently, if at all. The Nuns were 'Brides of Christ' but he did not provide for his harem as generously as he did for their male counterparts.

One of the first things we were taught when we were installed at St.Kevin's, was the structure of the Catholic Church governance, both locally and world wide. We looked up to the Catholic hierarchy, which was arranged in a pyramid above us. Catholic lay people were the ground-troops of the church, and they were below, and respectful of the brothers. The priests could say Mass and produce the Body and Blood of Christ, and could release sin in the confessional so they were at the next level up. They lived in reasonable comfort, and had a housekeeper and car. The Monsignors were one level above the priests, and above them came the Bishops, Archbishops, the Cardinals, and finally at the apex of the pyramid, the Pope himself. At each step in the pyramid the authority and influence increased exponentially. The Pope's power reflected that of Pontifix Maximus, the chief Pagan priest of Ancient Rome. The Pope's armies have now dwindled, and only the Swiss and Noble Guards remain at the Vatican. Surprisingly, the Pope's moral authority remains and is possibly enhanced in this day and age.

In contrast to the priests and the higher echelons of the church, the brothers had an abstemious life. Abstemious is defined in The Oxford Dictionary as "not letting yourself have much food, alcohol or enjoyment". They certainly didn't indulge in many of this world's amusements, as they had taken vows of poverty, chastity and obedience.

Meanwhile, the Pope, who was at the top of the pyramid of power and influence, inherited all the power of St. Peter who had been appointed by Christ to rule his Church. Christ had given the keys of the kingdom of heaven to Peter, so it seemed obvious that if one offended the Pope, or his local representatives, your chance of getting to heaven was minimal and hardly worth considering. You would be the candidate for the 'Big Hole' or the 'Black Hole' and most of us knew that at the bottom of either hole, Hell awaited.

Because the Protestants didn't believe the Catholic Church's teachings, they would be greatly disadvantaged when they approached the 'Pearly Gates' of the Heavenly Kingdom and few would be admitted to the Divine Presence. Some of the brothers said that only a small minority of non-Catholics were going to get to Heaven. I can't remember anyone telling us that all of the Protestants were going to Hell, but if they weren't going to Heaven, their options were very limited under the Catholic system. It was obvious that the unfortunate Protestants were likely to end up in a situation with more heat than light. I was getting a mixed message because my father remained tolerant of Dais's Catholicism, while retaining his somewhat nominal adherence to Presbyterianism. He did not seem to know that he was going to Hell and I, wisely, refrained from enlightening him.

We were also told that if we died with only modest sins then we would first go to Purgatory where there was some suffering till we were purified and we could then join the queue for admission into Heaven. And in the case of dead relatives, we were assured that we could shorten their time in Purgatory with prayers and by giving money to priests to say Masses for them.

The object of all this abstemiousness and self restraint was to get oneself to Heaven. In Heaven we would forever have the Beatific Vision of God in all his Glory. We would have heavenly music – harps seemed to be popular – and this was to go on for ever and ever. Due to my lack of musical appreciation I never got to grips with the attraction of an eternal heavenly choir. It seemed to me that I would be bored very quickly, and the prospect of the same diet for an infinite time ahead would probably lead to incalculable damage to my person. I did not look forward to what others thought would be a happy, prolonged holiday in Heaven. I was, however, kept in line by the fear of an eternal Hell, which was much worse. Father Wall and my various teachers had sketched out the general idea about both options, and I will have more to say about Hell in the pages ahead.

At that impressionable young age, I admit that I believed what the brothers told me. These respected adults presented those frightful teachings to me as incontestable fact, and there was no alternative dogma available to me at that time. I knew that if I faltered in the practice of my faith and fell into sin, then the jaws of Hell yawned as an inevitable consequence. It has taken fifty years for me to get away from the fear of the fires of eternal damnation and even now I still feel a modest amount of trepidation, dread, anxiety,

The 1938 'Class Leaders' photo, with the author at the top left.

apprehension, fear or disquiet, when I talk of these matters. Yes, there is still something there, but I will press on for your sake, and my mental health.

In my final term in the junior school at St. Kevin's, when I was twelve, I was equal Dux with Mick O'Brien, and we had our photos in the school magazine as class leaders. I sat the scholarship exam for the senior school and while they said I didn't win it, I was given a half scholarship by Brother Tom. I suspect that they gave the full scholarship to an outside student to bring a new pupil into the college.

The half scholarship meant that my parents were asked to pay twelve pounds school fees per term, instead of the usual twenty-four. This may seem a small sum now, but my father sold a pound (440gms) of beef sausages for sixpence (5 cents) and pork sausages for nine pence (ten cents) . Twelve pounds ($24.00) would have purchased 480 pounds(220kg) of beef sausages. Now that's a lot of sausages in anyone's currency, and the brothers expected payment in traditional pounds. Dais wrote a check for the twelve pounds, plus an extra thirty shillings a term for my laundry to be done.

In the third form, which was the first year of the senior school, it all turned to custard. I was picked out for bullying by the 'Southland contingent', some of whom came from the coalmining towns of Ohai and Nightcaps. These boys were all older than me and they could fight. They didn't beat me up, but the constant threat of a beating and continual harassing made my life totally miserable. I tried to work out why I was picked on, but could come up with no idea at the time. I offer an explanation now; most of the boys at St. Kevin's were members of a group, which afforded some protection for them. They either had older brothers at the school already, or were part of a group who travelled together from areas like the West Coast, South Otago or Central Otago. As a single boy from Kurow, with no brothers or comrades through geographical links, I had no one to stick up for me.

Most of the boys in my year had only a passing interest in the subjects that we were being taught. It was sad that some of their fathers were doing hard physical work to keep them at boarding school, while they had no interest in learning. Most of the conversations between students, in my year, revolved around their home towns and families. Another main topic of conversation was Jack Doyle's horse racing betting syndicate, which had a wide following of clients. They were forever discussing their bets and coming races. If I was included in any conversations, the bullies would not allow me to participate and would tell the other pupils not to talk to me. Because of this I developed no friendships, and remained at the bottom of the pecking order - everybody had the right to remind me what an outcast I was.

As the weeks and months went by I remained unhappy and isolated. The Brothers never intervened, or perhaps they never saw what a miserable situation I was in. I felt the whole world was against me, but hesitated to tell Arch and Dais of my unhappiness. I was very aware of the second bit of advice Arch gave me when leaving Kurow and I knew that there was five pounds, the equivalent of a week's wages, waiting for me when I returned home as long as I didn't complain about anything at St. Kevin's. Five pounds was a lot of money and although I was very unhappy about my situation I wasn't going to risk losing it by complaining.

Because of my total isolation, life became so intolerable that I considered suicide. I can't remember how I planned to kill myself, since there was no gun immediately available. Hanging would require a rope and the ability to tie a slip-knot, so that was off the agenda. Poisoning wasn't an option as I didn't know of any poison. Perhaps I could just will myself to die? My dilemma was that I knew if I did choose suicide it would be a mortal sin, and I would be cast into Hell for all eternity. I suspected that would have been even worse than boarding school. So there I was, stuck in a living Hell and I didn't have to die to get there.

The bullying and isolation went on all through that year and into the fourth form, when it took a turn for the worse. Our teacher in the fourth form was a Brother called 'Big Dig' (short for 'Big Digger'). He seemed to be in his forties and was of medium height,

A group photograph of the Christian Brothers from Dunedin in 1936. 'Big Dig' is on the far left and Br. Tom in the centre front.

but was at least 30 pounds over weight. A roll of fat had formed around his neck and his abdomen was stretching the front of his soutane. He had a depressive nature, and we used to watch his face as he entered the classroom each morning, to gauge his mood. When he was frowning we knew that we were in for a rough day. The boys used to say that he was a boxing champion before he became a brother, but I have no proof of that. He was pretty handy with his fists and we didn't have to be much out of line for him to smash us in the face or the temple. While we were under Big Dig's rigid discipline, one of our fellow pupils, nick named 'Pork Chops' could do no wrong. He lived close by, and could go home for morning tea and return 20 minutes late to class and nothing would be said. My mother was told by one of the domestic staff at the school that the boy's mother supplied Big Dig with an occasional bottle of whisky, but I have no proof of that either.

Apart from the usual curriculum, we also had half-an-hour of Religious Studies before lunch. Our text was taken from 'Power's Manual' which was a small book with about 200 words per page. We were told to memorize a page each day. I usually sat in the second row behind Mick O'Brien, but for Religious Studies Mick was told to move from his front row desk and sit at the back. Big Dig then sat on Mick's desk with his knees a few inches from my face. One day he said, "Put up your hands, all those who know their Power's Manual."

The next moment I saw stars and was unconscious for several seconds. Big Dig had smashed his fist into the side of my head. He was known to punch a pupil for little or no reason, but this was the first time he'd hit hard enough to render anyone unconscious. If I had hit him back, I would have had to leave the school and Dais would have found that impossible to handle. Her whole life would have been wrecked.

It is some little consolation to know that teachers have been hitting pupils since Roman Times. Even in more modern times, the Irish used this technique for 'knocking sense' into the senseless. Today, a teacher wouldn't get away with striking a pupil and knocking them out. I wonder, too, how much damage has been done to young men over the last 2000 years as teachers have taken out their frustrations on them with their fists. From what I'm told about the treatment of girls in convent schools, they seemed to have got away with fewer beatings. They must be the better for that.

In retrospect, I think I would have been better off if I had gone on to Waitaki Boys High School. They had qualified teachers and a better curriculum and overall programme. As Waitaki was a public school they were obliged to accept all pupils that applied. At St. Kevin's there was some selection because it was unlikely that a parent would commit to the expense of sending a non-academic boy to board.

St. Kevin's examination results were much better than Waitaki's. This was achieved by us learning by rote with the brothers making no attempt to get us interested in knowledge for its own sake, or develop a love for learning. St. Kevin's was a factory designed to get good examination results by insisting pupils memorised prepared answers to probable exam questions. We were able to pass the exams, but retained little knowledge permanently, so remained basically uninformed. The brothers did their best for God's sake but they lacked basic education themselves. If you feel that I am too critical of the brothers you could be correct, but bear with me.

The day after I was knocked out, there was the same set up with Big Dig sitting over me. Once again Big Dig said, "Hands up those who know their Power's Manual." When I put up my hand to defend my head, Big Dig said, "Don't put up your hand unless you know your Power's Manual!" That was his big laugh for the day, but he had discovered an effective technique to beat religion OUT of my skull. I'd never been an ardent convert to Christ's message, and after Big Dig's concussion I was even less enthusiastic.

For the rest of the year that fat, menacing bully hovered over me like a black cloud, but especially so during Religious Studies. Whenever he posed a question, whatever my answer, I was in danger of being hit on the head. I spent most of my Religious Study time that year composing myself so that Big Dig would not be in a position to deliver a knock out punch. Big Dig had been able to concuss me from a sitting position so I was fortunate that he had not been standing. If so, he could have killed me.

This anxiety about being hit, and possibly knocked out again, caused me to go to pieces in face-to-face oral examinations. Later on, during the oral exams at University and medical school, I would develop a fast pulse, break out in a sweat and stumble over answers. My anatomy professor at medical school twice told me that I was so nervous during the oral exams that he thought I should consider giving up on medicine. I was always able to cope with written exams, but oral continued to be a trial for me. I knew that Big Dig was the cause, and five years later when he was at the Christian Brother's School in Dunedin, I went to see him to tell him how his behaviour had affected me. He listened to me, but I could see that my complaints didn't touch him. I saw not a glimmer of compassion for the damage he had done to me. I can see now that he was a very unhappy man and should never have been allowed the responsibility of teaching boys in a boarding school.

Nowadays everybody seems to know about Manic Depressive Disorder, and being Bi-polar, but although I never saw Big Dig in a manic phase, I suspect he must have been a uni-polar performer in the dance of depression. He has since gone on to his final reward. If he does become aware of this book and makes comment I will let you know in the revised edition.

I was so unhappy at school because of being bullied, it began to dawn on me that I couldn't be less happy if I fought back. We were given some basic boxing skills at sports training, and in the previous eighteen months I had grown a few inches and, dare I say it, had developed a few muscles in my shoulders and upper arms. I knew enough to keep my left arm out straight and use my right arm to defend my face. Boxers who keep their right arm out are called 'South Paws'. I must have been a North Paw.

Halfway through this fourth form year, when I was fourteen, I was in the sixth form room with half a dozen others when Jim Muir, one of the sixth form students, decided to throw me out. Jim was two years older and four inches taller than me, but as he grabbed me to push me out of the room, I hit him in the face and his nose started to bleed. Soon, twenty or thirty students had magnetically gathered around as we continued our punch up on the grass outside the schoolroom. I can still feel my fingers slipping in his blood as I closed my hand to make a fist. I kept hitting his face and dollops of his blood flew into the air and down on to his shirt. After a few minutes my fear disappeared and I began to enjoy myself. While I was able to hit him on the face each time he came within arms length, I was not being hurt by any of his blows to my chest and shoulders.

For the first time I felt the power that comes with physical superiority in a fight. As Jim's enthusiasm for the contest waned mine waxed. The anxiety and depression I had endured for years dropped away in seconds and I began to feel half human. It was as if Christmas had come early yet it was only half way through the year.

We had been going at it for five minutes and the thirty spectators, were becoming vocal. Suddenly the head master, Brother Tom, walked around the corner and the crowd melted away like snow before the sunshine. It was still winter, but it felt like spring to me, and as a result of this punch-up my status in the school changed overnight. Life became bearable, or even enjoyable, and the boys who had talked down to me a month previously now called me "Champ" and praised my fighting ability.

While I enjoyed my new status, I also resolved never to use my physical ability to threaten or bully others. I don't know what became of the senior boys who had initiated and continued my bullying over the previous two years. I have not seen their names in the Queen's Birthday Honours list, but neither have I seen them in the 'Court Reports', so maybe their bullying tendencies were modified by the rough and tumble of life. Perhaps they are leading ordinary lives, reading the newspaper, watching T.V. and passing helpful comments to their family and friends about life locally, and what the government is doing centrally. They may be kind to children and little dogs, and help old ladies across the road and if they learned enough at school to read this book they at least remain literate; if they can't read for whatever reason, perhaps some kindly person might read it for them.

As I think about those dark years in my life, I wonder how many young people are permanently damaged from bullying by older students or teachers. Both the bullied and bullies must be damaged by it and could well carry the effects into later life. I was certainly affected, and the damage carried on through my eight years of medical school and junior hospital work. I think my scars have now healed, but then you might think otherwise as you read on. I also hope that the teachers these days are on the look out for bullying, and have the power and ability to detect it along with the capacity to stamp it out.

There was more to my life at St. Kevin's than being bullied. Big Dig, besides directing us in our spiritual life, gave us guidance on family life. He said that when we were married we should stay with one set of tradesmen and not switch around. He also said that we should be on our guard once we left school, as there were plenty of predatory Protestant girls out there, ready and willing to seduce good Catholic boys at short notice. I couldn't get out of school fast enough to find these girls who were waiting to throw themselves at me so willingly. Sadly however, I found these friendly and alluring ladies to be absent, both at university and in the hospital world. Later it dawned on me that since Big Dig was mistaken in this area, he could also be wrong about other matters of Christian dogma which affect the here and now, and the eternity that lies ahead for us all.

Emotionally and physically, I was in better shape when I was fifteen. As I moved on to the fifth form, the bullying was long gone and I was a bit of a star. 'Zeb' was our new teacher's nickname. He was a step up as teachers went, because he was doing a B.A. by correspondence, and he impressed me as being slightly more broadminded and better educated than some of my earlier teachers. He still relied on corporal punishment to focus our attention, if he thought that we were drifting off into a mild delirium.

Like most of the Brothers, he didn't show much enthusiasm for teaching, except when giving us 'six of the best'. The Brothers used a leather strap, which was two pieces of hard leather stitched together so that it was rigid. When using the strap, Zeb's eyes would light up, his breathing rate would increase and he used all the force he could muster when bringing that strap down in a large arc, onto our hands. It was important to keep your hand up as high as possible so that you didn't get the full benefit of his swing. On one occasion, the boy being punished simply moved his hand to the side as the strap came down, and it went on to hit Zeb on the knee. This led to weak smiles and suppressed giggles as we thought this was the best 'show' of the season. We were unable to display our approval in the conventional way by clapping or cheering, lest we be brought up in front of the class for a repeat session, to be part of the 'second act'.

Out of boredom one day in class, I made faces at Zeb. He called me out and gave me six of the best in front of the class. This enhanced my reputation, because they said I didn't even blink when the strokes from the leather strap hit my hand. The class was mystified as to why I had been attacked so unjustly, and I had their sympathy for days after that.

During that year, we attended a weeklong 'spiritual retreat'. For the whole week we had long sermons and a lot of time to meditate on life now and into the future. The retreat was always conducted by a priest. On this occasion we had a Dominican called Father O'Brien, who had been especially trained for this work.

He told us that the Dominican Order had been founded by St. Dominic in 1215 and was officially called 'The Order of Friars Preachers'. They were influenced by St. Thomas Aquinas who lead them to the study of Aristotle. They were heavily involved in converting the Albigensian heretics of southern France. Father O'Brien did not reveal to us that his order were entrusted with the execution of the Spanish Inquisition, which was characterised by brutal death and torture, after 1230. His Dominican legacy positioned him well to deal with wavering school boys at St. Kevin's in 1941. I can still see him walking around the college in his hooded robe and leather sandals without socks. He was a good-looking man in his early forties and he gave us 'the full treatment'. He let us know what it was all about to be a Catholic in the twentieth century. Briefly stated, he told us, "that before Christ died he said to his disciple, Peter "Thou art Peter (Latin for 'rock') and on this rock I found my church and I give you the keys to my Kingdom".

In this way, Peter had been given Christ's power on Earth and the right to allow the dead to pass through the gates of Heaven and enter God's presence. Peter's successor was the Pope, who wields Christ's Power through the same authority. This authority, in turn, transfers down through the Church's hierarchy until the priest in front of us was speaking with the authority of Christ himself. If we wanted to be happy in this life, and the next, we knew we should listen to him closely.

Whenever the Pope speaks Ex-cathedra from the Papal throne, his statements and rulings are infallible, or impossible to be wrong. Whatever the church proclaims on earth is 'God's will', and the Pope has the keys to the Gates of Heaven. If you were planning a happy eternity you knew where to place your bets to be sure of a dividend. Those outside of the Catholic church have a rock bottom chance of making it to Heaven as the Pope in Rome is unlikely to pull out his keys and open the 'Pearly Gates' for them.

This same priest also told us that there was an 'unforgivable sin' but never told us exactly what it was, and I don't know what it is to this day. However the sin that really got up his nostrils was the secret sin of masturbation. He said that men in mental hospitals "abused themselves" and inferred that if we continued our secret sins we would dilute our brain power and end up in mental institutions. Father O'Brien said that if we fell into 'mortal' or 'serious' sin, and if we died with any of these sins un-confessed, we would go directly to Hell and stay there for all eternity. If our minds strayed for only a few seconds to a forbidden sexual subject it was a mortal sin. I found it impossible to keep my thoughts off sexual things, so was forever worrying that I was in a state of mortal sin, and in danger of going to Hell.

Fr. O'Brien told us a story of two good friends who made an agreement that the first one to die would come back and tell the other about the after life. One died and came back on a night a month later, and (wait for it!) told his friend "There IS a Hell, and I AM IN IT!!!"

The concept of Mortal Sin in the Catholic Church was its greatest weapon in those days, and possibly still is. A Catholic, who remained in a state of mortal sin, went straight to Hell. To remedy this, you needed to be absolved, or find forgiveness, of your sinful action. There were two ways of achieving this; to go to Confession where the priest would give you a penance and then absolve you, or to make an Act of Perfect Contrition yourself, without the help of a priest. The catch was that you could not be sure if God had accepted your Act of Contrition. The priest's absolution at confession, on the other hand, was guaranteed.

If a Catholic was consigned to the fiery gates of Hell through dying in mortal sin he stayed there for eternity. There was no chance to visit Purgatory, where some blame could be worked off. It seemed to me that Confession was simple enough, and you knew that you were back in 'business' afterwards, It was safer to go to Confession regularly and be sure that we had, once again, escaped the fires that burn but don't consume. Since I was in a recurrent state of mortal sin, I might as well masturbate happily until I could get to Confession and once again get back in God's good grace and have a fresh start.

The priest in the confessional must have endured a boring repetition of adolescent confessions and I don't know how he avoided snoozing off. Most of my penances seemed to be "Three Our Fathers and three Hail Marys!" After each confession I knew that Hell was no longer looming for me and I would become quite ecstatic. It wasn't as big a 'high' as when I beat Jim Muir in a fair fight, but it was close.

Fr. O'Brien continued to reinforce our fears by explaining that Heaven and Hell were eternal and he explained eternity as follows; "If there was a mountain of sand and every hundred years a little bird came and took away one small grain of sand, when he had taken away the mountain of sand then ETERNITY WAS JUST BEGINNING!"

I've explained why the concept of an eternity in Heaven didn't appeal to me, but the prospect of Hell was not an attractive option either. Father O'Brien said that if we were confined to Hell for all eternity we were to have the exquisite pain of our bodies being burnt. However, the fires would not consume our flesh, so the pain would continue for ever and ever. He did not tell us if amputees had their limbs restored after they died, or comment on those who had lost an eye or an ear or a testicle or a breast. I was left thinking that they would be at an advantage in Hell since they would not have as much area to be burnt. I was left with a yo-yo choice between harp music and scorching flesh that stayed intact. Hearing Fr. O'Brien's description of Hell fires was enough to stop me masturbating, or even thinking about it, for the rest of the week.

Fr. O'Brien told us that Heaven and Hell were physical places, with Heaven being above the clouds and Hell somewhere below the earth. After Christ and the Blessed Virgin had died, their bodies were taken to Heaven, where they remain uncorrupted. One of the Old Testament prophets had also been given the same treatment. This was told to we students with the authority of the Pope, who when speaking on matters of doctrine was infallible. I found this confusing, as we were taught that God was in Heaven, but it wasn't clear if God was in human form. Since Michelangelo had personified God as an old man with a thick beard and Christ and Mary's bodies were intact in Heaven, I had no doubt that Heaven was a physical place.

Further confusion was presented in the concept of God's Trinity, 'The Father, The Son and The Holy Ghost'. We just had to believe that the Trinity was possible, and the details of how all this was accomplished would be revealed to us when we died. I just needed to have faith.

Then there was another place for babies that had died before they could be baptized. They were forever to be left in Limbo. More recently, I have read in my local paper, that the Catholic Church now says that Limbo is a mistake. I thought Limbo was part of the infallible teaching of the Pope, but if he is infallible how could this be wrong? I wonder what other infallible teachings will be found to be false in the future?

My life became an emotional seesaw. The brothers kept telling us to pray for the grace of a happy death, which meant dying in the arms of Mother Church. I'm not sure that death was a great threat to my fellow students, as most of them had no real experience of it. I on the other hand did. I knew, for example, that my father was always running over my puppies, and that sheep and cattle were being killed on a weekly basis, so death was everyday reality to me.

I was grateful for the emotional respite school holidays brought. At Kurow, I was able to ride my ex-racehorse called 'Money Spider' around the town and on the new farm that Arch had bought over the river, at Hakataramea. I felt like a prince as the cars from down country drove by. There were few vehicles in those days, and the well-dressed occupants seemed interested in the country boy doing his thing on a large horse, with three or four dogs in attendance.

When we were driving cattle and we needed them to move faster we would get the dogs to bark together. If that didn't work, the next stage was to persuade the dogs to bite the hocks of the cattle. After a while, when the dogs barked the cattle took notice, because they knew that if they didn't move their backsides their rear legs would be threatened. When the cattle kicked backwards the mature dogs had the sense to be long gone, but several younger dogs met their end when they were kicked in the head.

I was driving half a dozen big bullocks, over the half kilometre one way bridge to Haka during the holidays, when a car came towards me from the far side. There was a large notice at each end of the bridge telling drivers not to go on the bridge if there was a vehicle or stock already crossing. The car stopped thirty yards from us, on the bridge, and the occupants stared at the large bullocks with their impressive set of horns. I told the dogs to "speak up," and the cattle responded by leaping forward. There was only a three-foot space on the right side of the car and the bullocks tried to fit through it, two at a time, with only limited success. The last bullock decided to drag his hind hoof over the car's bonnet. I can still see the wide-eyed expressions of horror on the faces of the front seat occupants as this happened. I was able to get the horse past the car and the occupants didn't complain to me about their exciting unscheduled stop. Doubtless they made good currency regaling their friends about their adventure in the country.

When I was fifteen, I was on the 'first fifteen rugby team'. The main game of the season was against Waitaki Boys High School. We had never beaten Waitaki, because their school had five times as many students as ours, but in the last five minutes of the game, John Hughes dropped a goal that put us into the lead. I have never before or since been subjected to such rough treatment in the field, but we survived and won.

I wasn't so fortunate in my school boxing match that year because the same John Hughes, who was older, taller and stronger than me, knocked me out in the first round. Pampa Joe and my father witnessed my demise, and fellow students told me later that neither of them blinked an eye as I went down and out.

At the end of the year, I passed my 'School Certificate' and went on to the sixth form where our teacher was Brother Connolly. We called him 'Paddy' as he was from Ireland. He told us about the Catholic priests teaching the Irish children their 'letters' under the hedges, because it was illegal under English law for Catholic children to be taught in schools. He gave the impression that this had happened just the previous week, but now I know that Catholic emancipation occurred in 1829, and Irish Independence in 1922.

The Irish, many of whom had a high level of alcoholism, illiteracy and dyslexia had their work cut out to leave the label 'Bog Irish' behind. Those who came here in the late 1800s, must have had a dilemma working out their loyalties between Church and State. Paddy said that if English law was contrary to Moral law or Church law, then it was quite all right to ignore English Law. As Church law and the Moral Law seemed to run in tandem, a good Catholic could have the luxury of choice between the two. If he flouted the Church law he would be threatened with Mortal Sin, and the possibility of ending up in Hell. If he neglected English Law, he could well get away with it. English Law was often the loser.

In my final year at the college, Big Dig didn't allow me to fight in the school's Heavy Weight Boxing Championship. John Hughes had moved on, and I was the obvious candidate, but instead he chose two boys who had tried out for the event the previous year. I felt that I could have been the Champion had I been allowed to compete. I was never given an explanation for why I wasn't chosen, and it bothered me for years.

Big Dig's bullying and dislike (or possibly hatred) of me blighted my time at school. Just to give another example, I felt that I was by far the best contender for the 'Best all rounder Cup'. Big Dig changed the rules that year so that anyone who had already won a cup could not be awarded a second. I had already won the cup for speech, so the best all rounder was given to another student, who was a good sportsman and a favourite of the brothers, but didn't participate in three of the seven qualifying categories for the overall award.

The brothers continued guiding us in God's ways and reinforcing his message by putting the fear of Hell into us. They enjoyed few comforts and had to accept a small single room in an institution, indifferent food, social isolation and no consoling warmth in bed at night as their lot. It was hoped that they would inspire a superior generation of Catholic men. Sadly, I don't think this happened, as the students I know of generally made only average contributions to society.

The brothers might as well have trained as lay-teachers and lived an ordinary life in the community, without the constraints of the order. The experience of marriage, parenthood and familial warmth would have served them well and increased their chances of becoming well rounded adults, with positive experiences and qualities worth passing onto their students.

My time at St. Kevin's College finally came to an end. You will make your own judgement as to whether I was maimed or enlightened by my experiences there. At least it helped me escape a future as a butcher in Kurow.

CHAPTER 4

Otago Medical School
1943 – 1950

INTRODUCED CHARACTERS

DAVID, the author's friend from St. Kevin's who also went to Dunedin.
REVEREND HAROLD TURNER, who ran Arana, a boarding College in Dunedin.
MRS.DENMEAD, Arana's Matron.
HATCH FOUKES, a student doing the medical course.
DR ECCLES, Professor of Physiology and Nobel Laureate.
BILL ADAMS, Professor of Anatomy.
JIM GWYNNE, another student.
RON ELVIDGE, a student playing in the Varsity A rugby team who also Captained the 'All Blacks' (New Zealand's National rugby side).
GRAEME MOORE, the captain of the Varsity A rugby team who was also an All Black.
BETH GRAVES, a member of the Graves family with whom the author boarded.
TESSA, the author's dance partner and lady-friend.
PROFESSOR HERCUS, Dean of the Medical School.
MARION O'CONNOR (nee MAJOR), who married the author's good friend from Kurow, Kevin O'Connor.
JACK SKINNER, brother of Kevin who was an All Black.
MANAGER OF CLIFF HANNOM, who was a professional boxer from Timaru.
DID VORITH, an ex-All Black.

THE DECISION TO GO TO DUNEDIN WAS A TURNING point in my life and it was a good one. It certainly beat returning to Kurow to work in my parent's butcher shop. My school friend, David and I were accepted at Arana Hall, which had just been established as a new boarding college for men at the university.

The Reverend Harold Turner ran it, and the kindly Mrs. Denmead was Matron.

Dunedin had established New Zealand's first university in 1869 and the students were well accepted by the community, because the university was their biggest industry. In the first year we did what was called 'Medical Intermediate', where we studied physics, chemistry and zoology. At the end of the year there was a competitive exam. The students who had scored the highest marks then progressed to their second year at the medical school, situated next to the hospital.

I soon became intrigued with zoology and biology, and developed an interest in chemistry. However, physics was a problem for those of us who had not studied it previously, as we had no real understanding of the basics. We were reduced to memorizing the complex formulae and hoping we could reproduce them in exams.

Some of the students were servicemen coming back from WWII and were able to get preferential entry to the medical school with only a pass mark. The rest of us had to compete with them, but gain higher marks to be accepted for the second year. We didn't resent the servicemen who had borne the burden of years of active service, but the occasional one who had served only a few months of cushy service, but still enjoyed the easier entry requirement, did annoy us. There were a few young women attempting the course, but I don't remember any of them being military veterans.

At the end of the year I passed easily in the three main subjects, but only achieved modest marks in organic chemistry, which I had considered to be my strongest subject. I knew that I had done a good paper so I thought that perhaps part of my submitted exam material had been lost. I applied for a recount, but the numbers came back the same. As a result, I had to sit a special exam at the beginning of the following year. This time I passed well and was qualified to enter medical school, but the entry date was twelve months away. While I waited I took subjects towards a Bachelor of Science degree. I was only eighteen-years-old at the time and I hated wasting this year, but I now realise that the extra time to sort myself out was helpful.

The general public, and girls in particular, didn't acknowledge the existence of medical students in the early years. They only took notice of us after we were third-year or fourth-year medical students. By that time, they knew that we had a good likelihood of becoming doctors, with a reasonable earning capacity. They knew that, sooner or later, they would be in need of our services in the future, if only to sign their death certificate.

In the second year we went on to study anatomy, where we dissected human cadavers. The bodies had either been donated through wills, or were those of unclaimed paupers and had been preserved in large vats of liquid formaldehyde, suspended by their ears. They would be taken out of the vats and laid out on tables for us and covered with wet cloths so they didn't dry out.

I am intrigued that we all start our lives floating in our mother's uterus, suspended in amniotic fluid before birth and there is the possibility that some of us will end up suspended in another liquid after death.

When Lord Nelson's body was brought back to port in H.M.S. Victory after the British triumph at Trafalgar, his body was preserved in a barrel of rum. I suppose the anatomy department at Otago felt formalin was a better preservative and avoided the possibility of their medical students wafting rum through the streets of Dunedin.

Most students were shocked when they first walked into the large room with the ten bodies laid out on tables. I must have been immune to some extent, as I was forever seeing stock being killed and carcasses hanging and then being cut up in Kurow, and was not disturbed by the sight at all.

There were a number of stories that kept going the rounds during my time in medical school. One was about a student who looked out of the dissecting room window and saw a man in the grounds pushing a heavily laden wheelbarrow. The student called out, "Do you want a hand?" and when the labourer said, "Yes", the boy threw a dissected hand down to him. The second story was about Dr. Hatch Foukes, who was a prominent rugby player and took a leisurely twelve years to complete his medical training. During one of his oral anatomy exams, the professor came into the room holding a large human bone behind his back. He presented the bone to Hatch and said, "What is this bone Mr. Foukes?" Hatch replied, "It's a femur, Sir!" The examiner then asked, "Which side is it from?" And Hatch replied, "I'm not going for Honours, Sir!" Fouke's parents became fed up with supporting him at medical school, and told him he had to give up playing rugby for Otago and concentrate on his studies. As the story goes, when his parents listened to Otago rugby on the radio the commentator kept saying, "This Mr. Smith is playing brilliantly", referring to Hatch Foukes who was playing under an assumed name.

My parents were paying for my studies, but I consoled myself with the thought that I was a much better investment than the trotting horses that my father was training in Kurow. At this time he employed a young man full-time to exercise the trotters at the Kurow racecourse. My father's horse Ginger Joe won a few races but my mother's horse, Daisy Mae failed to win. Daisy Mae was sold to an Australian who used her as a brood mare. She was more successful in this line, and became a prominent breeder, because her progeny were all winners.

Professor Bill Adams, the Anatomy Professor, was of average height, with a hooked nose and fierce dark eyes that drilled into us. He was a dominant character and was known for handing out severe punishments if a student gained his displeasure. We had every reason to fear him, as our futures were in his hands. It was up to him to assess our papers and determine our mark. If we failed our anatomy exams in the second year, we could be thrown out of the medical school. We were careful to follow his rules. A student coming to the door late for a lecture would be greeted with a loud "GET OUT!" and have his way out pointed to by the irate professor.

I had no difficulty with the physiology course in the second and third years. It was less of a memory exercise and I coped with the reasoning well enough to be in the upper third of the class.

The Physiology Professor was John Eccles who was a tall, rather quiet man, who lectured us occasionally but spent most of his time and energy in researching the electro-chemical transmission of impulses in the nervous system. This study led to his being named as a Nobel Laureate, as he continued this research after he had moved on from Otago. He went to our local Catholic church and read from his missal during the long and dreary sermon given by our priest. I asked my confessor if I could read during the sermons too, but he turned me down flat. Perhaps he thought I wasn't as smart as the professor and deserved to be bored for Christ's sake.

I passed the second year exams and progressed to the third year, where we had the same subjects. At the end of the third year I failed the anatomy exam by two marks. Along with twelve others, I had to return for a repeat exam called 'Specials'. Only two of us passed the second time, and again, I failed by two marks. This high failure rate was unexpected, as normally only one or two would fail this exam. We soon learned that politics had raised its ugly head, and was the possible reason for the higher failure rate. Prof. Adams had been upset because a visiting professor from Hong Kong had been sent to his department, for a year's study leave. Bill didn't want another professor in his department, but had been overruled by university administrators the day before our exam. It seemed that we took the brunt of Bill's displeasure over this decision.

To fail us because of his personal upset was unjust. As I had to repeat the year, I took some more science subjects and made the best of a bad situation. Later, during the repeat year while I was sitting in the dissecting room Bill Adams came up to me and said, "Don't work too hard this year Mr. Valentine, you'll be okay at the end." I took this to mean that Bill's conscience had troubled him, and he regretted failing me and the others in the 'Specials' during the previous year. Fortunately, at year's end, showing less nervousness than the year before, I passed my oral anatomy exam. Bill did not repeat his advice, to "give up on medicine". I was now free to advance to the fourth year, where we were introduced to the clinical subjects of medicine, surgery and pathology.

One of my contemporaries, Jim Gwynne (who eventually became a professor of Pathology), told this story about a confrontation I had with Bill Adams in my fourth year. During first term, I had walked from the hospital and was entering the enormous swinging doors of the medical school. These doors must have weighed 300 lbs and had an 18-inch brass kick plate at the bottom and swung on massive brass hinges. I had discovered that if I jumped towards the door and put my heel hard on the ground and the ball of my foot on the door, I could flick it open. As soon as the door had burst open I could jump through, before it could swing back and injure me.

On this particular occasion I kicked the door open and jumped through, almost landing on the feet of my old antagonist Prof. Bill Adams. His eyes shot wide open and he burst out, "You will kill somebody doing that Mr. Valentine!" I retorted "I'm sorry I missed you Bill!" I headed down the corridor without pausing as I didn't want to continue the conversation. I later heard that Prof. Adams made a complaint to the Dean of the Medical school about the incident, but nothing more was said and it passed into history. The only reason I was able to get away without punishment was that I had already passed from third year, so had moved from Bill's realm of influence.

Very few students rented flats in those days and David and I stayed at Arana Hall for three years. One late night, some of the Arana Hall students planned a raid on Carrington Hall, which housed both men and women. We tried to arrange it so that we could get into Carrington, wreak havoc, and be out in ten minutes. I can still remember bursting into the Carrington Hall bedrooms and seeing the startled wide eyed students, as we threw them out of bed. Carrington authorities rang Reverend Turner to complain that the Arana Hall students were wrecking the place. Rather than rush over to the scene of the crime, he simply went into our bedrooms at Arana Hall and ticked off any rooms with empty beds. We were caught, and those of us on the raid were told we could no longer live at Arana Hall, although some of us could still take our meals there. David and I were able to get a basement room at a house

Hell-Bent for Life

down the hill. We were among those allowed to return for meals, but the room wasn't ideal, so we started looking for alternate accommodation.

Kevin O'Connor, my childhood friend from Kurow, had been at medical school for four years and heard that I was looking for board. Kevin had grown into a six foot two inches tall man and was built like a barn. He was playing for the Varsity A and Otago rugby teams. Kevin was boarding with the Graves family and he asked them to take me in as an extra boarder and they agreed to let me share a room with him. The Graves family consisted of three brothers and their sister, Beth. All were single and in their forties. Beth did all the housework; the cooking, washing, cleaning, mending and – can you believe it? – she also made our beds! Beth's brothers were not totally indolent and took turns at putting the garbage out once a week, and mowed the lawns when necessary. They all retained their sporting interests, and played cricket and rugby, so I guess they were too busy for the mundane work of housekeeping. During this time I continued to train at the university boxing club. Even now some of my friends tell me that I fought Kevin Skinner, the All Black Captain, for the heavy weight University Boxing Championship. In fact, it wasn't Kevin, but his brother, Jack Skinner. In that bout Jack was given the decision, but I wasn't knocked out, so that was a pleasant change.

A few of us from the University boxing club had been invited to spar with Cliff Hannom, a professional boxer from Timaru. Jack Skinner hit Cliff and stunned him. Cliff responded by knocking Jack to the ground. As I was next in the ring I saw a padded head guard there and said, "That looks like it would fit me" and put it on. When I went in to the ring I was very careful not to annoy Cliff unnecessarily and survived to fight another day.

When we were ready to leave the gym that day we were standing at the top of the stairs with our gear. Cliff Hannom's manager called to us and said, "Thank you boys, please come back tomorrow." We left, and when we got to the bottom of the stairs we looked at each other. I said to Jack, "Well, I won't be back." And he replied, "I won't be coming back either!"

Kevin O'Connor was talented both mentally and physically. He had a great pair of hands when playing rugby, and had won the mile event at his inter-secondary school championships while Ron Elvidge, who was another good all-rounder, won the shorter distances.

When Kevin took his French exams in his last year of high school, the examiners told him that he had obtained the highest marks ever awarded in that subject. Sometimes during the time we boarded together and shared a room, I would be restless because there was an important rugby match the next day. Kevin would come in at night, lie down and say, "Goodnight," and go to sleep immediately.

Sometimes on Saturdays, I would be mistaken for Kevin. Being mistaken for Kevin tickled my ego, until one day when I was a spectator at Carisbrook Rugby Grounds. As the Otago team ran on, a young man in front of me said, "Here comes Mr. O'Connor, the biggest and ugliest man in the Otago team!"

Most Saturday nights I'd go to Joe Brown's Town Hall Dance where I would try to keep my feet away from my partner's toes. The dances often ended at midnight, and I would sometimes offer to accompany one of my dance partners, Tessa, home. She lived in St. Kilda, one of Dunedin's outer suburbs. We would travel by electric tram and then I would walk Tessa to her house from the tram stop. On the tram, she would often let me cuddle her, and on most nights when we walked down the side streets to her home, she would kindly masturbate me. I can't remember getting semen over our clothes, so we must have been tidy little house keepers.

I had to catch the last tram back to town at about 2 a.m. to avoid the long walk home. One night, as I walked back to the tram stop near Tessa's home, I heard the tram coming and raced to catch it. I can still see this tram in my memory; it had not slowed for the empty tram-stop and was rocking along at full speed, a hundred meters ahead of me. I ran as fast as I could but had no hope of catching it so I had to walk the three miles to the town centre and a further two to get home. As taxis passed me they slowed, hoping I would hail them. I was stupid to continue walking, as I had the fare for the taxi. However, I consoled myself during this post-midnight hike by getting a meal of 'pea-pie-pud' at the central pie-cart. This local Dunedin delicacy was a dish made of peas, pie and potato and cost nine pence. I think I became less interested in Tessa after that incident. My elation at being ejaculated was well and truly dissipated after I had walked the two hours home.

I have heard that many male medical students donated sperm at various fertility clinics during these years. I don't think they were paid, so I suppose they did it for the common good; "Act locally, think globally." What a shame for me to have wasted all that semen with Tessa's benevolent help, but as my genetic makeup has tendencies to dyslexia, depression, dipsomania, asthma and obesity the infertility clinics would have been better to search elsewhere for their semen. I can't think of any good I would have achieved with a donation.

While we were boarding together, a scout from England offered Kevin a place in the Wigan Rugby League Club. He was to be paid eight pounds for a win, five for a draw and three pounds for a loss as well as being guaranteed a junior medical position at a local large hospital. In this way, Kevin would be available to play for the Wigan club and generate a good income while practising medicine. Kevin went to Professor Hercus, the Dean of the Medical School, who said, "Oooooh, Mr. O'Connor, that would be professional sport. Don't take it and maybe I will get you a hospital position later on, perhaps in North America." When the North American possibility eventuated, the salary offered was so poor it wasn't possible for Kevin to accept it. He would have been much better off going to Wigan.

Rugby writers wrote that Kevin was the unluckiest man "never to have been an All Black". One year they had picked the team and the selectors were tossing up the possibility of selecting either an extra forward or back. They took an extra back, but had they taken an extra forward, it would have been Kevin. Unbelievably the same thing happened next year. This didn't seem to upset Kevin and he took it in his usual gentle stride. Perhaps this lack of aggression in his personality held his rugby career back. Whenever he tried to push me around and I got ready to respond, he always pulled back and said something like, "I'll leave it for now and get you next time".

In the end, Kevin went off to England for three years. I didn't hear any news of him playing rugby, so perhaps he was injured. I suspect he may have contracted tuberculosis, as this was common in young doctors in those days. The more effective, modern treatments for T.B. had not been developed, and the tuberculosis patients were rested in beds in tuberculosis wards for months or years until the condition cured itself. Some of my colleagues were admitted to hospital with T.B., and one young man I trained with died from it.

Kevin was engaged to a tall and glamorous girl named Marion Major. They were married in England and spent their honeymoon in a multi-story hotel, where the washrooms and toilets were on the landing between the floor levels. Marion got out of bed during the night to go to the toilet. When she woke up in the morning she was in bed with a very large black man. Both of them were more than surprised, and rushed to get dressed. She had obviously returned to the wrong level and entered the wrong room – she'd slept the night with the wrong man! You would have to have known Marion to understand this. She was a dreamer who seemed to drift around in her own world, quite removed from reality. One Sunday, after she was married, she was talking to a neighbour over the fence. An alarm bell must have rung in her stomach as she said, "Oh dear, I haven't eaten since Friday!" For most of us, missing one meal would be significant, but by half a dozen we would be ravenous if not rabid. Kevin did most of the cooking and housework, which was unusual in a male in the 1950s. He was well prepared for domesticity, as my mother told me that "Kevin's father always opened the door with an apron around his waist."

In my fourth year, I started to play on the University B Rugby Team, and in my fifth year I played for Varsity A.

Eventually I started my sixth and final year of medical school. I kept up my rugby playing and at the beginning of the rugby season I had a run in with Graeme Moore, who was a fullback. At the time he was also playing for The All Blacks. Graeme's girlfriend was an attractive staff nurse in the emergency room at the hospital. She had started to show some interest in me, and that didn't suit Graeme at all. One afternoon at Rugby practice, when I came up to him with the ball he tackled me harder than necessary and we started to fight. Graeme was the Captain of the A Team and after that fight I was made a reserve, but this didn't suit me, so I went off and played for the B's. Graeme eventually married the lovely nurse that we had quarrelled over. I would like to be able to say that they lived happily ever after. I hope they did.

As the end of the sixth year approached the final exams loomed over us. We had to sit surgery, medicine, gynaecology and obstetrics exams. I still disliked oral exams, but was not as nervous as I had been when facing previous anatomy orals under Bill Adams.

All the students were highly agitated about the finals, because a failure in any one subject meant that we had to re-sit the exam. A failure in that second attempt meant waiting for another year to sit it again. That was a worst case scenario, as by then we had had enough of school and couldn't wait to get to paid jobs.

At last the final results were posted at the Medical School, and I found I'd passed! Since my Medical School days were now completed, the next step was to find a job at a hospital where I could do my first year as a junior doctor.

My choice was influenced by my desire to play rugby; it seemed to me that it would be a struggle to make it into the Otago rugby team, because most of the forwards were All Blacks. I thought I would have a better chance of being selected for the Southland Rugby Team. I applied for a first year doctor position at the Southland Hospital, in Invercargill. In those days I put thoughts of my rugby career before those of my medical training. Did Vorith, an ex-All Black who trained a local Dunedin team, told me that if I stayed in Dunedin, he would get me into the Otago Rugby team, but I still elected to go to Southland Hospital. This turned out to be a bad decision. Southland Hospital had a poor medical reputation back then. Colleagues even to this day ask me, "Why did you go to Southland Hospital?"

One of my younger football teammates in Otago went on to do his junior medical years in Auckland, and eventually captained the Auckland rugby team. He trained as an orthopaedic specialist in Auckland and his status and income surpassed mine for his whole life. I would have been far better to have stayed at the Dunedin Hospital or gone to one of the bigger hospitals in the North Island of New Zealand. I did not come from a medical family, so was unaware of the distinctions between hospitals. I knew that a Southland surgeon had left a large artery forceps in a patient's abdomen, as the x-ray pictures showing this medical 'fault' had been published in most of the newspapers. This didn't seem to ring a warning bell in me, and instead of opting to "Go South young man" I should have decided to, "Go North young man!"

The Southland Hospital had confirmed that I was accepted as a Junior House Physician, so I was committed to going to Invercargill.

I had been at the Southland Hospital in my sixth year and gained the impression that it would be good for me socially. In that year there were a lot of compatible junior doctors who had great parties most Saturday nights. There always seemed to be plenty of alcohol around, and if they ran low they would go to the laboratory and siphon off some of the ethyl alcohol to give orange juice a bit of punch. If the party was still flagging they went down to the anaesthetic room and brought up the nitrous oxide machine. Nitrous oxide is also known as 'laughing gas,' and certainly lives up to its name. I can't remember any severe hangovers, so my liver must have been in good shape in those days.

Arch and Dais came to Dunedin for my graduation ceremony. It would be hard to imagine a prouder mother than mine. 'Jack' Valentine had broken the family tradition of lower education, labouring and horse racing and a brave new world and future lay at his feet.

Hell-Bent for Life

Otago Universi[ty]
"A" Tea[m]

Back row: R.J. Cantwell, L.K. McIver, K.J. O'Connor (A
Middle row: O.M. Ellis, R.D. Fraser, J.D.K North, J.M. Tan
Front row: Mr J.E. Manchester (Coach and ex All Black Captain), J.J. Sullivan, I.J. Botting (Captain and All Bl

Otago Medical School 1943 - 1950

ootball Club
48

friend), P.B. Dignan, H.F. Drake, E.K. Hart, C.R. Moore
'alentine (Author), B.H. Doherty, C.S. Bayley, I.B. Cameron
ord University and England), Mr. C.L. Carter (President), G.J.T. Moore (All Black), T.F.C. Geary, J.T. Fitzgerald

CHAPTER 5

Southland Hospital
1951

INTRODUCED CHARACTERS

DR. HAYWARD HUTA, The superintendent of Southland Hospital in Invercargill.

DR 'MING' MENZIES, the senior surgical registrar at the hospital.

WHEN I ARRIVED IN INVERCARGILL TO START MY first year as a junior doctor, most of the good time boys had moved on and I was the only single doctor living in the junior doctor's quarters. I soon found out that my married workmates had better things to do than drinking high octane punch and sucking up laughing gas on a Saturday evening, so I had to face a lonely and solitary year. The symptoms of post-traumatic anxiety that Big Dig had caused by punching and knocking me out had lessened. One of the troubling symptoms that remained from my days at St. Kevin's was the tendency to break into a sweat when meeting new people. This too had eased, and I could function normally in most social situations. I perspired less if I did not wear too much clothing, but there were limits to how little I could wear and still be decent.

As I was sixteen stone, or 224 pounds (100kgs approx) and in training for rugby, the other house surgeons lost no time in calling me when they had difficult or possibly dangerous male patients. I always responded but took my time sauntering through the long corridors. Usually the crisis had passed before I arrived, but sometimes it was necessary to put a patient into a strait jacket. This was a canvas jacket that enabled the patient's arms to be strapped to their sides. On most occasions an intra-muscular injection of paraldehyde settled the patient. It was painful and took some time to work, but it was certainly effective. This was just as well, as I disliked having to wrestle recalcitrant male patients. I can't remember being given the opportunity to restrain any female patients, and perhaps that was just as well.

The superintendent at Southland Hospital, Dr. Hayward Huta, kept in touch with what was happening in the hospital by seeing every patient during ward rounds on alternate days. He did not have specialist qualifications but he didn't hesitate to interfere with a specialist's care of a patient. Occasionally when a specialist doctor had written a long protocol for a patient with cancer, Dr. Hayward Huta would put a long squiggle through the page and cancel the treatment. He would write on the treatment chart "a quarter of morphine every four hours" which was usually a pain management protocol for patients in the later stages of terminal illness. If any senior doctor challenged Dr. Hayward Huta's actions, they were in great danger of losing their appointment at the hospital. Howard tolerated no questioning of his methods and his domination of the medical scene was a major reason for the hospital's poor reputation.

He once told me about a very large and powerful Swedish sailor who was locked in a padded cell. He was tearing up the walls in the cell, and when Dr. Hayward Huta looked through the spy hole in the door a long splinter of wood was thrust through it. Howard still had good vision in both eyes when he told the story, so the sailor had missed his target.

At last the rugby season started and I was able to talk my way into the top team of the Marist Rugby Club. At the very first game, in the first ten minutes, I jumped high for the ball in a 'lineout'. I got the ball and as I came down I felt my feet go from under me as somebody from the opposite team lifted them up. This lifting tactic is illegal these days. I landed on the tip of my left shoulder and dislocated the outer end of the clavicle. I was taken off the field in the most severe pain I have ever felt. That was the end of rugby for that season. The collar bone was not broken but the outer end of the clavicle was poking up under the skin. The dislocation was not reduced or pinned and I walked around with heavy strapping for the next two months, unable to move my left arm more than six inches from my chest. This meant that I was only partly effective in the wards and unable to help restrain uncooperative patients. When I was fit again the rugby season was almost over, and my main reason for going south had vanished.

I regret to tell you that since the hospital's morale was poor, I was not motivated to do more than what was strictly necessary to do my job, and so did not lift the standard. Invercargill was cold in winter, and the walk along the estuary from town to the hospital was often shrouded in mist. I wondered if Dartmoor was like this, when Sir Arthur Conan Doyle wrote the Hound of the Baskervilles, with the hound looming out of thick mists. At the time, Invercargill was little more than a farming town and as I didn't come from local farming stock, my social life was a drag. In retrospect, I should have made a greater effort both socially and with my work. My feelings of isolation, in this small town at the last stop before Antarctica, was no excuse for being less than enthusiastic about my hospital duties.

I was still a practising Catholic and was having difficulties with assisting at the infrequent abortions in the operating theatre. If I was able I would get another junior doctor to replace me and I would do his duties. I liked assisting in the operating theatre, and occasionally we juniors were allowed to do minor operations. The senior surgical registrar was Dr. 'Ming' Menzies, and he was keen to get as much experience as possible, because he was studying for a higher qualification in surgery. He limited our surgical experience by taking most of the surgeries, leaving very few for we junior doctors.

During my time in Invercargill, a massive 12-foot shark was put on display in town. It was packed in ice but still smelled badly. It had been caught at Smoky Bank in Foveaux Straight. As I filed in to see the shark, a fifty year old man kept calling out, "Come and see

Smoky Joe from Smoky Bank, the one and only." From that time on, we juniors called 'Ming' Menzies "Smoky Joe from Smoky Bank" because, like that shark, he was predatory, and especially so when it came to doing surgery.

Dr. Menzies eventually qualified as a surgeon and became superintendent at a small hospital on the North Island. He learned to fly an airplane, and it is said that during the duck-shooting season he would fly a 'top-dressing' or crop-dusting plane over a lake reserved as a safe haven for the birds. He would drop rocks into the water to encourage the ducks to venture to other lakes where his friends were waiting to give the ducks a rousing welcome with their shotguns. I'm sure he did lots of good work in his surgical career but his exploits with the ducks are what he is remembered for.

At the end of 1951 and my first junior year as a practising doctor, I decided to leave Invercargill and go overseas. In those days there was no likelihood of a paying career in rugby as it was a strictly amateur sport. I was still inspired to experience overseas travel, having been impressed by my mother's envy of the Queen's travels to South Africa, and with this in mind, decided to look for a position that involved overseas travel.

I had come to Invercargill to play rugby, but my dislocated clavicle precluded that. I also thought the idea of Saturday night parties being on the agenda each weekend was attractive, but these didn't materialize. The married junior doctors were otherwise occupied and I approved of those who spent time with their young children, despite it leading to my social disappointment.

It was time for me to look further afield and investigate the wider world. Being aware of Dais' disappointment at not being able to travel in her early and middle years, I was determined to not miss out. I didn't have the constraints she did, so started looking for ways to combine my medical career with travel. A whole new experience awaited and I was very enthusiastic about the prospect of broadening my horizons.

CHAPTER 6

Colonial War Memorial Hospital in Fiji
1951 - 1952

INTRODUCED CHARACTERS

SAM, an acquaintance from the author's school days at St Kevin's.
MARTHA MORRISON, the author's landlady in Suva.
JOHN READE, the surgeon at The Colonial War Memorial hospital. In line with English and Antipodean practice, he was addressed as 'Mister' by his colleagues.
HAFIZULAH, an Indian patient.
VILAKESSA, the Fijian anaesthetist.
SEMESA, an AMP (Assistant Medical Practitioner).
RATU MARA, Polynesian Chief who attended Otago medical school at the same time as the author.
DR HARRY STONE, an American dental colleague and friend the author socialised with.
BETTY and BARBARA, two young ladies from the New Zealand Bank.

I TOOK THE BANANA BOAT TO FIJI. TRAVELLING WITH me was a group of twelve New Zealand army sergeants who were to lead Fijian soldiers in the Malayan Emergency, where Communists were active in the jungle. It was said that the Fijian soldiers would take off after their opposition and run them down.

I knew one of the sergeants, Sam, from my school days at St. Kevin's. He had been my first boxing opponent at school and I had won that fight. His uncle was a Monsignor in the Catholic Church and that was a prestige item for all of his days at school. Sam had a good memory so did well in all his exams. He was always talkative, even garrulous and most people got fed up with him after a few hours. He was accepted as a candidate for the Priesthood, but after two years he found himself in the street again. He then joined the army and became a sergeant in the New Zealand forces. I know that Sam continued in the army and remained a sergeant for twenty years, but it seemed sad that a bright man with a good memory could not find himself a better situation in the wider community.

When we got to Suva, I took a taxi to meet with the Chief Medical Officer for the Fijian Government. He kept me waiting for twenty minutes, even though there was nobody in his office. I was sweating in my heavy Harris Tweed coat in the poorly ventilated waiting room. When I was eventually shown in, he said there was only one vacancy. I later found out that there were vacancies for medical staff all over Fiji, but I presume they were running on a tight budget and saw no reason to engage more medical staff while there were no complaints from the public about the service they received. The job I was offered was Surgical Registrar at the Colonial War Memorial Hospital in Suva. I accepted happily, giving no thought to my having little experience of surgery.

I secured board at Martha Morrison's Boarding House, which was a short distance downhill from the hospital. Martha was a tall good looking woman in her forties who worked at Cable and Wireless in central Suva. This organization provided the transmission link for the undersea cable which carried telephone messages from Australasia to North America. As she was away all day Martha employed two forty year old Fijian housekeepers. They were both cheerful ladies with comfortable figures and smiley faces. It was their job to keep the very large house clean and provide meals for the Europeans. My enduring memory of them is that of them often sitting in the kitchen entertaining their friends and relatives. They must have done some work though, as the house was clean, the beds made and the food cooked. I presume they were pretty hard on the tea and biscuits. Whenever Martha had a visitor come to the front door she couldn't stop these two ladies coming up from the kitchen and shaking hands with the new arrivals and introducing themselves. It was a friendly, relaxed atmosphere and we slept under mosquito nets with doors unlocked and windows open. There was no air conditioning, but

Hell-Bent for Life

Medical students at the Colonial War Memorial hospital in Fiji.

we did have electric fans. We had no fear of being robbed at night, so the Colonial administration must have had an effective police department. When I returned fifty years later, that had all changed and the windows were well and truly barred and all doors were locked at night and air conditioning had arrived.

The Colonial War Memorial hospital catered to Fijians, Indians and Europeans alike, but most Europeans chose a private doctor in Suva, or hotfooted it to Australia or N.Z. by plane for specialist attention. The junior doctors had trained at the medical school in Fiji, and at that time were called Assistant Medical Practitioners, or AMPs. Many of them, after working as Assistant Medical Practitioners for some years, became very competent hospital and rural clinic doctors.

The senior nurses were Europeans and had been trained in New Zealand and Australia. The Fijian general nurses were graduates of the Nursing School at the Colonial Nursing Hospital, where a three-year course in general nursing was offered. These trainee Fijian nurses were smiling and joyous but with almost no sense of responsibility. If they passed me in the street they liked to draw their hands across their throats as I went past. This meant, "I would cut my throat for you", the implication being that "If I had intercourse with you I would die of pleasure!" They would then dissolve into peels of shy laughter. A variation of this was to whisper, "QUANA KANA Doctor," as we passed in the corridors. This meant, "I cannot eat," which would be the consequence if they cut their throats. "QUANA KANA" had the same sexual association as the throat cutting gesture did.

These girls were sent back to their home islands upon completion of their nurse training, where they would be in charge of small dispensaries. All the dispensaries that I saw in the outer islands were neat and clean. Most of the unmarried nurses had trouble with the chiefs of the islands who made advances on them, which were not easily repelled as these approaches were part of the island tradition.

The surgeon at the hospital was Mr. John Reade. Following the English system of medical titles, he was referred to as Mr. Reade. John was only employed part-time, so was happy to let me do whatever I thought I was capable of. When an elderly Indian man named Hafizulah came in with an enlarged prostate and his bladder distended up to his umbilicus, I went to see Mr. Reade, and he said "put a catheter in him and we'll do him in the morning." I said "Acute retention should be treated as an emergency" and he replied, "Well if he should be done as an emergency you go and do it."

Taking my courage in both hands, I went back to the hospital and had blood cross-typed in preparation for the operation. Vilakessa was the chief anaesthetist, and he came along to give the anaesthetic. In those days a prostate operation was done with a lower abdominal incision, opening into the distended bladder, and then shelling out the prostate to free it from the surrounding tissue, with a blunt dissection. The distended bladder contained two pints of urine and this was soon discoloured with blood. The gory mess was everywhere with the drapes and our gowns saturated. There seemed to be as much fluid loss as you would expect while performing a Caesarean Section.

I shelled out the prostate, inserted the various catheters and sent Hafizula back to the ward. To my great relief he recovered fully and was soon discharged. Most afternoons, when I was walking up through the Indian sector from the public swimming baths, Hafizula would call out, "Hello doctor!" even if he was on the other side of the street. He was happy with the outcome and my modest surgical career was continually advertised by Hafizula to his Indian friends.

Vilakessa, was a forty year old Fijian. Like many Fijians he was a large, massively muscular man and always retained his amiable disposition. He was a Chief from the Island of Ba and held a high position in Fijian society. When giving an anaesthetic, he used a nurse's cap to restrain his fuzzy locks. Vilakessa hated putting the patient too deeply under anaesthetic because it sometimes caused a respiratory depression. This could increase the chance of the patient being difficult to arouse or, in the worst case, dying. When a patient was under a lighter anaesthetic the abdominal muscles remained tense and made it more difficult for the surgeon to put his hand through the incision. Mr. Reade in turn would frequently shout, "For Christ's sake Vilakessa, put the bloody patient down!" Vilakessa would do his best and the operations went off satisfactorily, if not a little more slowly. Whenever I finished an operation, I would always say, "Thank you Vilakessa," and he would inevitably reply "Thank you doctor, a very good operation doctor."

Filariasis is a disease that was present in Fiji. It is caused by an infecting organism, Wuchereria Bancrofti, being introduced into the bloodstream by a mosquito bite. The microfilariae (larvae) enter the lymphatic system, and obstruct free flow of the lymph fluid. This

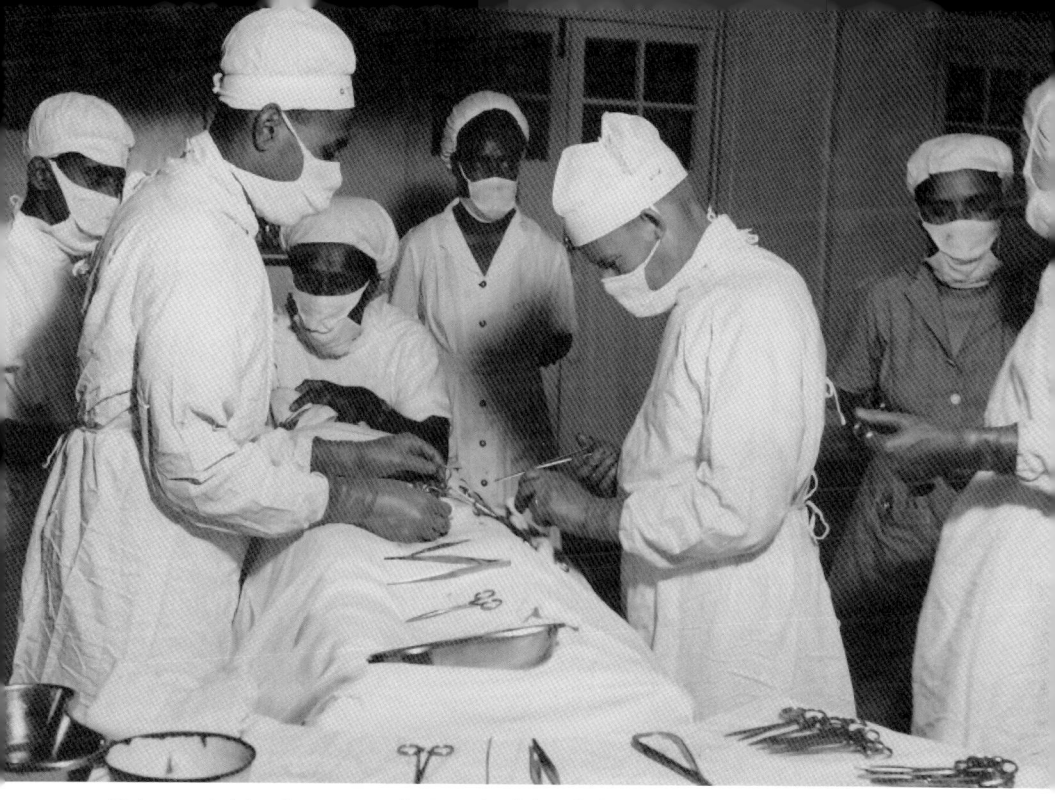

Vilakessa administering an anaesthetic at the Colonial War Memorial Hospital, Suva.

causes Elephantiasis, or gross swelling, and it sometimes affected the upper legs and, in males, the scrotum. I had a male patient with this problem, whose swollen scrotum measured 14 inches (35cm) in diameter. This restricted his walking, urination and all social activities, so it became necessary to operate to remove the bulk of the mass. After making the first incision I found a lot of hard, fibrous tissue, and there was a significant blood loss. The operation seemed to go on forever. Finally, after I had finished and looked into the blood sodden mass, I could see a near normal sized testicle sitting amongst the mass of diseased tissue that I had removed. The wound healed well and if the patient complained that he had lost a testicle, I never heard about it. This far on, I can't remember if the other testis survived.

    The operating theatre at the hospital was cooled, and this was a lifesaver for the European nurses and for me, during those hot, humid Fijian summers. Vilakessa often thought that the atmosphere was too cold, and sat at the head of the table with a blanket wrapped around his shoulders and his great shaggy head of frizzy hair sticking out, topped by a large nurse's cap. He would often say, "Very cold today sir!" Certainly it was cool, but the water had not been taken out of the atmosphere. This made it muggy and we would sweat under our operating theatre clothes. The Europeans found it preferable to be cool and sweating rather than put up with the Fijian heat. So Vilakessa had to keep himself warm with his woollen blanket.

The AMP's helped in all the usual hospital situations, but one of the Fijians had better English skills than his colleagues. As I was the "Police Doctor" he described a case that he was involved in where an Indian girl had been murdered. She was brought into the morgue with her head still attached to her body by only a small segment of skin. She had been entertaining her Indian boyfriend in her bedroom most nights, and her brothers told her that he wasn't suitable and she must stop seeing him. When the boyfriend came to her bedroom that night she gave him her brother's message. This was not to the boyfriend's liking and wasn't on his agenda. He showed his pique by using the cane knife he was holding to cut off her head with one sweep.

I said to the AMP, "He must have lost his temper," and the AMP broke into a great big smile and said, "Lost his temper very badly doctor." You can see from his humour around this murder that there was no love lost between the Fijians and Indians in those days. In the last fifty years I don't think much has changed.

Most of the stress between Fijians and Indians was based on land ownership. At the beginning of the 20th century, a small amount of land was freehold, but then the Government prohibited further sale of land to non-Fijians. Because of this, Fijians owned the land and the Indian businessmen, many of whom had significant finances behind them, couldn't get title to their properties.

If an Indian cane farmer asked the Fijian owner for a lease of land, the landowner might say something like, "Oh, you can have that ten acres on the hillside for five years, but the forest has to be cleared." The farmer would then negotiate a lease. When the land had been cleared and planted in sugarcane, the Indian farmer might again approach the Fijian owner for a lease renewal, and the Fijian owner might say, "Oh no, we want that bit, but there's another ten-acre block next door that you might like to clear." You can understand how this disadvantaged the hardworking Indian farmer.

Some of the Indians had the financial means to send their children to Australia or New Zealand for further education. When they had qualified as accountants, lawyers or doctors, these young people tended to stay overseas rather than return to Fiji. When travelling in rural Fiji, I would often see young Indian women clad in colourful saris waiting for the bus. The road was dusty but the girls remained beautifully presented despite some of the saris being quite lightly coloured. They must have spent ages keeping themselves and their clothes in such immaculate condition. When I looked up into the hills I saw the tin shacks they lived in on the hillsides and could see their brothers carting water up to the shacks, in 40-gallon drums, on sledges pulled by their horses.

It was part of my job to help tutor the student AMPs at the hospital. They came from islands all over the Pacific, including Micronesia. At that time the New Guinean people had their own training school. I taught my native students some radiology (or x-ray) and one of the young English physicians told me the material I had given them was too advanced. However, when they sat an examination he retracted and said that they had reproduced the material very well. I wonder if they could absorb even more advanced material if I presented it to them. At that time they were taught information comparable to that given to nurses in New Zealand, and after a few years in practice most became extremely competent doctors.

In the smaller district hospitals the senior AMPs were in charge of medical services. We knew of AMP Semesa, who was six-foot-six-inches tall, and worked on the West coast of the main island. When police brought in two Indians who had been fighting with cane knives he is said to have lifted both up by the scruff of their necks and said, "Fight you buggers, fight!" Semesa wasn't just a good AMP, he was a versatile one. Those who knew him said that he should have become a qualified doctor as he was an excellent practitioner. Many Europeans chose to consult him even when other Western-trained doctors were available. It was said that AMP Semesa, while working in the Pacific in WWII as an army doctor, had helped to pioneer the use of fresh coconut milk intravenously as a plasma expander when blood was not readily available.

Besides the inter-racial conflicts, there was considerable tension between the Fijian police and the Fijian Army. The majority of police and army were Fijians as they were given preference for entry by the Fijian authorities. Occasionally when the army played the police at rugby we treated multiple injuries at the hospital, because the participants thought of the encounter not as sport but as training for war. One week end a full-scale riot between the police and army went on in the town for several hours. The army kept sending trucks back to the barracks for reinforcements so that everybody had plenty of time to enjoy their recreation before they exhausted themselves. In the Accident and Emergency (A&E) Department we were conscientiously looking after the cuts and minor fractures of the participants. Nobody was killed, which was a bonus. I wasn't told the reason for the dispute but as the two groups were always antagonistic they didn't need a major reason to have a confrontation.

As Police Surgeon, I was called to any case where the police needed a medical opinion concerning injuries, so I was known to most of the police in Suva.

My mother came to visit me for ten days, and on most days we would walk from her hotel to go shopping. Usually there was a massive Fijian police sergeant on traffic duty who must have weighed all of 22-stone, or three hundred pounds (135 kg approx). He knew I was the police surgeon, and if he was on point duty when Dais and I wanted to cross the street, he would immediately stop all the traffic and signal us to cross. This impressed Dais, and no doubt added to the fund of stories that she would take back to Kurow. I'm not sure her audience would have remained interested after the first ten minutes, since it was well known that talking about me was the mainstay of her conversation. Friends told me that when they met my mother they had competition to see how long they could delay her talking about me. It's a pity that she only had one little bird in the nest, as lots of chicks would have spread her interests wider.

While Dais was in Fiji, I was invited out for half a day to the Andi Thaukambou Secondary School for Fijian Girls. This was the only secondary school for Fijian girls in the country, so they were the crème de la crème. I had met some of them when they had been patients at the CWM Hospital. It would have been difficult to have found a more attractive group of young people - bright-eyed, cheerful and obviously intelligent. Many would come from chiefly families, as the Chiefs looked after their own. My mother came with me on the visit. The main purpose of the afternoon was to entertain and introduce a school board member from New Zealand, who was visiting the islands. The Fijian students started performing the Fijian 'mekes', but the Polynesian 'hulas' done later, danced by the girls from the Polynesian islands to the east, were far sexier. The head mistress, who had a Master of Arts degree from New Zealand, pointed out that the girls gave me all their attention and neglected the board member. She said I had glamour, but I struggled to believe this unexpected compliment. If it were true it must have only been evanescent as nobody has repeated her assessment of me since, despite me having waited for sixty years; while there's life, there's hope!

Fijians, physically, are typical of Melanesians, with their dark skins, frizzy hair and heavy musculature. The Polynesians from Tonga and Samoa have lighter skin, finer features and straighter hair. Throughout most of the Pacific, Melanesians and Polynesians live separately in different villages. However, the Lau Group is an exception and adds to the area's anthropological and cultural diversity. Although Fijians are Melanesian, they have

Three Fijiian men. Their fuzzy hair and heavy musculature is typical of Melanesians.

adopted a lot of features from Polynesian culture, including the kava ceremonies and dances. This follows from raids that took place in the past between the Polynesians from Tonga and Samoa, and the Melanesians from the Fijian Islands. These inter-island incursions had been going on for hundreds of years, so there was plenty of interracial mixing. The descendents of these Polynesian invaders are scattered through the Melanesian Lau group, and a disproportionate number of the Lau chiefs are Polynesians. To this day, in Tonga and Samoa, you also see many people with the tight curls typical of Melanesians.

It astounds me that these fierce warriors undertook 300 to 400 mile journeys through one of the world's roughest oceans, in open canoes, without the benefit of modern navigational aids. They found there way with the help of the sun, the moon and the stars. In the daytime they could sometime see the green colour of the islands over the horizon, reflected on the base of the distant clouds. On rare times when clouds would obscure the stars, the men could ask advice from their wives and girlfriends who accompanied them on these voyages. Feminine intuition would prevail and guide them to their destination, hopefully as straight as an arrow. If all this failed, and they missed their destination, they were lost in the wide Pacific Ocean, with thousands of miles to contemplate where their landfall had gone. If they continued sailing into the sunrise, they would perish from thirst or starvation long before they came upon South America.

My friend Ratu Mara was a good-looking, six-foot-two-inch, straight-haired Polynesian chief from Lakemba in the Lau Group. We were at Otago medical school together until he was pulled out in the third year and sent off to do a political degree at Oxford. I met up with him again when he was a district officer near Suva. He later became the Prime Minister of Fiji in 1970. Ratu Mara was a Catholic, and he didn't play musical beds like many of the other Fijian chiefs. He remained married to a lovely Fijian lady, and one of his sons was a contemporary of my daughters at Otago University later on.

It was part of my police duties to examine the victim's body after a murder. I was required to go to the Lau group on three occasions. This group is a string of islands to the east of the main Fijian group. Like Fiji, the Lau Group is part of Melanesia. The first two times I went to the Lau group I was flown by the Royal New Zealand Air force in an old PBY, or Catalina flying boat. They were amphibious aircraft with retractable wheels, and could land and takeoff from both land and water. On the first flight, one of the officers said, "The last time we landed in this lagoon we hit a coral head that tore a hole in the bottom of the plane. One of us had to sit in the hole until we took off again." When PBYs take off they sometimes bounce high into the air, and then drop back down with huge impact. The person sitting in the hole would have had an exciting time until the lumbering giant was fully airborne.

On my third visit to the Lau Group, I was taken by sea to the island of Thithia. We travelled in a large police launch which was well equipped with cabins, a galley and other seafaring comforts. A part-European senior police officer and two other policemen came with me on the launch. One of the policemen acted as a batman for the officer, and it was his job to set out the officer's clothes and generally look after him. The senior officer was always well dressed and was very aware of his position. I was vaguely indignant about the whole situation, as the officer made it obvious that he was leading the investigation and I was just along to make up the numbers.

We sailed over at night, so there was plenty of time for discussion and I was told how we would proceed with the inquiry. We knew that the unfortunate woman victim, who was said to have been a witch, had been attacked with cane knives and killed. She had been buried eight days previously. The senior officer told us how we would proceed at the exhumation but emphasised that we would be looking for defensive cuts on the victim's hands.

When we got to the island we were received by the Chiefs and I was given a 'tambu' at a kava ceremony. As I had accepted the whales tooth I should have been obliged to do whatever the donors requested. Although no blatant request was made to halt the exhumation, I had the feeling this was the implication of the gift-giving. However, the law required that we go ahead with it. Although we dug up the body, I kept the tambu and still have it to this day.

Later in the evening we went to a "tra-la-la," which was a simple repetitive dance in the European manner, with the male and female dancing facing each other. The young women came and asked us to dance. The music, kava drinking and dancing went on until the small hours of the morning. I woke the next morning without a hang over, and keen to get started so I could examine the body.

At ten in the morning, twelve of us set off for the burial site. Our party was made up of the police officer, two policemen, eight local Fijians armed with shovels and myself. When we arrived at the burial site, the covering earth was removed from the grave, and the body was brought to the surface. It had been wrapped in many layers of beautiful woven mats, each tied with a handmade cord.

As each cord was cut and another mat came off, the smell became worse. In the tropics bodies decompose quickly. The attendants started disappearing until there was only the officer and myself left looking at the wrapped body. As we cut the last cord the covering mat rolled open and the skull rolled out and disintegrated into fragments at our feet. I looked at the senior officer and said, "Shall we look for defensive wounds on the hands?" And he replied, "I've seen enough if you have" so we set off back to the village and the villagers stayed behind to rebury the body. It took us another twelve hours to sail back to Suva, and during the trip everyone was very subdued.

One morning the operating theatre nurse and I were having a cup of tea between operations. While I had been operating, a strong wind had sprung up, and during our tea break the senior doctor appeared with the senior nurse. They were both excited and said there was to be no more operating that day as a typhoon warning had just come in over the radio. They hurried off to supervise the battening down of the windows, locking of doors and directing the staff to prepare and take shelter. The wind gradually increased in intensity, and it began to rain heavily. Soon pools of water outside the operating theatre were being whipped up and carried away in a heavy spray. The loud wind made it hard to hear anyone speaking. I had no family responsibilities, so I stayed in the hospital to experience my first hurricane.

Upstairs in the 'part-European' ward, water poured in through every small crack, and several times large plates of glass from the windows burst inwards and scattered over the floor. Some of the patients were moved to safer rooms, while the rest were put into the centre of the long ward. After about two hours everything grew quiet and it was almost completely still. I thought the storm was over, and since everything was in hand at the hospital I took the opportunity to go home for lunch. When I was half way down the hill the storm started again, and I was unable to stand without a hand holding onto something for support. By waiting between gusts of wind, I was able to make my way from telephone pole to

COLONIAL WAR MEMORIAL HOSPITAL
SUVA, FIJI

IN REPLY PLEASE QUOTE:

9th July, 1952.

Operations performed in the Operating Theatre by DR. J. VALENTINE in the six months 7/1/1952 - 7/7/1952.

ABDOMINAL
- Appendicectomies — 20
- Herniorrhaphies — 28
- Filarial abscesses — 2
- Umbilical sinus — 1

RECTAL
- Haemorrhoidectomies — 6
- Excision fistula in ano. — 9
- Pilonoidal sinuses — 2
- Wiring prolapsed rectums — 2

EAR, NOSE & THROAT
- Tonsillectomies — 7
- Antrostomies — 12
- Excision nasal polyps — 4
- Excision eye — 1
- Oesophoscopy — 1

ORTHOPEDIC
- Mid-thigh amputations — 3
- Syme's amputation — 1
- Amputation metatarsals & phalanges — 7
- Insertion Kirschner wires — 3
- Compound fractures tibia & fibula — 2
- Fractured vertebra — 1
- Repair cut Achille's tendon — 1

GENITO-URINARY
- Dilatations and curettages — 51
- Examinations under an anaesthetic — 8
- Excision of hydroceles — 9
- Cystoscopies — 9
- Supra-pubic cystostomies — 4
- Prostatectomies — 4
- Ectopic gestations — 2
- Repair 3rd degree perineal tear — 1
- Amputations of scrotum (filarial) — 5
- Excision of fibrous mass and repair of urethra — 1
- Urethral dilatations — 4

COLONIAL WAR MEMORIAL HOSPITAL
SUVA, FIJI

IN REPLY PLEASE QUOTE:

CONTINUED:

GENERAL   Excision of cysts, tuberculous glands,
          a wrist ganglion, and biopsies   29

The assistants were: Theatre Sister, Theatre Nurses,
                     Assistant Medical Practitioners,
                     and Medical Students

General anaesthetics were administered by A.M.P. V.Ramaqua

TOTAL: 240 cases - no operative mortalities

Post-operative mortality:
       After an E.U.A. & laparectomy for ectopic
                                   gestation........ 1
       After a mid-thigh amputation for gas gangrene .. 1

(T.A. DORAN, M.D. Medical Officer-in-Charge)

(D.W. GIBBONS, Theatre Sister-in-Charge)

(V. RAMAQUA, Assistant Medical Practitioner,
                                      Grade A)

A record of operations and duties carried out by the author between 7 January, 1952 and 7 July, 1952 at the Colonial War Memorial Hospital in Suva.

telephone pole until I made it to our boardinghouse. There was a light lunch provided, but Martha was upset because the tin roof that covered the servant's bathroom was starting to disappear into the air. I helped to nail up the doors and windows, and then spent twenty minutes on the porch, on the lee side of the house, watching debris and pieces of tin being carried high above the trees. I looked away from a large Indian house on the side of the hill for a few seconds, and when I looked back half of the roof was gone.

Late in the afternoon when the storm had begun to abate, I went back to the hospital. People soon began to arrive and in no time there were almost 100 people awaiting attention. The hospital electricity was out, so no more surgical supplies could be sterilised. The operating theatre had had its windows blown in and was swimming in water. The Assistant Medical Practitioners, nurses and a European doctor on vacation worked willingly and effectively in these less than ideal conditions. As one AMP was cleaning up a head wound, he called me across and showed me a crack in the bone at the base of the wound. This patient did well, but incredibly, an x-ray taken of the skull ten days later showed no sign of a fracture. As there were many fractures and dislocations to be taken care of, I spent much of my time sending inpatients home in order to make way for the treatment of more urgent cases. One young woman turned up with her baby because it was constipated. I sent her off. On the other hand, an older European lady came in the next morning, a little apologetically, because she knew we were very busy. She had had the end of her finger amputated during the storm and just wanted to see that the dressing she had put on at home was satisfactory. I was very proud of her.

During the storm, several of the staff lost control of the situation, becoming overwhelmed, and working inefficiently. As time went on, others showed the same inability to cope. After dealing with a large number of serious cases with grossly inadequate facilities for three days, I started to develop a mild tremor and found it hard to make decisions. During the week after the typhoon, we had 120 different fracture cases to deal with. Eli Singh, a bright Indian AMP in his middle twenties, was the fracture expert. Although he was much better at reducing fractures than me, he always insisted I check his work. He told me later this was in case legal matters came up later. I had overall responsibility during those difficult days, and learned a lot from working in the clinic. I suppose, from a medical point of view, I was lucky to be in Fiji when the typhoon hit. We were without electricity for five days, and although we treated many open wounds and compound fractures with non-sterile dressings and equipment, surprisingly, there were no post treatment infections.

The Australian government later flew in supplies for us, so for a short time we were better off than usual. The Fijian Health Department usually ordered replacement stock from Britain, and there seemed to be a two-year gap between ordering supplies and receiving them. If I was operating, it was unusual to be able to get a suitable gauge of catgut for suturing; in the middle of an operation we would take what we could get. Near enough had to be good enough, and to this day I feel resentful hearing people demand exactly what they want and not making do with a less than ideal alternative. This delay in supplies was worse in the anaesthetic department. If an anaesthetist ordered some complex equipment, when it turned up two years later, he would be long gone. His successor would either not be interested or not familiar with the equipment, so it was added to the stores. Poor old Vilakessa was still stuck with the 'rag and bottle' technique and was still juggling Mr.Reade's need for the patient to be fully relaxed, with his responsibility to give a safe anaesthetic.

Our Fijian patients were so stoical that they wouldn't complain, and so we had to be careful not to neglect them. It's hard to take a good medical history from a patient who refuses to complain. This was complicated by the language problem, but fortunately there always seemed to be somebody around to help me out.

In contrast, the Indian patients let us know loud and clear when they had pain and what their problems were. The part-Europeans' tolerance of pain was half way between the Fijians and the Indians. We had to remind ourselves to keep a close eye on the Fijians in case we missed something serious.

The Indians were always anxious to have themselves and their relatives treated in the European wards. They were very aware of social distinctions and discrimination. These social differences in patients were reflected in the peptic ulcer rates. Peptic ulcers were fairly frequent in the European community, but I only saw one case in the Fijian community. This Fijian male was high up in the police hierarchy for the then British colony of Fiji. He was a very intelligent and ambitious man who worked as a superior officer to many Europeans. I presume that with the change from his traditional village lifestyle he was subject to the influence of the tension and anxieties found in our modern life.

While working in Fiji, I got to know Dr. Harry Stone. He had been a dentist in the U.S. Navy during WWII, and had come to Suva, as an employee of the U.S. Government, to help upgrade the local Fijian dental school. Harry was fifteen years older than me and was of medium height, was overweight, and always wore an open shirt and shorts. He had an open and chatty personality and we became good friends. I continued to correspond with him for many years. At the time Harry lived at The Old Central Hotel in Suva. Here we met Betty and Barbara who were bright New Zealanders in their early twenties. They had been brought to Fiji by the Bank of New Zealand to be employed as bank tellers. They were both personable and good company and we made a good team. Betty kindly gave me free access to her playground. I did not want to convert it into a nursery, so wore a condom at all times and we got along quite nicely during those lovely tropical evenings. Contraception in those days was pretty rudimentary, and her friend, Barbara, became pregnant. Barbara did everything in her power to seduce Harry, but this was probably to provide her child with a name and financial security. Harry didn't cooperate, and I wasn't in Fiji long enough to find out the end result of Barbara's plight. The banking administrators must have had a tough time keeping up with the turnover of female tellers from New Zealand. Maybe they learned to send out male clerks because even if their reflexes weren't as quick at counting notes, their turnover rate would have been slower without the problem of missed periods.

I don't know if there were any illegal abortions done in Fiji at that time, but no abortions were carried out at the Colonial Memorial Hospital where I worked. Many Fijian girls lived with Indian men, and it was said that the Fijian girls in early pregnancy boiled up hibiscus leaves and drank the concoction to end an unwanted pregnancy. They must have had an effective contraception or method of abortion, since there were very few mixed-blood children. I can't imagine that all of these young people were living celibate lives, as 'brothers and sisters'.

Harry was my best friend, but I hadn't developed other close friends and I was dissatisfied with the Fijian Colonial administration. I was running out of steam and enthusiasm for the place and felt that it was time to leave. I took out my list of the one hundred and fifty operations that I had done while there, and had it signed by Mr. Reade. I thought that it would be a good reference when I was looking for another job, but I have never had to show it to any prospective employer. I keep it in my desk for old times sake and fifty five years on, the paper is getting a little brown and wrinkled around the edges. I've no doubt that the same could be said about me.

Sometimes I would go down and sit on the wharf, which was close to the baths. Most days, I saw a twelve-foot shark glide silently past, every few minutes. It is hard to believe, that few Fijians are killed by these great creatures. As I considered my future plans, it occurred to me that it was time for me to adopt this creature's style, and without causing any ripples, leave.

CHAPTER 7

Micronesia

August 1952 – August 1953

INTRODUCED CHARACTERS

DR. CHUNG-HOON, Medical Officer in charge of the Leprosy Programme in Hawaii.
DR. MARSHALL, Chief Medical Officer of the U.S. Trust Territories (USTT).
DR. TINTINGER, Head Medical Officer in charge of the hospital on Saipan.
DR. RICHARDSON, the head doctor from Truk, who was visiting Saipan.
MR. HEDGES, the District Administrator for Saipan and Tinian.
MR. TROUT, the Administrator of the Tinian Leprosarium when the author arrived on Tinian.
MISS JESSIE LINDSAY, the Tinian Leprosarium Secretary.
DR. ARMER, the half Japanese and half Tinian Leprosarium doctor who had trained locally.
MR. EAST, the administrator of the Tinian Leprosarium under Mr. Hedges.
DR. NORMAN SLOAN, a world famous Leprologist who was employed as the consultant leprologist from the South Pacific Commission.
CAPTAIN HEINZMAN, Director of Naval Medical Services on Guam.

MARGARET, an American woman who was a former girlfriend on Tinian.

DR. STONE HAD INTRODUCED ME TO DR. MARSHALL when he visited Fiji in May 1952. Dr. Marshall was the Chief Medical Officer for the U.S. Trust Territories of the Pacific Islands (USTT) and at that time was visiting from his base in Honolulu. He told me that he was responsible for the medical administration of the USTT in Micronesia. These were the islands in the West Pacific, to the north and south of Guam. The Japanese had occupied the islands of Micronesia after World War I then after the Allied victory in World War II, the United Nations appointed the U.S. as Trustee of the Micronesian islands until their final granting

THE HONOLULU ADVERTISER, SUNDAY, AUGUST 24, 1952.

Young New Zealand Medico Eager For Work at Tinian Leprosarium

There's a little dot of land, virtually unheard from before World War II, that has become vastly important in the Pacific these past 11 years.

It is the island of Tinian, south of Saipan in the Northern Marianas, and the home for the next two years of an eager and ambitious 26-year-old New Zealand doctor, John Valentine.

Dr. Valentine has been in Honolulu the past two weeks for a briefing by the department of public health, trust territory, before he takes over the post as physician in charge of the Tinian leprosarium, described as "Kalaupapa on a small scale," but doing yeoman service for those inflicted with Hansen's disease.

* * *

THE YOUNG doctor—for the record, born 26 years ago in Kurow, New Zealand, and a graduate of Otago university medical school in Dunedin—received his appointment Aug. 18, was briefed here for two weeks and left by Transocean Air Lines yesterday en route to Tinian.

In the next two years Dr. Valentine will probably do more air travel than any doctor in the South Pacific as the trust territory involves a great deal of water and considerable land in an area wider than the United States (excluding the Territory of Hawaii and Alaska).

Dr. Valentine was 24 when he finished school, an age considered extremely young for a young man to complete medical training. He explained the stepped-up system in New Zealand, however, as a six years' highly intensified course.

BUDDING MEDICOS might be interested in the program. During the first year all persons admitted to the school are privileged to undertake the premed course. But at the end of the first year only 15 to 20 per cent have made the grade and enter the second year where that year and the third are devoted to anatomy and physiology.

The fourth and fifth years embrace clinical and ward work, medicine and surgery, pathology and bacteriology, a course stringent enough to make the layman grab onto the first pole and wait until the earth stops whirling.

In the sixth year clinical work is stressed and the seventh corresponds to our year of internship.

Dr. Valentine interned at Kew hospital in Invercargill, N. Z. From there, in 1951, he moved to Suva in the Fijis to a post at Colonial War Memorial hospital, attached to the Central Medical school where native boys are trained as assistant medical practioners.

This system of assistant medical practioners, shortened to AMP's, is a boon to the trust territory of the Pacific, particularly valuable to the isolated areas of the vast sweep of island and atoll as it is physically impossible for medical men to "cover" the field.

* * *

WHILE IN Honolulu Dr. Valentine has stepped up his interest in Hansen's disease, this attributed to two persons. One is Dr. Eleanor Alexander-Jackson of New York City, the first bacteriologist to make a pure culture of Hansen's bacillus, and Dr. Shuji Hasagawa of Tokyo, who has perfected the drug cepharanthine, developed from the root of the stephania cepharantha and the stem of stephania sasakii, both plants members of the menispermaceae family, native to Japan.

Dr. Valentine is anxious to team cepharanthine with sulpha which he thinks will aid Hansen's disease sufferers, his primary patients in the Marianas. He will use Dr. Alexander-Jackson's stain methods in his work and considers her achievements of top order in the field of bacteriology and a potent step in understanding Hansen's bacillus.

The Tinian leprosarium is the site of the only Hansen's disease settlement between Hawaii and the Philippines. It had its beginning in September, 1948, when 63 islanders, the majority from Yap in the Western Carolines where the disease is most prevalent, were admitted as patients.

THE NAVY at that time was the administering authority and chose the site on what was considered the most practical island for the sanitarium. It is only three miles from Saipan where the best hospital in the trust territory is located.

Establishment of Tinian marks a long stride forward in treatment of Hansen's disease in the Pacific. At present there are 109 patients at Tinian, the majority ambulatory. During the past year, 28 patients were discharged. The settlement is a cluster of little white cottages resembling a typical tropical village. The patients, nearly self-sufficient, live independent lives within the confines of a 900-acre area.

Dr. Valentine was eager to get on with his job. He is young, resourceful and particularly interested in the surgical end of Hansen's disease. He has spent considerable time on Molokai, visited the Pearl Harbor leprosarium, Hale Mohalu, and all-in-all, has seen a great deal of the Island of Oahu during his stay.

IT WILL be interesting to watch the progress of his work on that tiny bit of land in the Pacific, a vital link in the trust territory chain and now detailed to do a humanitarian job without precedent in the history of the South Pacific.

An article about the author from the Honolulu Advertiser (August 24th, 1952).

TO SOUTH PACIFIC ISLAND—Dr. John Valentine of New Zealand points to a tiny dot of land in the Marianas, the island of Tinian just south of Saipan, where he will serve as physician in charge for the department of health, trust territory of the Pacific, for the next several years. Dr. Valentine, 26, and two years out of medical school, is vitally interested in the work ahead of him, primarily the care of Hansen's disease sufferers at the Tinian leprosarium. (Advertiser photo.)

of independence.

When I asked Dr. Marshall if there were vacancies in the Trust Territories he said he couldn't employ me while I was working in Fiji, but to come and see him when I reached Honolulu. All of my worldly possessions fitted into one large suitcase, so it didn't take long to pack and catch the bus to Nandi, where the Fijian international airport was located. I boarded a huge aircraft, ready for my first plane flight. I found myself seated next to a very large man whose forearm seemed to take up the whole space between us. He said that he was a professional wrestler and kindly bought me as many drinks as I could cope with. He kept saying "I've had a good season in New Zealand so don't worry about the expense." I arrived in Hawaii in great shape, on the 29th of July, 1952.

All the passengers were taken to a large hall where U.S. Citizens were called up first. Then the non-U.S. passengers were called by name, until I was the only one left. Before leaving Fiji I hadn't been able to obtain an entry visa for the U.S. as there was no U.S. Embassy in Fiji. I was apprehensive about being sent back, but at last a man in military uniform called me up to his desk at the other end of a very long room. I covered the distance to his desk and explained that I couldn't get a visa in Fiji. He opened my passport, picked up a large stamp and brought it down on my document with a resounding thump and said, "Have a good time doc." I was now in U.S. Territory and it was necessary for me to get a job if I was to survive.

Micronesia

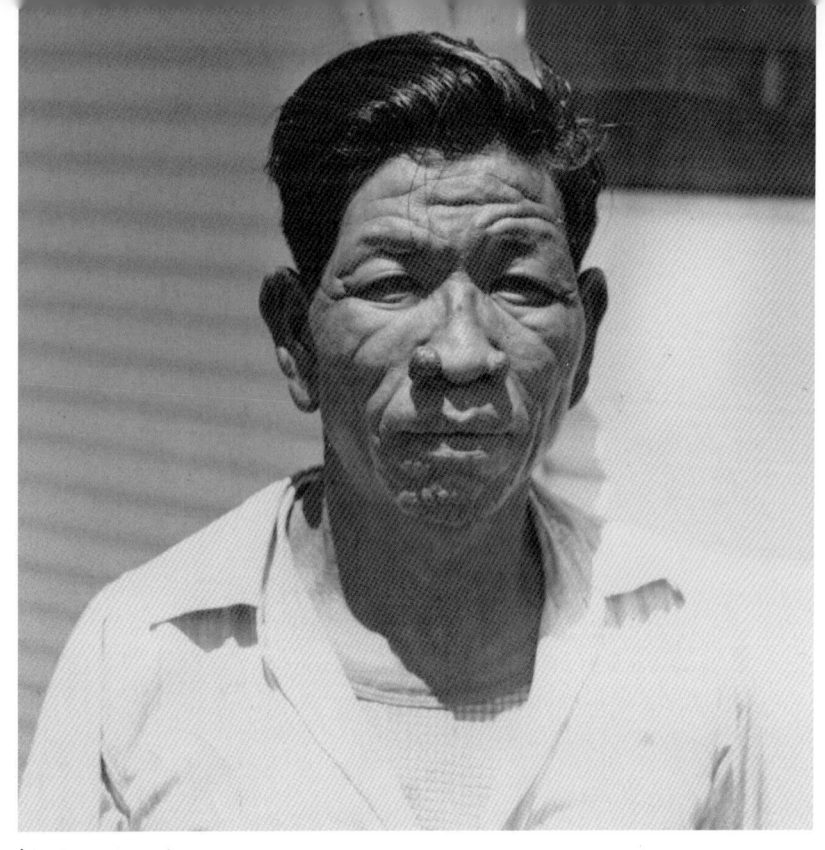

Lepromatous patient.

As a taxi took me in from the airport I was excited by the large American automobiles in the many car lots - mile after mile of them. In New Zealand we had seen very few American cars in the war years, or subsequently, and here they were in abundance. I was used to little old Morris Minors and Austin Minis, and seeing so many of these great, finned American behemoths told me I was now in a different world.

Pampa Joe and I had been watching movies for half my life and I thought that the U.S., with its giant cars and glamorous people with exotic accents, was typical of the wider world outside of North Otago's wastelands. Well here were the cars and I was surrounded by people speaking with different accents. It only remained for me to find the glamorous people doing interesting things. Keep reading; don't skip pages or even paragraphs, or you might miss the action!

Micronesia August 1952 – August 1953

I was able to get a room at the Army/Navy YMCA, which was close to the standard of a first class New Zealand hotel. When I went to see Dr. Marshall at the U.S. Trust Territory medical building, he said that he had recently received a resignation from the doctor in charge of the Leprosarium at Tinian, in the Mariana Islands north of Guam. I did not realise that Honolulu was two thousand miles east of Guam, but if I had, it would not have influenced my decision. By taking the job I would be paid more than in Fiji, and they were offering me a month's training with the leprosy department in Honolulu. I accepted the job gratefully.

Dr. Chung-Hoon was in charge of the leprosy programme in Hawaii and he was a prominent medical advocate for the programme. He told me that leprosy was an infectious disease caused by Mycobacterium leprae, an organism resembling the tuberculosis bacterium. He pointed out that there were two basic types of leprosy: the Tuberculoid type is confined to the skin and superficial nerves. It has very few leprosy bacilli and is mildly

Hands of a chronic leprosy patient.

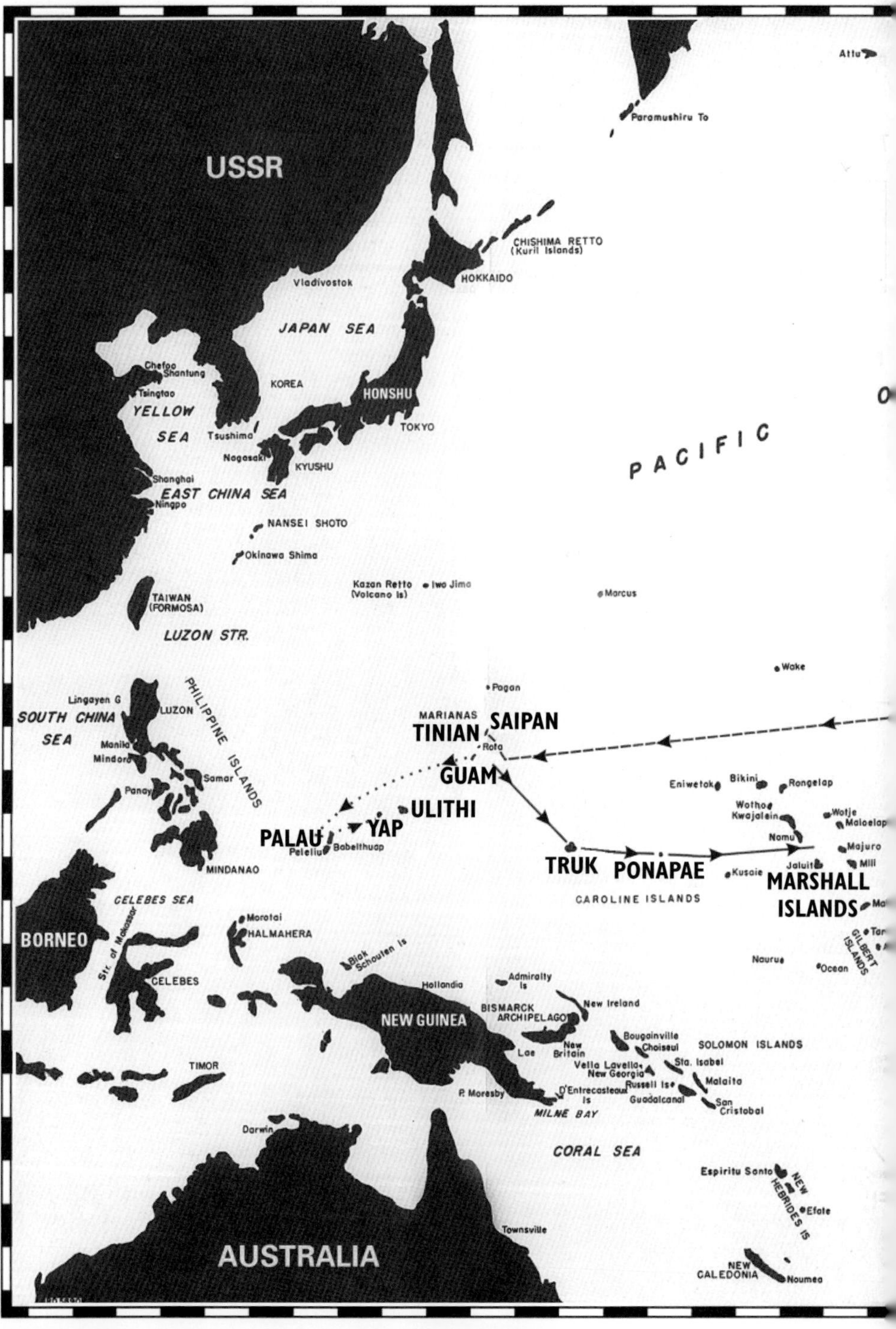
USSR
Attu
Paramushiru To
CHISHIMA RETTO
(Kuril Islands)
HOKKAIDO
Vladivostok
JAPAN SEA
Chefoo
Shantung
Tsingtao
YELLOW
SEA
KOREA
HONSHU
TOKYO
Tsushima
Nagasaki
KYUSHU
PACIFIC
Shanghai
EAST CHINA SEA
Ningpo
NANSEI SHOTO
Okinawa Shima
Kazan Retto
(Volcano Is)
Iwo Jima
Marcus
TAIWAN
(FORMOSA)
LUZON STR.
Wake
Pagan
Lingayen G
LUZON
PHILIPPINE ISLANDS
SOUTH CHINA
SEA
Manila
Mindoro
Samar
Panay
MARIANAS
TINIAN
SAIPAN
Rota
GUAM
ULITHI
YAP
PALAU
Peleliu
Babelthuap
Eniwetok
Bikini
Rongelap
Wotho
Kwajalein
Wotje
Maloelap
Namu
Majuro
Mili
Jaluit
TRUK
PONAPAE
Kusaie
MARSHALL
ISLANDS
CAROLINE ISLANDS
MINDANAO
CELEBES SEA
Morotai
HALMAHERA
BORNEO
Str. of Makassar
CELEBES
Biak
Schouten Is
Hollandia
Admiralty
Is
GILBERT
ISLANDS
Nauru
Ocean
NEW GUINEA
BISMARCK
ARCHIPELAGO
New Ireland
Lae
New
Britain
Bougainville
Choiseul
SOLOMON ISLANDS
Vella Lavella
New Georgia
Sta. Isabel
TIMOR
P. Moresby
D'Entrecasteaux
Is
Russell Is
Guadalcanal
Malaita
San
Cristobal
MILNE BAY
Darwin
CORAL SEA
Espiritu Santo
NEW
HEBRIDES IS
Efate
Townsville
AUSTRALIA
NEW
CALEDONIA
Noumea

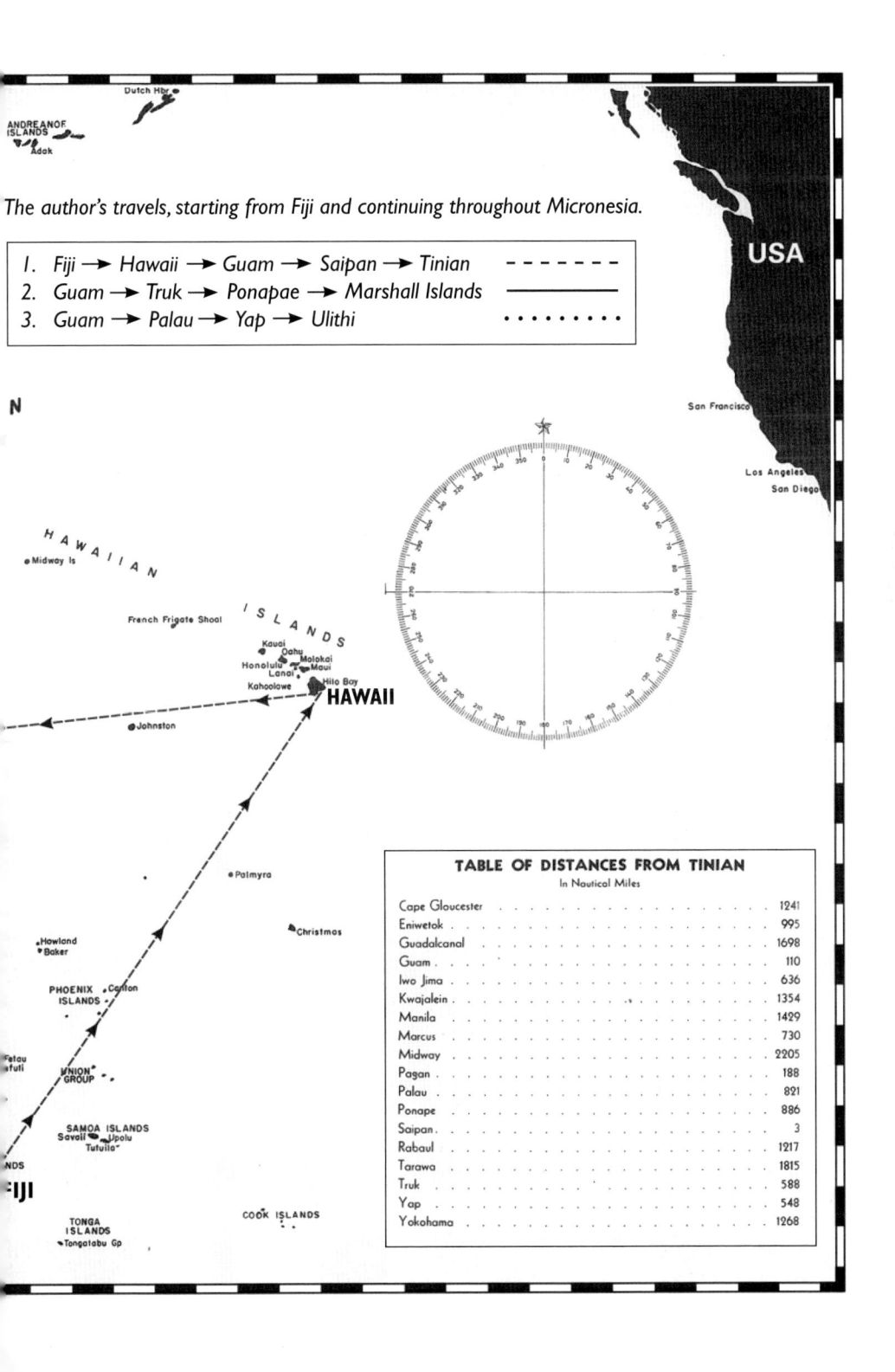

The author's travels, starting from Fiji and continuing throughout Micronesia.

1. Fiji → Hawaii → Guam → Saipan → Tinian   – – – – – – –
2. Guam → Truk → Ponapae → Marshall Islands ─────
3. Guam → Palau → Yap → Ulithi   · · · · · · · · ·

TABLE OF DISTANCES FROM TINIAN
In Nautical Miles

Cape Gloucester	1241
Eniwetok	995
Guadalcanal	1698
Guam	110
Iwo Jima	636
Kwajalein	1354
Manila	1429
Marcus	730
Midway	2205
Pagan	188
Palau	821
Ponape	886
Saipan	3
Rabaul	1217
Tarawa	1815
Truk	588
Yap	548
Yokohama	1268

infectious. Once it has come under treatment it is safe to assume that most cases are no longer infectious. The second type, Lepromatous leprosy is the more generalized form and the whole body may be involved. The skin lesion is a macule or lump and the ear lobes are enlarged early on in the course of the disease. The skin on the face is thickened, especially on the cheeks and around the eyes, which has led to the condition being described as 'the lion face'. There are many leprosy organisms in the skin biopsy of lepromatous patients, making them the more infectious cases.

Dr. Chung-Hoon gave me every assistance, and with his help I was able to see the local leprosy programme in Honolulu. He flew me to the old Leprosarium at Kalaupapa on the island of Molakai. Here I found many old 'burnt out' cases of the disease. Most were no longer infectious, but because of residual deformities or because their relatives and friends had died, they had decided to remain in Kalaupapa.

Thirty-percent of these patients had cars. There was a foot and horse track up a high cliff to the main island, but only three miles of road in the leprosarium, so their opportunities for touring were limited. They could cover the three miles of road in five minutes without breaking any speed limits. I did not inquire how their fuel arrived, though I imagine their need was modest. I didn't know how they coped when the cars broke down either, as there weren't many mechanics in this tiny, isolated community.

Dr. Chung-Hoon's medical officers in Honolulu had developed a programme that allowed the non-infectious cases to be discharged or treated as outpatients. This took away the fear of hospitalisation and allowed the patients to lead near-normal lives.

After a pleasant month in Hawaii, spent becoming more familiar with the disease, I was all set to go to Micronesia.

Before I left, I was sitting on a stool at the bar and a young sailor next to me must have been homesick or wanting company. He asked "Where are you from?" and when I replied "From New Zealand", he looked at me blankly. He obviously didn't know where New Zealand was. He didn't ask, and that was the end of the conversation.

Micronesia August 1952 – August 1953

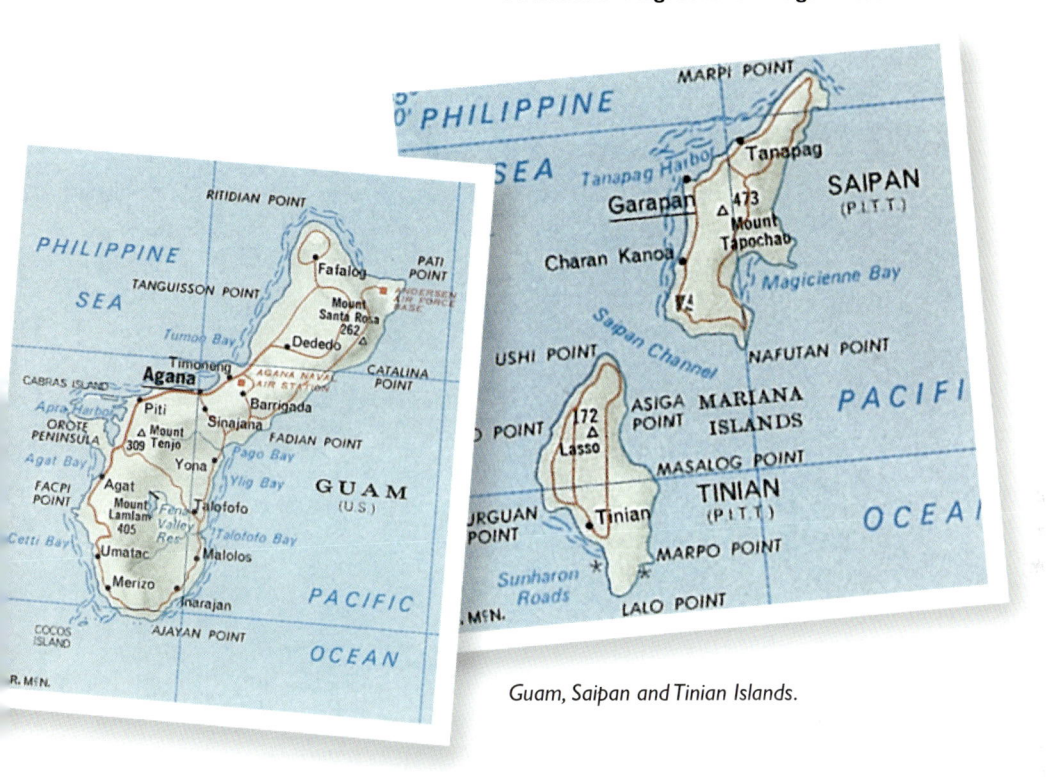

Guam, Saipan and Tinian Islands.

On the last night before leaving for Saipan, I went out on the town with Dr. Marshall's daughter, her boy friend and a young female companion for me. We went around half a dozen bars and asked for 'rum and raspberry', which was the latest drink in Dunedin. They had rum, but nobody had heard of the raspberry cordial flavouring, so as 'beggars can't be choosers' we made do with whatever alcohol they had. When we at last drove up to Dr. Marshall's house, at 3 a.m., we found Dr. Marshall walking up and down outside his gate carrying his suitcase. He was to accompany me to the Trust Territories, and our plane was due to leave in one hour. His daughter said "We've been all over town looking for rum and raspberry for Dr. Valentine, but they didn't have any raspberry I'm afraid." This put me on the back foot with my new boss who was a Mormon, and they disapprove of drinking alcohol.

We hurried to the YMCA to pack my belongings. The man at the front office said that I couldn't take the daughter's boyfriend upstairs with me, as two men were not allowed in the room at the same time. Being a Christian organisation I suppose they didn't want any same sex relationships on their conscience. We said it was an emergency and he permitted us to both go upstairs to do the packing job in extra quick time. Dr. Marshall and I made a dash to the airport and caught our plane to Guam. We were seated side by side for the eight hour flight; Dr. Marshall seemed strangely silent all this time and I knew that I'd made a poor start to my new job.

We changed planes at Guam, and then set off for Saipan. Again there was a strained silence until we were on the ground at the Saipan airport. Dr. Marshall preceded me down the steps where a group of men and women were waiting to meet us. Saipan had a massive airport which had been built in WWII as part of the final offensive against the Japanese mainland. I took in the large Quonset hut with the sign "Welcome to Saipan", in large letters across the front.

I saw about 20 vehicles, of all shapes and sizes, lined up with their waiting owners standing around them. Most of the vehicles were Jeeps which had been left by the U.S. military, but were becoming difficult to service because the American forces had thoughtlessly failed to leave enough spare parts to maintain them.

As the new doctor for the Tinian Leprosarium, I was the centre of attention. Among those waiting was Dr. Tintinger, who was in charge of the hospital at Saipan. Dr. Richardson, who was visiting from Truk, welcomed me heartily and impressed me as a personable and alert individual in his early thirties. Dr. Titinger was also in his thirties, but was a little overweight and slower in manner. My feet were on the Trust Territory at last. I could now start my new job in this remote part of the Pacific Ocean.

I was next introduced to a large man with a huge cigar pointing out from under a very large straw hat. This was Mr. Hedges, the District Administrator for Saipan and Tinian who was an engineer and owned a factory in Chicago. He and his wife had tired of their bourgeois ways amid the industrial city smoke stacks and dreamed of sailing to the South Seas in their own yacht. Thousands, or perhaps millions of us, have had similar dreams. Mr. & Mrs. Hedges differed from the majority in that they actually made their dreams real by purchasing a yacht and setting sail for the South Pacific. They had put a manager in their factory and told all of their friends that Bora Bora in the Tahiti group was their next port of call. In Bora Bora they learned to speak the language and employed a young Tahitian man who helped them sail their yacht to Saipan. There had been a change in administration after elections in the U.S, and as is usual, many new appointments in public offices were made. During this post-election period, Mr. Hedges was appointed Administrator for Saipan and Tinian. I was surprised to learn that while I was on Saipan I was to stay with the Hedges, in their own home. They were good hosts and for our first night in Saipan they held a party for the medical people on the island. At the party we were invited to have an alcoholic drink. In response Dr. Marshall said "I don't take alcohol, but if you have some rum and raspberry Dr. Valentine would like some."

This broke the ice and the next day, while I was seeing Dr. Marshall off at the Saipan airport, he told me that he was very worried about the leprosarium on the neighbouring island of Tinian. He said "It is a big responsibility for a young man, but I think you can do it." Dr. Marshall was relying on me to improve the situation at the leprosarium and I hoped that I would not disappoint him. I already knew that all was not well on Tinian. The doctors and hospital administrators told me that Miss Lindsay, the Leprosy Hospital Secretary, was neurotic. Furthermore, the patients were working, salvaging scrap metal left from the war, and were wandering all over the island. As if this wasn't enough, to add to their difficulties, it was common knowledge that the hospital Administrative Assistant, Mr. Trout, drank too much. This begs an observation that I can't let pass by; Mr. Trout drank like a fish!

The Mariana Islands are volcanic, and Mt. Tapachau on Saipan, at 1,500 feet, is a prominent feature. These islands are high in contrast to the sea level coral atolls which most of us visualise when Pacific Islands are mentioned. Both Saipan and Tinian are close to 15 miles long and 6 miles wide at their widest part.

On Saipan, everything was being reclaimed by the jungle.

Most of the local people lived in small houses constructed from scrap, salvaged from the wrecked buildings that were left after the Japanese/American battle of Saipan in June 1944. Along the road from the airport many of the houses had small shops attached, which sold basic necessities. Most had "Millars High Life Beer" signs prominently displayed.

Having been only a day out of Honolulu, where all the modern amenities were on hand, I thought this was the end of the earth. The doctors told me that the Island of Saipan was fiercely fought over when the Americans invaded from the south in the last year of the war. The Japanese military and the civilians were forced up the island towards the high cliffs in the north. Rather than surrender or be killed by the advancing Americans, most of the Japanese civilian men threw their wives and children over the steep cliffs. They then jumped themselves. There were 30,000 Japanese military and 20,000 civilians who died and only 600 Japanese survived to be taken prisoner.

Mr. Hedges told me that the Saipan/Tinian district had a population of about ten thousand people. Most were native Chamorros whose blood was now mixed with that of the Spanish, German and Japanese who had controlled the islands at different times. The Japanese, who were there between 1914 - 1944, were the only occupiers who really developed the islands economically. They had thousands of Japanese and Koreans working sugar cane farms on both Saipan and Tinian.

On Saipan, I was taken to the local hospital, which was made up of 20 large Quonset Huts left by the U.S. forces. Dr. Richardson said that few local patients were seen, as the Chamorros did not like Dr. Titinger, who was reserved and did not inspire their trust. Another doctor had, quite unprofessionally, told me that Dr. Titinger was "fat and lazy", so that may have had something to do with it too.

My colleagues knew that I was keen on practising surgery, so Dr. Marshall had asked Dr. Titinger to call on me should any surgery be needed. Having visited the operating theatre, I was pleased at the prospect and hoped that I could get the nursing staff to help

Tinian harbour in 1953. Note the large airfield which was one of many on the island. This was the largest air complex in the world at the time and were built in preparation to service the U.S. military's attack on Japan.

Aerial view of the U.S. settlement on Tinian. The Leprosarium is the lowest group of buildings.

me. I was soon to learn that the Island of Tinian was almost two hours away by boat, and as there was no aircraft at the time it would be impractical to get across in time to do urgent surgery.

The next morning, accompanied by Doctors Richardson and Titinger, I set off for Tinian. We went down to the dock where the boat was waiting to take us across the narrow strait and down the west coast of Tinian. An 'M' boat left over from the war was lying at the dock. It was old and oily, and rather than having seats, passengers had to stand on an open platform, unprotected from the blazing sun. Several young men came down to the wharf to see the boat go out and they looked as if they expected it to never return from 'The wilds of Tinian'.

After two hours on the small boat in the choppy sea, my face was sun burnt and my stomach was churning. Sailing almost the full length of Tinian Island was an interesting experience in spite of this. Signs of the Japanese occupation were everywhere. The bright green of sugar cane farms covered the island. There were now six hundred people living on Tinian, but during the Japanese occupation, five thousand people lived there, with three quarters of the island under intense cultivation. Now their sugar cane fields had gone to rack and ruin and reverted back to dense green jungle.

We passed the small beaches where American forces had come ashore in July 1944. The invaders had really 'slipped in the back door' because the Japanese weren't expecting them to land on these two narrow beaches. Obvious landing points further south had been fortified, but the two tiny beaches on Tinian's rocky western coastline to the north remained unguarded. After Saipan had been taken by the Americans, Tinian was 'softened up' by U.S. planes, which by then had complete control of the air. Tinian's five thousand military defenders were disorganised and uncoordinated, but were as willing as ever to die for the Emperor. A large U.S. Naval force then shelled Tinian Town, but this was only a cover for the real landings. Soon thousands of marines were pouring onto the undefended beaches, closer to Saipan. It was their job to establish a beach head by that evening. The marines held their positions against spasmodic Japanese counter attacks during the

Micronesia August 1952 – August 1953

Tinian Leprosarium patients' quarters.

An overview of the Leprosarium. The hospital, housed in quonset huts, is in the foreground.

night, and the next day the tremendous job of getting men and supplies over the reef and up the beaches really began. The supply lines never failed and Tinian's battle became a classic example of a well organized, amphibious operation.

Each day the marines pushed the defenders further down towards the rocky south end of the island. Here, in caves in the high coral cliffs many soldiers holed-up. Once again the Japanese civilian families threw themselves to their deaths on the rocks at the foot of the cliffs because they believed the Japanese Army propaganda about their fates if the Americans captured them. The soldiers that remained in the caves were dealt with by flame throwers and explosive charges. Many were filmed as they came out covered in flames and screaming as they died. I am grateful that the priest who told us about Hell while I was at school did not know about this or he would have had another powerful tale to tell.

At long last our small boat came into the port of Tinian Town. It had previously been an active port, but was now disintegrating. Old hulks lay around and two lone Chamorros looked at us from the wharf. We waited for twenty minutes, and eventually were met by the local Methodist Missionary and his smiling wife. He was a young, lean man who looked about eighteen but claimed 24 years and one year of college at home in the U.S. He kindly took us to Tinian's hotel where we had a meal. This building had originally been built to house General Underhill, who was the General Commander of Tinian after the Japanese defeat. At some stage his former residence had been converted into a small hotel, where you could buy meals and cold beer. Mr. Flemming, a half European, ran this place with his Chamorro wife and their attractive daughter Daisy. Most of the islanders on Tinian at this time were Chamorros, who had previously lived on Yap. The U.S. Navy had relocated them from there to Tinian, after the war ended. Daisy was a sweet young woman, and Mr. Flemming was his usual polite self and gave us unimpeded views of his one remaining tooth, whenever he smiled.

My quonset house was next door to the hotel. It was large and roomy and when we looked inside there were many womens' nylon or silk stockings strewn about. I was to learn that my predecessor consoled himself with the comforting presence of local ladies. Sadly, all the women he entertained were gone, with only their stockings to show that they had been there. The place was a shambles, and the water supply was off and wasn't to be repaired for another two weeks. The doctor had a Jeep, and earlier that day the crank case had broken. It was to be four weeks until it was on the road again.

After lunch the missionary took us down to the leprosarium. The roads on Tinian were beautifully surfaced by the U.S. Seabees, but trees were growing over the previously wide thoroughfare and there was only just enough room for a Jeep to get through. Soon we came to a notice almost concealed by the high grass, saying "Tinian Leprosarium - no admission except by permission of the Medical Officer".

A queer feeling crept over me as we bumped over the short road leading to the colony. On our left were small houses which had been painted white two or three years previously. They had been used to house Japanese Prisoners of War. Some of the houses had windows and doors missing. Two or three apathetic patients stood around as we drove in. They watched listlessly as we got out and went into the office. This was an old Catholic church with its steeple still intact. Here I met Jessie Lindsay, the old lady about whom I had been warned. Jessie was in her fifties and she greeted me politely, and appeared slightly nervous as she rustled papers. Then Mr. Trout, the hospital administrator, came forward. He was a small, round man wearing a tooth-brush moustache and an airy 'certainly-doctor-we-can-fix-that-up-straight-away' attitude. I was shown my desk, which was partially partitioned from the church cum office, and we set out to inspect the rest of the leprosarium.

A middle aged patient called Ben ran a store where the other patients could purchase nick-nacks; small bottles of perfume were a popular item he told me. I looked at the bottles which were sweet smelling bottles of hair lotion. Ben's face had the lumps of advanced lepromatous leprosy. Although he didn't understand English well, he was highly intelligent, and his figures were always correct.

Next we went to the treatment room. This was a small building

Hell-Bent for Life

where the patients came each morning for their tablets or injections. The injection given was called Promin and there was a sign, 'Promin Room', above the door. We went through a screen door into a small waiting room. Eight patients sat around waiting, along with two dogs for company. A young man and an eleven year old boy were giving intravenous injections to two older people, who sat with their arms out in front of them. The Promin solution was injected into the vein in front of their elbows. I was amazed that the eleven year old could do the technically demanding procedure. The cloth on which the patients rested their arms had seen better days, and rather than being white, it was almost grey. The interior of the building had once been white but was now also a shade of grey. I did my best to smile at the people and as we went out the door Dr. Richardson commented, "A little paint would brighten it up." We next went to the hospital, where 15 people were in bed in the Quonset hut wards. Visitors sat around on beds and dogs lay on the floor. An atmosphere of dirt and neglect was everywhere. I put on a brave face and smiled at everyone I met.

The doctors I had travelled with had to return to Saipan on the boat, but before he left Dr. Richardson assured me that I only had to ask for whatever I wanted and it would come. That night I went to bed after dinner at the hotel a very thoughtful person. I was a long way from home and in US territory with less than $200 to my name. On the other hand I had more responsibility than I had ever known, and the Leprosarium was in a disgraceful state. I knew that it was going to be a challenge, but I did not realise just how difficult it was going to be. I know that you are waiting with bated breath so I will press on!

The next day began with an early start and as patient morale was low, I exaggerated my cheerful veneer to draw a reluctant smile from those I met. Jessie Lindsay was as helpful as she could be and I soon suspected that she was not the neurotic I'd been led to believe. Mr. Trout was lazy and incompetent, but he gave signs of regeneration. The native doctor and head nurse did everything to help too and the patients seemed pleased to see someone who would take an interest in them.

My first problem was to assure good and adequate food for the leprosarium patients. I discovered that no rice had been delivered for two months. Rice was the patients' basic staple, and as there was almost nothing else to give them it was a grim situation. The store rooms were almost bare. The Protestant missionary had been buying rice and seeing it was distributed to the patients. There was a Catholic Priest on the Island and most of the patients were Catholic, so this situation was awkward. I was told that the previous doctor and Mr. Trout had been asking for rice for two months and the radio log bore this out. I sent two dispatches asking that rice be sent over, and when this brought no result I went over to Saipan. Mr. Hedges, the District Administrator, was properly dismayed when made aware of the situation. He called in the supply officer and I was assured of a regular delivery. It was two months before the adequate supplies appeared, and in the mean time I had to arrange, at two week intervals, for stop-gap supplies from Saipan. Whenever I went over to Saipan, the Hedges accommodated me at their home and the two day break was always most welcome. It was still not quite 'urban civilisation' but it would do until something better turned up. It soon dawned on me that the social situation on Tinian, amongst the few Europeans, was torn apart by misunderstandings, personal dislikes and antagonisms bordering on hatred. The previous doctor had been a chronic alcoholic. He had entertained everybody in the small community who wished to be entertained, at frequent parties which went on half the night. His liquor bill for one month was $200, which was a lot in those days. He was a good entertainer and most people liked him socially. However, when he went to the leprosarium he rarely stayed longer than 15 minutes and sometimes did not re-appear for a week. That didn't seem to bother the local Americans too much. Compounding the problem was the fact that Mr. Trout, the administrator, was also an alcoholic and drank over ten ounces of ethyl alcohol from the hospital stores each day. He supplemented this with beer bought at the hotel. He too was a fine talker but very seldom did the job he was paid to do.

Jessie Lindsay was a Mormon, and all of this bothered her. She spoke about it to those involved and to visitors, and although her own life was impeccable, she became the whipping post for the Tinian community. When I was in a house with three or four others, half the conversation was directed at pulling Jessie down. I was surprised that the missionary and his wife were also involved in this. All the while Jessie worked away conscientiously and did her best to help me. I soon found it embarrassing to listen to this talk about Jessie as I respected her much more than the people who were criticising her.

I suspected that Dr. Armer was also an alcoholic. On most occasions, when I got to the hospital at eight, only two or three members of the staff were about. The others would appear an hour later with sleepy expressions and red eyes. The doctor confided that he was upset about his wife, who lived in the Marshall Islands, and was having trouble with her third pregnancy. I sent a dispatch to the doctor at the Marshalls asking about her condition, and found that she was healthy, but that the baby had died. I told the intern and he seemed relieved that at least his wife was well.

In the storerooms, there were many ten gallon jars of ethyl alcohol which had been ordered by Mr. Trout. It became obvious that this wasn't used for cleaning microscope slides, but was siphoned off daily by Mr. Trout for his own use, and any surplus was handed around to his co-workers. I called the staff together and showed them that I was injecting a solution of corrosive sublimate into the bottles of alcohol and told them that it was now a deadly poison.

I had a medical emergency on my hands in the American area. I was called to see a seriously ill two year old girl at the hotel. I don't remember how her illness had started but this was the first time I had been asked to see her.

When I went to see the child in the bed room I was surprised by the crowd of Americans and Chamorros gathered in the room. Before I examined the child I asked them all to move out, which is standard medical practice. Some people thought that I was unreasonable and unsympathetic to insist on this and disliked me because of it. As the child was not improving, we arranged for a U.S. Air Force plane from Guam to come and pick her up and take her to the hospital there. She eventually recovered, but some of the Americans maintained their dislike of me from that time. The situation wasn't helped by the fact that while I was preoccupied by the child's illness, and absent from the leprosarium, Mr. Trout had taken a case of beer to one of the patients' houses and staged a party. It was a standing rule that there was to be no alcohol given to the patients.

At this time I was having difficulty sleeping. Some of the patients were still without adequate food and some were resentful that I had stopped them working for an American scrap metal company. They had been employed, along with Filipino labourers, to break up aeroplanes that had been left after the war ended. Most were parked on the tarmac but others needed to be dragged from the cane fields where they had crashed. The planes were cut up and melted into aluminium ingots for sale overseas. If collectors could get these planes for restoration now I presume they would be worth mega bucks. In the meantime this scrap metal could well have been used to make your cooking utensils. We are all familiar with the phrase 'swords into plough shares', but it's a new twist to have 'aeroplanes into pots and pans'. My patients were working for the scrap metal merchants and it was my task to stop them. I assured them that we would get their gardens and a fishing boat going, so they could put their time and energy into getting food for the whole leprosy community. They seemed keen to make a start.

In all this stormy blackness there came a ray of sunshine. Mr. Trout received a despatch from his sister, saying his mother had been admitted to hospital and that he should come home. It was part of our contract with our employers that they would pay for our return trip home if there was a family emergency. Mr. Trout had been sending out his belongings for several weeks before his recall, so we were sure he had planned his departure. There is a poem referring to 'Remittance Men', who were sent away from England, usually because of some social embarrassment they had caused their families. These Remittance Men would receive monthly payments from their families at home. Most would spend it on alcohol, and live in pecuniary need until their next payment arrived. The poem describes these men as; "True patriots they, for be it understood, that they left their country for their own country's good." This may be interpreted quite differently in Mr. Trout's case. The U.S. would be worse off and Tinian the better, for Mr. Trout's exit. I was pleased to see him go and ensured that no obstacles were put in his way. I felt sorry for him, as I stood on the dock, with only three others there to wave him goodbye.

As Mr. Trout had left, I hoped his influence would weaken, and called a meeting of all staff members after lunch. They all appeared for the meeting, except for Dr. Armer who had a headache. I told those in attendance that Mr. Trout had been a bad influence, and that now he was gone they should develop some real sense of responsibility. My pronouncement was not taken badly and two of the boys thanked me on their way out.

I went straight to Dr. Armer's headquarters afterwards and told him the next time he let me down I would bust him at Headquarters or bust him with my fist. I asked him which he preferred but he didn't give me an answer. In some ways, I really felt sorry for this half-trained, half-Japanese doctor who felt so superior to the islanders with whom he had to live and work. He called them 'Kanakas'.

The administrator on Tinian was Mr. East, who was awaiting the arrival of cattle from America. He needed to make yards and fenced areas pending their arrival and asked me to let patients do this work. He promised that in about two weeks, when that was done, he would be free to spend almost all of his time on hospital projects. The cattle duly arrived but after many long weeks there was still no help forthcoming for leprosarium grounds or gardens.

Before he left, Dr. Marshall suggested that I publish a small newsletter about the work at Tinian, and I decided to go ahead with this. Jessie Lindsay persuaded some of the patients to tell their stories in Japanese, their common language. I asked that she have their stories translated into English but kept as close to the original intent as possible.

Here is a summary of two of the stories; Venito E. Gurtamag told his story. He said that in 1925, when the Japanese found leprosy they held a meeting with all the district chiefs to decide where they would establish a leprosarium. The chiefs suggested Pekel Island (now called Leper Island) about 20 minutes by canoe from Yap. The Japanese accepted this and sent carpenters with lumber to build three buildings. Eventually there were 30 patients on the island including three from Saipan and three from Rota.

The patients on Leper Island were not allowed to leave their island, so the chiefs sent a man called Falameyog to care for the patients, and the Japanese sent supplies once a month. At the beginning of the war the Japanese Government were not able to continue supplying the island so the island chiefs sent food. As the war progressed there was so much disruption that no food arrived and the patients were reduced to eating leaves off the trees to keep themselves alive. Some of the patients left Leper Island and hid in the various districts on Yap; when the Japanese found any of these escapees, they were shot at once.

When the Americans arrived, they gave food and medical supplies to those on Yap Island and the 20 patients left on Leper Island. On 23 September 1948, the American doctor on Yap asked the chiefs to gather all the leprosy patients from the district, to be sent to Tinian and on the 7 September 1948, 65 people arrived at Tinian.

Paulos M. Smith also told his story to Jessie. He said that in 1929, when the Japanese were in possession of the Palau Islands, a Dr. Isek discovered several cases of leprosy. They consulted the chiefs and elected to establish another leprosarium at Ngurur Island, about one hour's ride by canoe from Koror. They built nine buildings for the patients and the helpers who were to work among the patients.

When the first patients were about to go to the new leprosarium on 10 January 1930, they held a farewell party. It seemed that the families of the patients were finding this looming separation harder to face than the patients, so they were given permission to go to the island to live for a few months.

NOTES FROM TINIAN LEPROSARIUM

1 January 1953

STORY OF THE LEPROSY ISLAND IN THE PALAU ISLANDS
(NGURUR ISLAND)

by

Paulos M. Smith

In the year 1929 the Japanese were in possission of the Palau Islands. Dr. Isok discovered several cases of leprosy, so 15 September 1929 he met with all the District Chief's to report his findings and to decide where a Leprosarium should be established. The Chief of Koror District, Mr. Tom, suggested "Ngurur Island". It is located near the Western end of Koror, about one hours ride by Canoe.

The District Chief sent laborers and lumber enough to build nine houses and the Japanese Bovernment sent labor and lumber to build four houses. The nine buildings were for non-lepers who were to work among the patients and care for them, while the four buildings were to be used as follows: three for Hospital wards and one for storing medical supplies. The buildings were completed by the 30th of November 1929.

The date for the first patients to go to the new Leprosarium at "Ngurur Island" was set as 10 January 1930. At this time the friends and families of the patients gave a farewell party. As the time drew near for the parting it seemed that the families of the lepers were taking it harder than the patients themselves. They were crying so much that the Doctor gave them the permission to go with their loved ones to "Ngurur Island" to stay for a few months.

The following 18 patients were the first to be admitted to "Ngurur Island Leprosarium" on 10th January 1930

Ngirasuh, male from Babelthaup
Rimireh, male "   "
Bokerruul, male "   "
Poroniga, female "   "
Uerriang, female "   "
Odiurenges, male "   "
Oterriil, female "   "
Ngirasakadoi, male from Koror
Marsil, male   "   "

Oligong, male from Babelthaup
Skang, male   "   "
Onlei, female "   "
Mosiuet, male "   "
Brass, male   "   "
Mesengei, male "   "
Ronguul, male "   "
Ngiraurur, male from Bililicu
Themleu, female "   "

The Japanese government sent them food and medical supplies once a month. Medical treatment consisted of one Capsule per day probably Chaulmoogra Oil.

After being on the island one year and finding that the disease was getting no better by the treatment they were receiving, some of the patients became despondent and took their own lives by hanging themselves on the trees of the island.

Then the effects of World War II was felt by the natives of "Ngurur Island". Supplies became slack and they soon used up their supply of vegetables in their little gardens and then as had been done in other islands, they resorted to leaves of the trees for food. Conditions steadily grew worse for them and many left "Ngurur Island" hiding in the Districts on Babelthaup where most of the patients were from. A few of these were found by the Japanese and killed.

The story of 'The leprosy Island in the Palau Islands (Ngurur Island)' and a short history of Tinian Leprosarium (dated 1st January 1953).

Micronesia   August 1952 – August 1953

In 1945 the Americans brought food and medical supplies to the island. Only three lepers and two non-lepers of the former 20 inhabants of "Ngurur Island" were left by this time.

In 1948 the American Doctor examined the five inhabantants of the island and the two non-patients returned to their home island.

I was admitted 26 August 1932 from Babelthaup Island to the Leprosarium on "Ngurur Island" and I am the only patient alive of the former patients. The Americans closed the Leprosarium when they sent all leper patients of the Trust Territory to Tinian Leprosarium, in the Mariana Islands. I arrived 7 September 1948 on a large Navy boat, which also took other leper patients aboard from the "Loper Island" near Yap, Western Caroline Islands. We were met on Tinian by Dr. Jack Millar.

....

TINIAN LEPROSARIUM

The Tinian Leprosarium was established September 1948 under the U.S. Navy. At this time all patients known to have active leprosy were brought in from all parts of Micronesia.

Dr. Jack Millar was the first Doctor and was replaced 1950 by Dr. Gordan McNeilly, who was replaced 1951 by Dr. William deShazo. When the Trust Territory took over 1 July 1951, Dr. Raymond W. Dowidat replaced Dr. W. deShazo. August 1951 Dr. Dowidat was replaced by our present Physician, Dr. John Valentine.

January 1, 1953 the Navy is again taking over the Islands of Saipan and Tinian so once, again at least for the present, the Navy will have the Administration of the Leprosarium.

At this date the Tinian Leprosarium has 108 patients. Many of these are now elegible for discharge.

From 5th December 1952 to 26th December 1952 Dr. Morman R. Sloan, Lererologist fuu the South Pacific Commission Has been visiting Tinian Leprosarium. With Dr. John Valentine accompanying him he will visit all the Districts of the Trust Territory in the interest of Leprosy.

In 1945 the Americans brought food and medical supplies to the island. Only three lepers and two non-lepers of the former 20 inhabants of "Ngurur Island" were left by this time.

```
          NOTES FROM TINIAN LEPROSARIUM
                    1 November 1952
```

YAP LEPER ISLAND
by
Venito E. Gurtamag

During the Japanese time in 1925 the Doctor on Yap Island found People who had leprosy so he held a meeting with all the District Chief's to decide where they could establish a Leprosarium. The Chief of Weloay District by the name of Waayan, suggested "Pokel Island" (now called Leper Island), located at the east end of Yap Island, a distance of about 20 minutes by Canoe from Yap.

The Japanese accepted the Chiefs suggestion and gave some lumber and sent carpenters. The District Chief's of all the Districts on Yap furnished the labor to help the carpenters. They built three buildings - one for the women's Ward - one for the Men's Ward and one for a store room for medical supplies.

The work was finished on "Leper Island" 16 July 1925 and the District Chief's gave a grand opening party. Games, dancing and plenty of good food was enjoyed by all present. Ten patients were the first to be brought there, four women and six men as follows:-

   1. Looyun   (female)   1. Fanoy   (male)
   2. Manna   (female)   2. Faloyog   (male)
   3. Ruamtin (female)   3. Gilbuuo   (male)
   4. Lockthin (female)   4. Waathangig (male)
                               5. Falosongon (male)
                               6. Yirig   (male)

This number increased until there were about 30 on the Island, three from Saipan, Valontin; Jose (later killed by Japanese) and Lodrigo. Three from Rota, Josus; Marry and Mosesh. One from Okinawa, Angkiga (names unknown). Others coming from Ulithi (working on Yap.) At that time the Japanese had three leprosariums - one on "Leper Island" which took in the Marianna Islands and Yap; one on Ngurur Island in the Palau's which took in only the Palau Islands; and one on Ele Island in the Marshall Islands which took in Truk, Ponape and the Marshall Islands.

The patients on "Leper Island" were not allowed to leave the Island, so Chief Waayan sent a man by the name of Falamoyog, from the village of Kaday in Weloay District, a non-leper to live with the lepers and to see that they were properly taken care of. The Japanese government sent supplies once a month and he issued them. When an emergency would arise he would go to Yap and get the needed supplies himself.

During the war the Japanese government became short of supplies so the District Chief's supplied the lepers. Then the war became so intense that it was impossible to get supplies to "Leper Island" so the patients had to eat leaves off the trees to keep themselves alive. Some of the patients deserted "Leper Island" and hid themselves in the various Districts on Yap but when the Japanese found any of those they were killed at once. This kept up until the Americans occupied the Island of Yap in 1946. The Americans gave food and Medical supplies to the people on Yap Island and also to the 20 patients now left on "Leper Island". The buildings had been damaged by bombs dropped by planes so the District Chiefs sent men over to repair them.

An article reporting the history of the Yap Island lepers published in 'Notes from the Tinian Leprosarium' (3 November, 1952).

Micronesia August 1952 – August 1953

September 3rd 1948 the American Doctor on Yap Island asked the Chief's to get all the lepers from the various Districts and they would send them along with the patients from "Leper Island" to the Island of Tinian. About 65 were located and arrived 7 September 1948 reporting to Dr. Millar on Tinian. From that day until now they have received free Medical care and are a very happy people. Since receiving Diasone and Promin drugs many have been able to return to their families and friends, for which they are grateful to the Trust Territory.

****

BIOPSIES

Public Health memorandum No. 13 deals with leprosy in the Trust Territories. It states correctly "The cardinal points for which he must constantly be looking for are:—
(1) Sensory, trophic or color changes in the skin.
(2) Thickened and tender peripheral nerve trunks.
(3) Presence of acid fast organisms in "snips" or mucous membranes."

It says "since tuberculoid lesions are often bacteriologically negative a biopsy of the infected area may be necessary." The memorandum requests the biopsies be sent to Dr. George Fite, National Institute of Health, Bethesda 14, Maryland.

Among the many reports received here from D. Fite, in only one has he made a diagnosis of leprosy without having seen the leprosy organism.

In the last six weeks we have received five biopsy reports from the Guam Memorial Hospital. Each case has been diagnosed as leprosy and in no case is mention made of the leprosy organism!

Please Doctors send your biopsies to Dr. Fite.

John Valentine

****

THE FOLLOWING PATIENTS HAVE RETURNED TO THEIR HOMES SINCE 1st. Sept. 1952:

Sitauo to Truk
Sien to Truk
Tipas to Majuro
Madarian to Koror
Maile to Yap
Layag to Yap
Gopin Niga to Yap
Buu to Yap
Rosa Isaxiki to Guam
Falanug to Yap
Elkinwer to Majuro
Soinu to Ponape
Ekar to Ponape

Kadmo to Truk
Nuial to Majuro
Francisco Cruz to Guam
Garad to Yap
Flagru to Yap
Labelon to Yap
Gillian to Yap
Peter Rumon to Yap
Jesus Paulino to Guam
Giminong to Yap
Sokisi to Ponape
Aketa to Ponape
Consolacion Kitugua to Saipan

****

Published irregularly by the staff and patients of Tinian Leprosarium, Saipan District, Mariana Islands, Trust Territory of the Pacific Islands.

Eighteen patients were admitted to the new leprosarium. Treatment consisted of one capsule a day of Chaulmoogra Oil, which was a plant extract that had questionable effectiveness as a treatment for the disease. After being on the Island for one year, and finding their disease was getting no better, many of the patients became despondent and took their lives by hanging themselves from trees.

On Leper Island, in the Yap district and on Ngurur Island the Japanese Government sent the leprosy patients food and medical supplies once a month, but those shipments were also disrupted by the war. Soon they had used up all of the vegetables from their little gardens and to survive they also had to resort to eating the leaves from trees. As conditions steadily grew worse many of the patients left the island and hid on Babelthaup, their home island. Once again, if found by the Japanese, these escapees were killed. When the Americans came the few remaining patients were transferred to Tinian.

We sent copies of these rather unsophisticated efforts to all the Trust Territory doctors and to the head offices of the American and International Leprosy Association. Perry Burgess, President of the American Leprosy Association wrote back and sent me a signed copy of his book 'Who Walk Alone'. This is the story of an American who developed signs of leprosy after exposure while in the Philippines at the time of the Spanish-American war in the late 1800s. At that time there was little chance of arresting the disease, and the story of his separation from his family and sweetheart is very moving. Doctor Wade, President of the International Leprosy Association and doctor in charge of Culion Leprosarium in the Philippines, wrote enthusiastically and asked to have a summary of the notes printed in the International Journal of Leprosy. Some of the doctors in the district wrote to say how pleased they were that someone working in the area had found a way of making the wider medical community aware of the problems of treating leprosy patients in our remote area.

For many years it had been thought necessary to put every

person diagnosed with Leprosy on an isolated Island so that they would not infect others. I had been told in Hawaii that many cases of Leprosy were not infectious, while others had healed without treatment, so there was no need to keep all patients in isolation. Those that did not need isolation could be treated as outpatients in their own districts. When reviewing the patients already at Tinian, I was distressed to find many who, in my opinion, were not infectious or did not have the disease, so should never have been sent to Tinian. As I had only a few months working with the disease I wanted someone with more experience to support me in my assessments.

Most of the patients on Tinian did not like being separated from their families. They came from Islands widely different in physical character and culture and were not used to the food supplied at the leprosarium. On their home islands they had a defined place in the community and were under the leadership of the family head and the village chief. There they had fixed duties for growing vegetables and fishing. On Tinian they were lost, with no family or chiefs to guide them, and in this strange environment they found little to do but write letters and flick through Sears Roebuck Mail Order Catalogues. Their meat and rice was given to them so why should they work? As leadership and motivation was lacking in our patients, we found it impossible to get them to keep their living quarters clean and tidy.

It was clear to me that bringing patients to Tinian, some hundreds of miles away from their homes, was an unacceptable solution for the leprosy control programme. I suspected that people in the outer districts were concealing their disease for fear of being directed to come to Tinian. In a few cases patients, now at Tinian, had had the last rites of the Catholic Church performed for them before they left their home islands. Much of the distress caused by isolation would be taken away if the patients could be kept in their own districts. Their relatives could visit them and they could have their own gardens and go fishing. The chiefs could be called in as necessary to exert moral pressure on the patients to work in the village, keep the place clean and help their chances of their condition improving.

A CHANGED ATTITUDE TOWARD LEPROSY

By John Valentine, physician in charge, Trust Territory Leprosarium, Tinian

In 1873 Father Damien arrived at the leprosarium at Kalaupapa on the Hawaiian Island of Molokai, and recently, on my visit, the life of the patients and staff there seemed to move on as usual. But Kalaupapa as an institution may be said to have aplastic anemia, i.e., no new patients have been received at that isolated hospital for two years.

During all past years the principal of complete segregation of leper patients has been accepted. The state has separated the patient from his family and friends and taken complete charge of his material welfare. That this has been well done is seen by the fact that among the 250 patients on Molokai today, 140 patients own cars.

But the effects of segregation have been reflected in a high divorce rate between patients and their healthy partners on the outside. Moreover, a patient who was finally discharged was frequently refused by his family. Many patients, cured but with residual deformities, were afraid to face an unfamiliar world and preferred to remain, completely cared for, in the leprosarium.

Today in Honolulu bacteriologically negative cases are being treated as outpatients. They take the sulphone drugs at home and return to the clinic for adjustment of the dosage and blood estimations.

"Open" cases are still admitted to an institution called Hale Mohalu (Happy Home) on the outskirts of Honolulu. Here "open" cases undergoing treatment may receive their friends during generous visiting hours. A special bus is available to take patients to see sights and parades in town. Those able and willing to work are paid and encouraged.

A special office of the Health Department encourages the public to accept Leprosy, or Hansen's Disease as it is called in Hawaii, as a curable disease and not as a Biblical scourge.

When the patient is cured and becomes a "closed" case, it is expected that he will be accepted back into his home and into society as a useful member.

I owe a debt of gratitude to E.K. Chung-Hoon, M.D. and G.H. Hedgecock, M.D., both of the Department of Health, Territory of Hawaii, for making it possible for me to observe and study their cases and their program.

* * *

An article written by the author titled 'A changed attitude to Leprosy' (September 1952).

On Tinian I was in a hopeless position. The Public Works foreman told me, when I first arrived, that the patients' fishing boat would be operable in two weeks. Although I had frequently asked about it, it still lay, un-repaired, at the wharf. During a rainstorm it had filled with water and sunk to the bottom.

While the patients were willing but unable to use the boat for fishing, we were supplying them with 2½ pounds of meat each week. They preferred fish, rather than the meat which was imported from the States at great cost. With the agriculture and fishing programme at a standstill after three months, I was ready to put in my resignation.

Then, unexpectedly, a bomb shell was dropped into our small community. The U.S. Navy was taking over Tinian! The Guam military needed the magnificent airfields to be available in case they were required to support the Korean War effort and it would be relatively easy to bring the airfields back into operation. Naval Officers would soon be responsible for Tinian, but as the patients at the Leprosarium came from other parts of the Trust Territories, they would have to go back to their own districts.

One week later we were told that the Navy would take responsibility for everything starting on 1 January 1953. The navy would run the Leprosarium for the first eighteen months, and then the Department of the Interior would be obliged to move the patients away.

Relief was in sight, and soon I wouldn't have to worry about the sub-standard food, lack of medical supplies and the general difficulties caused by our isolation. One weekend while I was on Saipan, the office staff told me that they were finally receiving medicines and other supplies that had been ordered 15 months previously.

Doctor Norman Sloan, a world renowned Leprologist, was coming to visit Tinian before he inspected the leprosy programme in the rest of the Trust Territories. When Dr. Sloan arrived at the beginning of December he handed me a letter. It said that I was to help him as much as possible during the remaining month before the handover to the navy. I was then to accompany him through

```
TRUST TERRITORY OF THE PACIFIC ISLANDS
    Saipan District, Mariana Islands
         Tinian Leprosarium
                                    2 September 1952
```

THE TRUST TERRITORY LEPROSY PROGRAM

Upon Dr. Marshall's suggestion I am putting down some opinions held by prominent people which may apply to the Trust Territory Leprosy Program.

Dr. Eleanor Alexander-Jackson is widely known because she has cultured the leprosy (or Hansen's) bacillus. She has developed a triple stain technique in order to show the non-acid fast rods and granules in smears. She not only considers that this technique can be used in the Trust Territory but has given us the materials. The older stains are still to be used but the new method, I hope, is of more than scientific interest.

While in Honolulu I was fortunate enough to meet Dr. Jack Millar. He was the first Doctor at the present Tinian Leprosarium after World War II. He has spent two years studying leprosy in the United States and is now loaned by the Navy to the Leonard Wood Memorial Foundation. He will study the latest therapy research in Japan, the Philippines and South Africa. Dr. Millar is still very interested in Tinian and the staff here hope for an early visit from him. He considers that if the Trust Territory is to play a part in the rapidly advancing world Leprosy program, it will be best done in the epidemiological field. This is helped because of the relatively isolated populations within the Trust Territory. To quote the booklet "Hansen's Disease," published by the American Leprosy Foundation: "Epidemiological work of a more intensive type than that heretofore carried out is necessary. This should be especially directed towards study of conditions prevailing in houses in which transmission has recently occurred, as evidenced by discovery of lesions in young children known to have been exposed in the household. Household contacts should be examined on report of the first case and examination should be repeated at intervals which need not be more frequent than once a year." It is thought that most people are infested as children in a leprous household and that adults are relatively immune.

Dr. Chung-Hoon and Dr. Hedgecock report the following from Kalaupapa Leprosarium, Molokai: "Experience over a period of three years with the Sulfone drugs in the treatment of 346 patients has convinced us that they constitute the best treatment for leprosy now available. We believe that they are effective in tuberculoid as well as lepromatous cases. They are certainly more effective in early cases than in later ones. Thus it is now more important than ever to diagnose cases of leprosy early and to give them prompt treatment."

The Honolulu Public Relations Office of the Health Department is very active in respect to leprosy. I quote a late publication for issue to the public: "Hansen's Disease can be eliminated in two generations when and if the disease can be handled as a medical entity on a basis of an intelligent understanding of the public health needs, and not in response to popular fear and superstition."

```
                                    (signed)
                                    John Valentine
```

A report by the author on the Trust Territory Leprosy Programme (dated 2nd September, 1952).

TRUST TERRITORY OF THE PACIFIC ISLANDS
Office of the High Commissioner
3845 Kilauea Avenue
Honolulu 16, Hawaii

Ser 4044

October 1, 1952

To All Public Health Department Personnel
of the Trust Territory

Dear Colleagues:

    There is reason for satisfaction in the way Dr. John Valentine is taking hold of Tinian and the Trust Territory leprosy problem. Though ultimately headed toward a career in surgery, John has seen considerable leprosy in the Pacific before joining us. He was fortunate in spending a month of intensive study at Honolulu at a time when several visitors notable in the field were here.

    Nineteenth and Twentieth Century medicine left leprosy largely by the wayside in remote and neglected places. That situation is now being rapidly altered. Thoroughgoing interest and research is at last evident. Yesterday I talked to Dr. Badger of the United States on his way back from attending the international leprosy meeting in Tokyo. The South Pacific Commission has employed Dr. Sloan of New York as its consultant on leprosy. Trust Territory has applied to the Commission for his services. He is expected to spend about three months with us during 1953, at which time many of our problems, including treatment of the tuberculoid cases locally, will be considered.

    It has been suggested to Dr. Valentine that an occasional informative letter from him about leprosy, the Tinian situation, and the patients, will be welcomed by all of us. His letter attached may be considered as the first installment.

                                     Sincerely,

                                       H. L. Marshall

                                     H. L. Marshall, M. D.
                                     Director of Public Health

Enclosure

Distribution:
  Each District and Tinian (4)

A letter from H.L. Marshall (dated 1st October 1952) introducing the author's previous report (of September 2nd 1952) to other colleagues in Micronesia.

TRUST TERRITORY OF THE PACIFIC ISLANDS
Office of the Liaison Officer
Agana, Guam

In reply refer t

March 11, 1953.

To Whom It May Concern:

For the past three months I have been closely associated with Dr. John Valentine, at the Tinian leprosarium and in a general leprosy survey of the Trust Territory. He possesses a basic knowledge of clinical leprosy which has made him a valued colleague throughout the study; he is well able to carry on the leprosy program here or elsewhere. It is also my impression that he is well grounded in general medicine and surgery, but my observation of this was limited.

Very truly yours,

Norman R. Sloan, M.D.
Leprosy Consultant
South Pacific Commission

A reference attesting to the author's abilities from Dr. Norman Sloan (Leprosy Consultant for the South Pacific Commission).

all the other districts during his inspection tour of the Leprosy programme.

At the time, I could not imagine anything better. Dr. Sloan had been a medical missionary for ten years in Africa, and had then been in charge of the Kalapapa Leprosarium on the Island of Molokai. I have mentioned that I had visited Kalapapa while in Hawaii, and that it was famous because of its association with the heroic work of Father Damien, who had been assisted by the Catholic Sisters. Perhaps the Sisters should be accorded similar kudos and remembered alongside Fr. Damien.

Dr. Sloan was in his sixties and was a very tall thin man. He was serious but aimiable and helpful. He was employed as the consultant Leprologist for the South Pacific Commission, and was brought to the U.S. Trust Territories to give advice on our Leprosy programme. He had been a medical missionary in Nigeria for many years and retained many missionary attitudes. However, he had a tremendous fund of knowledge in the Leprosy field and was exactly the person I needed to teach and advise me.

He told me that there were approximately six million leprosy patients worldwide, but only one million were under treatment. At that time the tablets cost 4 cents a day so it was sad that so few were getting the help they needed.

We do not know when leprosy first came to Micronesia. Guam has been a dependency of the U.S. since the Spanish American war at the end of the 19th century. In 1902 the first four cases of leprosy were recognized on Guam, and by 1907 there were 87 cases. At that time the patients were sent to Coulion in the Philippine Islands, but after WW II all leprosy cases were sent to Tinian, as this island had been designated the sole isolation centre for American Micronesia.

Sometime after the Japanese first occupied Micronesia in 1914, they established three leprosy Islands. One was at Yap (in 1925), one in the Palau Islands (in 1929) and the other in the Marshall Islands (in 1927). In September 1948, the U.S. Navy established a leprosarium on the Island of Tinian and patients from all districts were taken there. Today it is agreed that any leprosarium should be established near a centre of population with easy communication and accessibility to needed supplies. This was recommended by the 5th International Congress of Leprosy, held in Havana in 1938.

By the time Dr. Sloan arrived, I had already discharged 28 patients to their homes and then he and I systematically reviewed the 100 patients who remained at the leprosarium. To my great relief he confirmed my suspicions that many of the remaining patients had no signs of leprosy and many of the other cases who did have leprosy were not infectious.

We prepared summaries for 46 patients who were considered ready for discharge. When the people found that they were being considered for release, they broke into shy smiles. I felt tremendous compassion for these patients who had been taken from their homes and deprived of their liberty. I now realise that my part in the release of these patients from Tinian, which enabled them to return to their families and friends, was the highlight of my medical career. It had been traumatic enough for all the people who had come to Tinian with leprosy, but for those who had never even had the disease, it was more so. Some of the patients had Yaws and various fungal infections of the skin. Yaws is a spirochetal infection resembling a mild form of syphilis and produces skin lesions. It is not venereal and is cured by a single injection of penicillin. Many doctors believe that if a patient has Yaws, then they have a natural resistance to infection by syphilis.

I was acutely aware that we were fortunate to be living at this time in the history of leprosy treatment. For the first time the disease could be accurately diagnosed and effectively treated. It was now possible to treat the majority of leprosy patients, in their own homes or close by. The new treatments are safe and cheap and there is no reason why they should not be available to all leprosy sufferers.

You, the reader can forget about Biblical leprosy, and leprosy in the Dark and Middle Ages. God knows what these diseases actually were, but they were often mistakenly given the blanket description 'leprosy'. There would possibly have been other diseases like Beri Beri, psoriasis and syphilis which all exhibit skin deformity and lesions.

The Encyclopedia Britannica, considered by many to be the ultimate source of esoteric wisdom, tells us that before 1500 A.D. 'Leprosy' in Europe, was considered highly contagious. It was associated with sexual contact and apparently responded positively to mercury therapy; this sounds more like syphilis.

In England, between the 12th and 15th centuries, 30% of the 700+ hospitals were leprosaria. In Paris, at the beginning of the 14th century, there were 80 hospitals and half were leprosaria. As patients in leprosaria had declined markedly in Europe by the 19th century, it is probable that this was due more to accurate diagnosis of medical conditions, rather than a decline in true leprosy cases. It is possible that many cases thought to be leprosy were actually syphilis. Yes, syphilis gave leprosy a bad name.

My last month on Tinian was made bearable by the appearance of a young single, American woman named Margaret. She worked for the Department of the Interior and was bright and cheerful. I was able to take her to parts of Tinian that I had been exploring alone or with the local Catholic priest, Farther Marcian.

One Saturday, while tramping through low scrub, we came upon the fully clothed skeletons of eight Japanese soldiers with only their rifles missing. They were on the higher part of the island where the Japanese had made their last stand. The bodies wore belts with anchors on their buckles, and I assumed they were marines, possibly members of Captain Goichi Oya's 56th Naval Guard Force (Kaerbitai) who fought in the July 1944 offensive. These men must have been 5' 10", which was quite tall for a Japanese person at that time. We all know that with better nutrition Japanese men have a tendency towards being much taller than their fathers. Having seen the bodies, I respected the courage of these men who had died fighting with minimal support, so far from their homes. I don't know why this group was together like this. I presume they had been killed by the Americans or had decided to suicide together.

Hell-Bent for Life

The roads on Tinian were almost overgrown with wild sugar cane but wherever we went we saw signs of the farms the Japanese had developed before the war. Often in the ruins of an old Japanese house were the remains of the tiled baths and the sliding wood and paper partitions so characteristic of Japanese homes.

On the high part of the island there was a 300 bed American hospital which had been prepared for the casualties expected in the final assault on the Japanese mainland. After the dropping of the atom bombs on Hiroshima and Nagasaki and the capitulation of Japan this hospital was not needed, so was never used.

At the northern end of the island were the atom bomb houses where the bombs were stored and assembled. They were loaded onto B-29s for the flight to the mainland of Japan. At that time Tinian was the largest and busiest airfield in the world. The runways were still intact and one could drive for miles along deserted concrete strips which were all the more lonely because they had once pulsed with activity. In some tall concrete towers which had been colonised by bees, there was so much honey that it was breaking through the wall linings and flowing to the ground. The bees did not object to an intrusion but if we heard the buzz of the large yellow native wasps we got out of there in record time. Father Marcian advised us to run straight for thirty meters and then change direction. His theory was that the angry wasps were conditioned to stay on a straight course and when we turned they lost us.

The road from the bomb houses to the loading pit, where the bombs were lifted into the belly of B-29s, were rough and overgrown. I felt the contrast to the energetic military security which must have enveloped the area before those bombs shook Hiroshima, Nagasaki and indeed, the whole world.

Scrap dealers had taken the heavy trailers which had been used to carry the bombs to the loading pits: I had seen these rusty iron vehicles lying at the wharf ready to be broken down and shipped away. They had been made so that the bombs fitted between strong uprights and were in no danger of rolling off. The actual loading pits had been filled with earth, and now bushes sprouted from the top. The bomb houses had been insulated and had air conditioning, which was unusual at that time. The heavy pulleys used to move the bombs were still in place, below the steel girders along which the bombs were pushed, before being placed in cradles for transport to the planes. Heavy mounds of earth had been built up to roof level on all but the seaward side of the building. Barbed wire fences still surrounded the area, but the gates were falling off their hinges.

A notice at the main gate read 'Restricted - keep out'. I took the 'No Smoking' notice from the bomb house as a souvenir. This notice seemed ironic as the bombs turned two large cities into smoking ruins.

Margaret and I were enjoying each other's company, but the other American women kept telling me that I shouldn't marry her. I was never given any good reason for this but it was advice easily accepted, because there wasn't any way I wanted to make a nest in Tinian, or Micronesia.

Soon the navy brass began to arrive to make arrangements for the take over of Tinian. Captain Heinzman, Director of Naval Medical services on Guam, came to see the leprosarium. He was keen that I should stay on some time after the change-over, but I was anxious not to miss the survey trip through the rest of the Trust Territories. Dr. Sloan and I told him that we would tell the incoming doctor as much as possible about the leprosarium before we left, but to please have the new doctor in Tinian before January 1st. He promised to do his best, and sure enough a week before the take-over, a huge Navy PBY dropped out of the sky and Doctor Devine appeared. He was young and alert, and I felt pleased to be handing over to him. He'd come down to visit the leprosarium two months previously, and when I was taking his party back to the plane, my Jeep had a flat tyre. Dr. Devine noted that the Jeep had no spare, and that the other tyres were worn out. Imagine my surprise when one week later, eight almost new tyres arrived from navy stocks on Guam.

After a month of uncertainty, Dr. Sloan and I boarded a plane for Guam on 3rd January - two days after the official take-over. I can't remember ever being so pleased to leave a place as I was to leave Tinian. I knew the remaining patients were in good hands and soon the leprosarium would be dispersed.

I liked my work and was very fond of the patients but I had to communicate through interpreters, because the majority of the patients understood Japanese, but not English. They were lovely, smiling people, like all Island people, and I was very satisfied when Norman Sloan and I were able to discharge many of them back into the care of their families on their own islands.

If I had a favourite prayer then, it would have been "Lord protect me from the workings of the U.S. Department of the Interior!" A difficult situation was made almost impossible because of the isolation, poor communication and infrequent freight deliveries.

There may have been deficiencies in my performance but this all happened a long time ago and time is a great healer, if not teacher. I was in my mid twenties then, so almost all the people involved will have passed over the great divide into Elysian Fields, so I don't expect my complaints and reminiscences will bother them.

CHAPTER 8

The Micronesian Leprosy Survey, Yap & Japan.
1 August, 1953 - 28 August, 1953

INTRODUCED CHARACTERS

DR. NICK BILLS, the District Director of Public Health at Ponape.
DR. CULION, a native medical practitioner at Pinelap.
SALOME, a 10 year old girl living on Pinelap. She became the author's self-appointed Guardian while he lived there.
DR. JOHNSTONE AND DR.KENNEDY, doctors on Koror Island.
ESTER EVANS the Nurse Administrator on Yap.
DR. MALNIKOFF, the author's deputy Medical Officer on Yap.
CAPTAIN EVANS, (Motor Vessel Errol) who died in a plane crash near Wake Island.
EDDIE, the Chief Officer on the Motor Vessel Chilcot.
MICHICO, Eddie's Japanese girlfriend in Kobe.
YOKO, Capt. Evan's Japanese girlfriend in Kobe.
MAMASAN, Head Hostess and Supervisor of the hotel the author stayed at in Kobe.
ECHO, a supervisor at the hotel, who spoke English. She and Mamasa 'adopted' the author, while he was in residence.

HAVING CONCLUDED MY RESPONSIBILITIES AT THE Tinian leprosarium, Dr. Sloan and I set out on our leprosy survey trip through the major island groups of the Trust Territories. Our first stop was the Truk District. Since then, there has been a name change and on modern maps the spelling has changed to 'Chuuk'.

Truk is a group of small islands within a lagoon and surrounded by a reef, with the district centre on the island of Moen. The Truk Lagoon is well known for the fleet of Japanese ships that were sunk there in WWII. For many years after WWII, there were very few fish in the lagoon, and it is thought that toxic chemicals leaching from decomposing ammunition on these sunken ships was poisoning them. Nowadays the lagoon swarms with brightly coloured fish and is known as an underwater diver's paradise. I presume the chemicals are dissipating and the water is once again closer to pristine. Like alcohol, it could be that a little explosive is good for you while a large amount is not. Those of us who are prescribed Nitroglycerine, and put the small tablets under our tongues to relieve angina pain, can confirm that small amounts of this usually explosive substance are beneficial.

On Truk we were greeted by Dr. Lahr and Dr. Hagentornas who were interested in our work and made us welcome at the hospital and in their homes. We found ten tuberculoid leprosy cases in our brief survey. If leprosy here was to follow the usual distribution, then there were almost certainly lepromatous cases waiting to be diagnosed.

My friend Margaret had left Tinian a month before and gone off and found a new man. They married on Guam, and had come to Truk, where he worked for the U.S. Government. We met them both and the new husband suggested that I go for a walk with him in the hills over looking the town. He explained that after their marriage he expected Margaret would forget me, but this had not happened. He then said that they were prepared to separate and that I should marry her. This was a dilemma, since I was still a practising Catholic and the Christian Brothers had told me that marriage was permanent as long as both partners were alive. They didn't tell me however (perhaps they didn't know), that marriage was not declared a sacrament until four hundred years after Christ. Margaret and her husband were alive, so her marriage was intact as far as I was concerned. While I was getting reasonably adept at removing girls' clothing, I was reluctant to start preparing to dress them. My travels were just beginning and there was no place for marriage in my itinerary. While in many cases it was easy to get into relationships, I found it was traumatic getting out of them. I was always left with a feeling of guilt that the female had been left high and dry. As the guilt stayed with me for weeks or months,

The Micronesian Leprosy Survey, Yap & Japan.

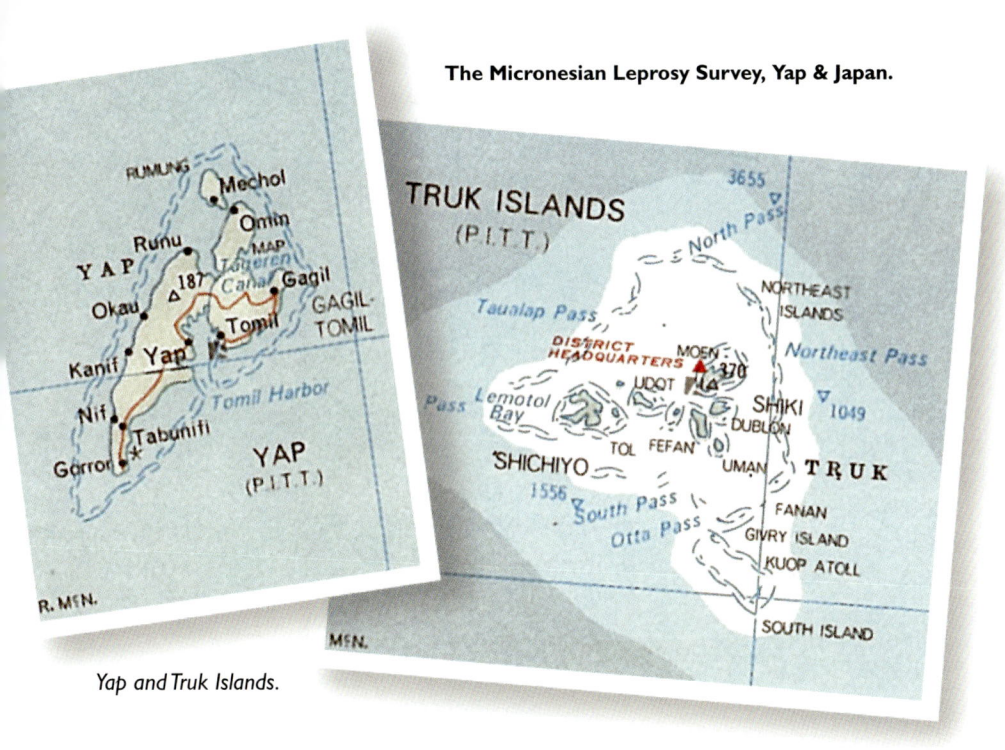

Yap and Truk Islands.

I felt a bit of a bastard as I moved on. As far as I know, none of my relationships resulted in pregnancies, so that left one less complication to face when exiting. I wasn't in Micronesia long enough to know what happened to Margaret and her new husband, but I do hope all ended well for both of them.

Norman Sloan and I had to move on with the leprosy survey, and I was grateful for this, since there was no time to stop and sort out my emotional tangles. If Norman had known what was going on he would have come down on me like a ton of bricks. I'm glad that I spared him all of that as he probably would have called me a disgrace to the human race, and I would have been hard put to defend myself.

Norman and I then flew on to the Marshall Islands. Since we were unable to reach the more remote islands in this group, it was the least satisfactory of all our surveys. We were able to visit the major inhabited districts of the group and examine half the population, and we found no new cases, but couldn't be sure that there weren't any.

Before the U.S. started testing atomic weapons on Bikini Atoll,

147

Native children on Pinelap.

the U.S. Navy removed all the natives to other islands. They were not given a choice in the matter, and once the testing was over, they asked to return. Their request was denied, as their islands remain contaminated by radiation. This remains a sad chapter in island history to this day. After the aerial explosions the Bikini and Rongelap Islands were showered with radioactive materials. The seas were affected and the world's atmosphere was debased with strontium 90 and caesium 137. If you were breathing air after the 1946 tests you will have some of this material in your bones, and it is likely your parents would have had their dose. We are all interconnected so this is concerning, but I will elaborate more about toxic contaminates in my second book.

The few known leprosy cases from the Marshall Islands were from the outer atolls, and a thorough study of the whole district was badly needed - I don't know if this was ever done.

Norman and I then flew to Ponape. We worked with the District Director of Public Health, Dr. Nick Bills, who was a single

The author with children on Pinelap Island. The whole island is coral with almost no cultivatable soil.

American from San Francisco. He was a keen sailor and took me out sailing in his outrigger canoe. An unexpected gust of wind flipped the canoe over but he was able to get it back upright with little difficulty. Nick was very interested in our work but was about to return to the U.S. We examined all discharged patients, known contacts of patients and school children at the Ponape Hospital. We visited the island of Sokas, where we examined 255 out of an estimated 300 people on the island. Out of all of these, we found two active lepromatous cases who would be sent to Tinian for further treatment, until the local leprosarium was built.

Next, we boarded the motor vessel Errol for the island of Pinelap. We knew that this was a focal area of leprosy infection in Micronesia as many of our Tinian patients had come from there. There were 800 people on Pinelap, and it was our hope to examine them all.

There was no air service in those days, so we had to go on the Errol. It was a small diesel powered ship that did a tour of the

The author on Yap Island, with a young patient from the hospital. Note the Japanese built breakwater dividing the bay. This afforded protected anchorage for their boats close to Yap Town.

islands every four months. At each stop it took on modest amounts of copra (dried coconut) that the islanders had produced, and in turn delivered supplies for the island. Other freight and mail sent by the Trust Territory Administration was unloaded as well.

As we approached Pinelap, the sun shone brightly and the wind blew softly, with the sea moving in great slow swells. This was the usual conditions found in these glorious islands. The first signs of landfall were the tops of coconut trees, and then the island gradually came into view, with the white surf beating against the reef. The sea turned to green as it burst over the coral reef and passed slowly to the white-sand beach behind.

The large whaleboats that came to greet us pitched up and down on the broad surface of the Pacific, and people soon appeared from the thick coconut trees lining the shore. We anchored a hundred yards off the reef, because the captain knew that the coral heads could rip holes in a ship's keel.

Norman Sloan and I were to go ashore in the natives' boats to

The author with a small boy on Pinelap. Note the typical native dwelling in the background.

do the leprosy survey over four or five days. The Errol would pick us up on the return trip from Kusaie a few days later if the weather was favourable. If there were storm conditions then we would be on Pinelap for the next four months. Imagine two doctors living on fish, coconuts and taro for one hundred and twenty days. The U.S. Trust Territories could not hold up an expensive ship just for a couple of leprosy surveyors.

The whaleboats were already alongside and we were directed to scramble down cargo nets into one of them where men were taking the mail on board. I looked down to see how Norman was getting along and saw that he was not getting along at all! In fact, he had one foot on the rope net and the other on the boat, which was drifting rapidly away from the ship. The next moment Norman was in the sea, somewhat slowed by the photographic equipment around his neck. Everybody was very helpful and they hauled him up into the boat, before it could swing back and crush him against the side of the ship. I was next in line and was fortunately able to get into the boat with dry feet and clothes and my dignity intact.

While we were on the island, we were to be under the guidance of Dr. Culion, a native practitioner, who gave whatever medical assistance he could to the islanders. He had some minimal medical training from the Japanese when they occupied this part of the Pacific and he carried on after they left, to the best of his ability. He was sitting at the end of the boat we had boarded, smiling nervously at Dr. Sloan who sat dripping wet at the other end, wondering what had happened to his camera and his dignity. We learned that Dr. Culion was half Japanese, and his constant smiling was a typical Japanese characteristic, and an expected courtesy in those days.

After stepping ashore, we were taken to a small infirmary where the chief and his council of six were waiting for us. Here we were received with quiet courtesy, which remained a constant feature the whole time we were on the Island.

We worked through interpreters, since most of the council spoke Japanese, Marshallese and their own native tongue, Ponapean. We were assured that half the village would parade for examination the next day, and the rest on subsequent days. We explained that not every case of leprosy was infectious and required isolation. We expected the distribution of the disease to be similar to what we found in other parts of Micronesia. If this was so, we could leave most cases on the island. We would do our best to bring Dr. Culion up to speed with current treatments over the following few days, and on the next ship we would send a supply of anti-leprosy drugs. Then Dr. Culion could supervise the more modern treatments while the patients remained on their home island. The Chief and his council discussed this for a long time and ever so slowly they formulated their reply. There was no concept of urgency or a high value placed on achieving outcomes quickly here or anywhere else in Micronesia. There was no hurry or bustle, or sign of the strain that was inseparable when living in the machine age. However, at the end of the day there was just as much, or just as little, accomplished.

At last the interpreter told us that leaving the patients on Pinelap was not an important consideration, as the food supply was marginal and a number of people had to leave the island each year and go to Ponape, which was a 'high' island, where they could grow more food.

Pinelap is a 'low' island, being only a few hundred meters in circumference and two or three metres above sea level. It frightens me to think of what will be happening to the island now that rising sea levels are occurring. Pinelap's coral sands are infertile and plants grow very slowly. Meagre amounts of soil are carefully husbanded in small depressions, to grow taro. A few bananas grow in the sand beneath the coconuts. The natives rely heavily on their modest agriculture but are vulnerable to tropical storms. Any damage to this extra food supply worsens their marginal existence.

Living was not easy for these polite and seemingly carefree people. We would see later in the day that the men who had spent the sunlight hours sailing their fragile outriggers on the broad Pacific outside the reef returned without a single fish, or at best one or two small specimens. Every day is a long day on Pinelap, because it is only five degrees north of the equator, and the tropical sun burns brightly and swings a broad arc through the heavens for the whole year.

After the preliminaries, we were shown to our residence. The house owners were in the process of moving out, and I protested that we did not want to be moving a family from their home. The interpreter brushed our concerns aside - after all, we were their guests.

The house was built in the Japanese fashion. We were told that a Japanese weather station had been on the island during the war, and the Japanese had taught the men to build in the Japanese style. Most of the houses were built in the same manner and were well suited to the climate. My problem was that I hit my head on the low doorways if I forgot to flex my knees as I passed through them.

Norman Sloan had acquired gastroenteritis from somewhere and stayed in bed until it passed. Sanitation was not good on the island; the islanders used the sea to attend to their natural functions, which was satisfactory as a strong current ran along the beach and carried away the sewage. At any time of the day you could see people sitting out by the reef, passing time. The teenage girls seemed to be particularly addicted to this, although the habit is not exclusive to island teenagers, as it is well known that our own teenagers retire to the bathroom when routine chores start to pile up.

It soon became obvious that one of the village men had been charged with watching over us during the daylight hours. Whenever we put our heads out of the house he was there. The children were especially interested in us, but whenever they gathered to watch us, our guardian would appear to move them along. "No loitering, move right along please," just like a London policeman.

One of the ten-year-old girls was particularly bright and attractive, and seemed to be a leader amongst her friends. She told us that her name was Salome, and she appointed herself to be with us whenever we left the house.

The second day on the island, I went for a walk after work. This tiny, low island would be continually overwhelmed by the massive ocean swells if it was not protected by the coral reef. Thankfully the waves break on the reef and the white spray fills the horizon at all times.

We were also taken into the trees and shown the foundations of the former Japanese weather station. The islanders had long carried off the superstructure, but you could see that the foundations had been well constructed and had been built to last.

As we returned through the village, I saw Salome, my little guardian in the doorway of her father's house. I offered her some candy and her shy acceptance began a lively friendship. She had learned some English in school, but was shy about speaking it. Salome was highly intelligent and it was not long before we understood each other completely. Whenever I was not working, Salome would be nearby. In the evenings we would sit on the beach with the other children and I would encourage them to sing for us. At the beginning they sang their hymns but with a little encouragement they went on to their Ponapean songs. They also sang songs from Kapingamarangi, an island 400 miles to the south, where the people are Polynesian and speak a Polynesian dialect. They are the remnants of the early Polynesian migration from South East Asia into the farthest reaches of the Pacific.

Now that we had gained their confidence, the children delighted in following us around. The little boys took great pride in showing us how they wrestled and there was competition to get into the centre of the circle to compete against the previous winner. The little girls watched and cheered the contestants on, but did not physically take part in the sport.

Some of the younger men had angulated fractures of both wrists after falling from the tall coconut palms when harvesting coconuts. Some of these palms grew to sixty feet high so to lessen these injuries, coconut trees which did not grow so tall were being introduced, with the hope that people wouldn't be injured so badly if they did fall.

In Sumatra in Indonesia, the men train monkeys to climb the coconut palms and twist the ripe coconuts till they fall to the ground. There are no monkeys in Micronesia so they just had to wait until the safer pigmy coconut palms arrive.

In other parts of Micronesia they cut the stalk that nourishes the coconut and allow the juice to drip into an empty coconut shell. They then leave it high in the palm to warm and ferment the liquid. A few days later, they collect the coconuts containing the juice, which by then contains various amounts of alcohol.

After the survey we explained that it was necessary to take two of the children with leprosy back for treatment. This did not seem to disturb the parents. The island was chronically short of food and they knew that friends and relatives in the leprosarium would look after the children. The parents, like all parents elsewhere, hated to see their children go, but realised it was for their ultimate benefit. We tried to bring them some comfort by telling them it would not be long until a leprosarium was established on Ponape. They would then be able to visit the children with relative ease.

Soon our ship appeared on the horizon and the men made haste to load their small amount of copra into the boats and take it out through the gap in the reef to the waiting vessel. With the money they received, the men would purchase supplies they needed from the outside world. All of this had to be done in the space of a few hours, as the captain did not want to lie off the treacherous reefs for any longer than was absolutely necessary.

Norman and I were grateful that the ship returned and we weren't to be stranded on Pinelap for four months until the next one arrived. It occurred to me that I might have needed to find a suitable female companion had I been stranded. A four month diet of fish, coconuts and taro would have reduced my waist line, but a lack of female company would have destroyed my sense of humour. Norman had been a Christian Missionary and was already long and lean and celibacy did not seem to bother him.

An American on the ship, who spoke the local language, came ashore and I introduced him to the children who were around. As a joke, I asked him if he would ask Salome if she would come to the outside world with me, and to our surprise she nodded her pretty head, looked to the ground, and answered, "Yes." I wished that I had not asked the question, as I knew how much the people loved their beautiful, if isolated island. It would be a difficult life for them in our world even if they were assured of enough to eat. We, of course, have the opposite problem; perhaps we could send our obese to Pinelap where they could feast on fish and taro for a year. They would return lean, brown and fit to face the rigours of life in the West, but they wouldn't want to eat fish and coconuts again.

Soon we were walking down the beach to board the waiting boats. We emptied our pockets of any small coins, but could not repay the children for our wonderful experience. As I looked back I saw that Salome had followed us fifty yards out into the lagoon. I did not look back, but some day I hope to return to Pinelap. They now have an airstrip with occasional flights coming from Ponape, so it will be easier to get there if there is a next time.

On the return trip to Ponape, the ship stopped a few hours at Mokil Island. We anchored fifty meters off the surrounding reef and the whaleboats came out through the gap in the reef, transporting copra to the ship. They then loaded their needed supplies and took them back to the island. While Dr. Sloan went ashore in the boat, I

A child with a banana on Yap Island.

decided to swim the 200 yards to shore through the thirty to forty-foot-wide gap in the reef.

    We were able to examine a group who had been in contact with leprosy patients, but no new cases were found. While there, we were introduced to one of the older islanders who had captained a large canoe for a journey lasting several days to another island. I knew about Polynesian navigation and had asked him how he knew the direction and his reply came back through the interpreter "We followed the compass." I asked him why they had undertaken this hazardous journey, and he replied, "We were short of tobacco."

    I decided to take the boat back to the ship, and as we sailed out through the crystal clear water, in the gap in the reef I looked down. There, twenty-feet below me, was a shark gliding ever so languorously about its business. It was approximately the same length as the boat I was in, and I made the resolution there and then never to repeat my swim in tropical waters.

    When we got back to Ponape, we examined a proposed site

for a leprosarium at the old Japanese airstrip. There were existing building foundations and fertile land, but the area was used as a water catchment for the town's central administrative area, so this made it unsuitable.

We then took the aircraft to Palau. The administrative centre was on the island of Koror. Here, two American physicians, Dr. Johnstone and Dr. Kennedy, looked after us. There were two cases of leprosy in the hospital. One was a lepromatous case and the other turberculoid. This latter patient had a crippling foot deformity, which made institutionalised care desirable, so both were booked for Tinian. We examined half a dozen groups on Koror, and then I travelled to three villages on the larger island of Babelthuap. Altogether we found ten cases (six of them on Babelthuap), and this convinced us that further study was needed.

The final district we were to visit was Yap. Here the U.S. authorities gave us every assistance to carry out our survey. Once it was completed, and Norman Sloan had left, I was to remain on Yap and be in charge as the District Director of Public Health. This left me to be in charge of the District Hospital.

On Yap, Dr. Sloan and I examined three groups of school children and the people of three villages. During the process I was surprised at the cooperation and social discipline wielded by the chiefs. A chief might say, "We have 79 people in the village, and 77 are awaiting you here. There are two others, both confined to their beds in huts nearby." We found ten tuberculoid cases and no lepromatous cases. This surprised us, as Yap had been long considered another focal point of leprosy in Micronesia. If the island had followed the usual distribution trends of leprosy cases elsewhere in Micronesia, we should have found three or four of the infectious lepromatous cases here as well.

We were much encouraged by the cooperation of the local chiefs. They came to us and requested that we put a leprosarium on Yap, and offered their help as much as possible. One of them said, "It used to be that when one of our people had leprosy, he went away to die. Now we see them come back well."

A mother and children on Yap Island with Fei (Yapese ceremonial money).

We believed that Yap was the logical place for a leprosarium for the Western Districts, and were shown a site that seemed satisfactory. It extended from the former German radio station to the sea, and there were good fishing and agricultural areas available, and it was in easy reach of Colonia (or Yap Town), the administrative centre. The Chief of Public Works also assured us that abundant subsoil water was available, and the area did not drain to the town.

Dr. Sloan then flew away to his next assignment, and I was left in charge of the Yap district. The hospital was in reasonable shape, and we had an efficient nurse administrator, a U.S. nurse named Ester Evans. She kept in touch with her son who was in the U.S. Armed Services and she had recently bought him a car. This surprised me, as there were few cars in New Zealand at this time, and I couldn't imagine being given one. Ester carried most of the administrative burden for me and we settled into a good working relationship. My deputy Dr. Malnikoff, was an Eastern European graduate who was already working at the hospital. This was fortunate, as it gave me access to his already established local knowledge. He had come to Yap at the end of World War II, but since the U.S. authorities distrusted medical degrees from Eastern Europe, he was not given the position of Medical Director.

The Yapese men wore a loin cloth which was a piece of cloth wrapped around their hips that then went between their legs and was tucked up into the waist again. The women wore very thick grass skirts that were worn low over their hips. Although they were naked from the waist up, it was considered immodest of them to show their thighs, although their bosoms were exposed to public scrutiny. This was in direct contrast to conventions in the West. I still remember these ladies in the sea fishing with their grass skirts floating around them. Their skirts were so thick they must have taken forever to dry out afterwards.

Recently, I noted in an Australian documentary that the social mores of the islands were being disrupted because the Yap people were viewing TV documentaries where they saw Californian beach beauties with their breasts covered but their thighs exposed. I hope they can resolve the dilemma between their traditional values and those from the Western world.

Yap is a series of small volcanic islands inhabited, in those days, by less than a thousand people. The Yapese are well known for their large discs of stone money which are called "Fei." Some of these discs are eight-feet in diameter, have a hole in the center and weigh a ton. They were cut from rock 200 miles away in the islands of Palau. The Yapese people transported these heavy discs back home on rafts pulled by canoes. In rough seas they were in great danger of tipping over and losing everyone, and everything to the sea. This meant that the Fei discs, which involved huge effort and danger to obtain, were held in high regard. The discs were not usually moved around the island as their ownership changed from village to village. Everyone knew who the owners of each disc were. One disc is submerged in water fifty metres deep at the entrance to the Yap Harbor. It is only visible on a clear day when the sun is directly overhead. This piece has an owner and it changes hands from time to time.

An old Yapese man with Fei.

The same Yapese man's foot on a Fei. This deformity of the foot is congenital.

Various colonial powers have had stewardship over the islands, and an old chief once said to me, "When the Spanish were here they said Pesos are good. When the Germans came they said use Marks as Pesos are no good. When the Japanese came they said use Yen as Marks are no good. The Americans came and said use Dollars, Yen no good. But doctor, Fei good all the time!" The Fei is more a ceremonial currency, and villages hold singing and dancing competitions for their ownership.

In the 19th century, an American sailor, O'Keefe, came to Yap. Some say that he was washed ashore after a ship wreck but others say he arrived in the conventional manner. No one suggested he was transported by an angel or aeroplane. He became a prominent leader on the island and established a shipping line. Some people called him the "The King of Yap." He got the Yapese people to work for him producing copra and harvesting Beche de mer from the shallows. (Beche de mer, or sea cucumber is used as a flavouring in soups and was sold to the Chinese market.) In return, he took the Yapese men to Palau where they cut the stone discs with milled steel chisels and transported them back aboard his ships to Yap. As it wasn't as dangerous to get the Fei anymore, it depreciated the value of the newer stone discs. The ancient discs, obtained at great risk, still retain their value. The story is told in the book "His Majesty O'Keefe".

Most of the inpatients at the hospital were being given canned orange juice yet right outside the windows to the hospital, oranges were dropping off the trees unused, so we were able to economise on that. Most of the patients had relatives with them, and they did cooking for them on open fires in the hospital grounds.

Ester Evans and I lived at the European hostel, where we had our own rooms. Unfortunately the food was terrible and I can still remember the taste of half-rotten chicken that had been inadequately refrigerated. We had both been promised houses that were being repaired, having become derelict during the war. During the month that I was there the houses were not touched and I began to despair of ever getting one.

One of my patients came from the island of Ulithi, which

A family on Ulithi Island, near Yap Island.

was a hundred miles northeast of Yap. He had a massive tumour in the abdomen from an un-descended testicle that had become malignant. With Dr. Malnikoff giving the anaesthetic, I was able to remove the tumour and found it measured twelve inches by eight inches. The patient did well and returned to his island. Later, when I visited Ulithi, he came to the beach to meet us and presented me with carved wooden statues of himself and his wife. He was anxious that I did not show the carvings to the U.S. servicemen who manned the weather station on the island, as they were always bothering the islanders to get souvenirs of their stay.

Another of our patients came from an outer island where it was traditional that the females, while menstruating, went to a menstruation house and stayed there until it was over. This woman

Hell-Bent for Life

A patient who had his testicular cancer removed, made these carvings and then gave them to the author in way of thanks for his treatment.

A Ulithi man with the same tattoos as my patient.

A family group on Yap.

had a cancer of her uterus, and as she never stopped bleeding she was spending all her time in the menstruation house. I didn't have the courage to attempt a hysterectomy on Yap, so sent her off to Truk, where there was a more experienced surgeon and better conditions.

I then struck up a relationship with the Yapese hospital laundress; she had a rudimentary knowledge of English and an attractive personality. Some evenings we went for a walk in the hills behind the town. The prominent feature was a Japanese gun emplacement set in the hillside for the defence of the harbour. She would let me embrace her, but would not let me take off her clothes. Instead, she would masturbate me for perhaps five or six times. She would lead me down the hill, past the Japanese gun, a tired but happy man. I suspect providing masturbation for the males may have been a cultural thing among the Yapese people to avoid unwanted pregnancies and keep the men relaxed and happy.

One evening instead of going up into the hills, we went into the abandoned house that was supposedly being repaired for the doctor. We were sitting on the ground in one of the rooms and we heard some movement at the doorway. I pointed my flashlight at the door and a young Yapese man was standing there. He then turned and fled, which was for the best, as I have since thought that if we were otherwise engaged I could well have had something unpleasant happen to me while my mind was distracted. I had always presumed my companion was single, but it could have been that she had a partner or family members looking out for her interests.

Although I got on well with Ester, and the hospital was running smoothly, my living conditions were not tolerable, so I sent in my resignation and prepared to move on. When I arrived at the dock to get on the seaplane, one of the two Catholic priests who lived on the island shook hands with me and thanked me. I presume that was for getting off his patch, as I would no longer be disrupting a member of his flock. The Catholics presence was strong in the western parts of Micronesia, as the Spaniards had been the major influence there until their defeat in the Spanish American War at the end of the nineteenth century.

The author with an achondroplastic dwarf on Yap.

    When I got to Guam, I went to the building in Agana which was the social centre for Trust Territory people. After having spent time in the outer districts, we loved getting to Guam, because there we could get ice cream and milkshakes and all those lovely things associated with civilisation that we couldn't get in the outer islands.

    On Guam, I met Captain Evans from the M.V. (Motor Vessel) Errol, which we had sailed into Pinelap. He was fortyish, well-built and a good-looking man. He was a magnificent swimmer and used to join the crew of the ship diving and capturing turtles. Back then, this was considered good sport, but now turtles are an endangered species so it would be frowned upon. While we were on the Errol, he told me that when two nuns were taking three of their senior school girls back to their islands, he invited one of the girls to use his bathroom. He conducted an affair with the girl, not quite under the eyes of the nuns, but almost. He was returning to North America and said that if I flew with him to San Francisco he would show me some of the bright lights. On the very day that we were to fly out to Hawaii, and then go on to San Francisco, I was offered a berth on the M.V. Chilcot to travel to Japan. Because of this I did not take up his invitation. Captain Evans boarded the plane and somewhere near Wake Island the plane blew up, leaving no survivors. This was not to be the only time I avoided death by plane crash.

Still happy and healthy, I set sail on the M.V. Chilcot with six other passengers. We had our meals with the officers and one of the other passengers was the wife of an officer who was sailing on another ship. She told us that she was going for a holiday in Japan, and her husband had told her that when she arrived in Kobe, she shouldn't stay at the hotel he used. Instead, he had arranged for her to stay at another one, which was more suitable for her. The other officers told me that the husband's hotel wasn't a good choice for her because it was used as a base for prostitutes. We never did tell her why she shouldn't go to his hotel.

She and I became good friends, and we used to spend a lot of time on the flying bridge. This was an accessory control room above the active bridge, which could be used in an emergency. There was no roof and cruising through the tropical nights with the moon reflecting off the rolling waves, it was the most romantic situation possible. She would let me cuddle her but that was as far as I could get. I was tempted to tell her that her husband was not behaving in Kobe, so that she might participate in fun and games with me in my cabin. Alas, I never did and she never did.

We landed at the wharf at Kobe that was used almost exclusively by American vessels, and went through the usual customs routine. The Customs officials were a little confused, as I was travelling with a British passport, which associated me with the Sterling area and 'pounds, shillings and pence', but I carried American currency, was in the company of 'Yanks' and was travelling on an American run vessel. There seemed to be a lot of Japanese around, and I vaguely thought that it made sense that the Americans would be administering the Japanese ports and other interests after WWII.

I was told to go to the plush Oriental Hotel, and then down to the bar to meet my officer friends from M.V. Chilcot. They had a flying start, and were drinking cocktails at $1.50 each. I could see that was a place where I could only afford to stay briefly.

Eddie, the chief officer, took me in a taxi to the tourist centre of Kobe, where Eddie's girlfriend, Michico, worked. We found her in a small bar down an alley. Michico was electrified at seeing him, and shouted and hugged Eddie enthusiastically. We three found another taxi and went to a Japanese hotel, high on a hill overlooking the town. After a stiff climb, the taxi entered the old Japanese gates, and then swung around to the front entrance. Here, standing on the step behind a long row of slippers the woman in charge, Mamasan, greeted us. We took off our shoes, gave them to the doorman, and put on the slippers provided. Eddie was a little drunk and demanding which embarrassed me, but the lady was sweet and obliging and we made arrangements for rooms.

I was hot and needed a bath. The hostess called a smiling girl in a kimono, who laughingly took my hand and led me to the bathroom. This was a tiled room with a big square bath in one corner that had a number of small wooden bowls sitting on the ground beside it. She showed, by signs, that I was to take one of the little wooden bowls provided and dip water from the larger bath and soak myself. I was then to rinse off with clean water and get into the large bath. I never did get into the large tub because the water was too hot for me. I had taken off all my clothes but was not sure what to do next. One of the senior women from the hotel walked in to sort out some problem. I was not completely embarrassed at having a stranger find me thus, as I was holding a tiny towel over my pubic area. It seemed to be a matter of routine for her to walk in on naked clients. She slid a small slide in the wall and called out to a man who was outside, whose job was to stoke the fires to heat the water for the bath.

Most of the officers from the M.V.Chilcot were still socialising downtown at the Oriental Bar, so we returned there. There I met up with the captain who took me to find his girlfriend, Yoko, who worked as a hostess in a 'taxi dance' hall. This was a wonderful place, with 200 beautiful Japanese girls all dressed exquisitely in long white formal frocks. Men came and bought dance tickets and when they finished the dance with their chosen hostess they gave her a ticket. We found Yoko and sat talking and drinking hot sake. Sake is a fermented rice spirit with high alcohol content. You take a small porcelain cup with the hot sake, lick a little salt off the back of your hand and drink the sake down in one swallow. After a few of these, despite any ailment, you begin to feel half human.

Yoko said, "Captain-san, you haven't been replying to my letters."

The Captain then said, "Where did you send the letters?"

"To the company office on Guam," she replied.

The captain then realised that one of the office staff would have been re-addressing her letters on to his home address. His wife would have been opening and reading the letters, so the Captain faced a trip back to Guam, where he would meet up with his wife and face the music.

Yoko could not get off work until the hall closed at 11 p.m. She explained that there was great competition for the taxi dancer jobs, and the girls had to pass in a certain number of dance tickets at the end of the evening. Even though the Captain was willing to buy her all the tickets needed, she was still not allowed to leave before closing time. He promised to come back for her later and we set off back to the Oriental Hotel

The Kobe taxi drivers must have felt that all their Christmases had come at once with all of our backwards and forwards travel. The alcohol was doing its job, and by the time we got back to the hotel, we were feeling very fine indeed. We arrived to find that the evening meal had already started and the diners seated on soft cushions around two low tables. A metal plate filled a hole in the table center, which had a charcoal brazier underneath and acted as a frying pan. A girl in a kimono officiated as cook and entertainer. She motioned for me to sit besides her and soon presented me with a bowl of cooked food with two chopsticks. It would be better to draw a veil over my first attempt at their use. Being hungry, I eventually managed to put away four bowls of food. We had some more hot sake in the tiny cups, which were continuously replenished from earthenware bottles.

The working girls who entertained us in Kobe.

A Kobe labourer pulling a cart laden with metal pipes. Immediately after WWII there was great poverty and few vehicles so this was not an uncommon sight.

There seemed to be plenty of girls around, and two in green dresses appeared to be unescorted. The smaller of the two was pretty, so I went and sat beside her. She smiled coyly from behind a fan, speaking English hesitantly. She told me she had learned some English at school and agreed that she would be my companion for the night. After they had sung some English and Japanese songs, somebody said that we were going to a Geisha house, so we called a taxi once again.

Right down in the crowded section of town we ascended a flight of stairs and entered a small room where we were invited to sit on cushions on the floor. After fifteen minutes, a girl came in dressed in full Geisha costume. She was smiling gently, knelt on the floor and bowed to each side of the room, saying in a high voice, "Cumbawa," or good evening. Another Geisha joined the first, backed by an older woman strumming away on a four stringed instrument. They sang and danced for us for two hours. My lack of interest in the music offered at St. Kevin's in Oamaru must have been eased by the hot sake, warm companionship and heady excitement of the evening.

My little Japanese girl pulled me to my feet and danced me around and around until my shirt was wet with sweat. The girls were chatting away very animatedly and it was obvious they wanted to stay and have a good time, but we protested and said that we must return to the hotel with the others. At last we were on our way and the girls remaining in the Geisha House came to the foot of the stairs to see us off. I told them that the two Geishas were the prettiest I'd met, but didn't tell them that they were the only Geishas I'd seen. The Geishas smiled and laughed in a most spontaneous manner.

The next morning three of the girls came into my room and shared breakfast. They appeared quite at home, and giggled and laughed happily. I showed the girls some photos of Yapese people and their stone money. The girls were interested in fundamental things such as, "What was their housing like?", "How old were they when they married?", "Were those banana palms?" Echo, the hotel hostess kept coming into the room to look at the photos.

Soon taxis came and with many farewells and waving of hands the girls were gone. I must apologise for not telling you about my nocturnal activities here, but I think the tone of the book is quite sexually overt enough as it is!

An hour after the girls had left the hotel the hostess came and talked about the evening. She told me that when we returned to the hotel the girls had made lots of noise and talked in the hotel corridors for thirty-minutes before collecting their sleeping kimonos from the girls on duty and taking their customary bath. She then said in her broken English, "Too much yak, yak, yak. How much did they charge? Those girls only care about the money." I could hear my mother and her friends saying the same thing, "Girls nowadays are not what they used to be. All they want is the money".

From then on Mamasan and her assistant, Echo, began to take a personal interest in me. They improved upon their already indulgent Japanese hotel service, and I was very happy in this mountain retreat.

The hotel was set in a big garden with small statues and ornamental pools on every side. In the evening, it was Mamasan's or Echo's duty to sit with me while I ate my meal. They mostly stayed until it was time for me to go to bed.

After breakfast each morning, I took a taxi downtown where I explored the poorer quarters of the city. All sorts of merchants displayed their wares in tiny stalls in the caverns beneath the elevated railway lines. Here it always seemed to be wet and cold, but the people seemed just as cheerful as any I had seen elsewhere. Considering most Japanese had a bad time at the end of WW II, and many had lost close relatives, they showed surprising resilience.

I seldom saw another European in Kobe, and the people stared at me, possibly because I am six feet tall. Japanese men seemed to be just over five feet in height in those days, so I stuck out a good 'head and shoulders' above the rest of the crowd. I had to remind myself that the Japanese soldiers travelled down the Malay Peninsula on bicycles, fuelled by only a handful of rice a day, and had beaten us in Singapore, (the Gibraltar of the East). Nowadays with better nutrition, each generation is taller and they would need bigger bicycles and more rice if they elected to repeat their Singapore campaign.

When I looked in through the open doors of some houses, I got the impression of deep poverty. Echo confirmed that frequently girls had to work as prostitutes to support themselves and an aging parent. Echo herself had to support her old mother who had just spent three months in hospital. One month in hospital cost the equivalent of two months wages for Echo, and like most of us today, she complained of the high cost of medical services.

Echo often came to sit and talk with me, and told me in halting English about her desire to go to Honolulu, where her grandmother had died. Echo had been married but when her husband returned from Korea they divorced, and both Echo and Mamasan had a poor opinion of Japanese men. Often while sitting and talking in my room we would hear sounds of male laughter, and Echo would make a face and say, "Japanese men." I found the Japanese women sweet and obliging, but if I had been a prisoner of the Japanese during the War, would have had a much lower opinion of Japanese men.

Many Japanese maids hurried around the hotel corridors, and their kimonos were very picturesque. In the morning, the girls wore European style cotton dresses because they were cooler and more convenient to do housework in, but at 3.30 p.m. they bathed and changed into kimonos. They kept these on for the rest of the day. Most maids would finish duty and go to bed at 1 a.m., but sometimes when there were customers drinking and partying, they had to stay up later.

Echo took care of the foreigners because she spoke a little English. She frequently didn't get to bed until 4 a.m., and had to rise at 6 a.m. to call the officers to go back to their ships. She was always tired, and for very good reason. After dinner she sometimes lay on my bed for a short nap while I kept look out for the manageress, Mamasan. She was supposed to get one day off a week, but if there were many foreigners at the hotel she would have to stay on duty.

The morning that I was to leave Kobe, both Mamasan and

Echo were anxious to have their photographs taken and wanted to pose in their kimonos. The sun was shining, and I posed them in front of a statue of a terrifying war god in the hotel garden. They changed their kimonos quickly and when the taxi came for me they both climbed in beside me. Echo explained that they were coming to the train station to see me off. They came inside the station, and I expected them to say goodbye at the ticket barrier, but no, Echo went and brought platform tickets and they came and stood with me until the fast electric train came in. I was taking my time boarding the train, but they made me hurry, and pushed me and my suitcases through the door and onto the train. In a few seconds the doors closed and I was only able to get a glance of Mamasan and Echo waving goodbye on the platform.

The train sped on to Osaka, and I marvelled at the high standard of service and friendliness provided by the railway employees. I took another train from Osaka to Tokyo, and although it was a second-class carriage it was equivalent to first class in New Zealand at the time.

After a few days in Tokyo I went on to Hong Kong and I was able to get passage on a freighter to Sydney. We called at Rabaul, where I was apprehensive of the venting volcanoes, but enervated by the steaming heat of the tropics. It wasn't long after my short visit that the volcano burst into life, killing many people and destroying part of the town. Some of the black people in the street were the darkest people that I had ever seen. They seemed to be a deep, shiny purple. I was told that they were not locals but came from a remote part of New Britain.

After two years of life in the tropics, I was on my way home. I looked forward to enjoying simple, familiar things like wearing an overcoat, sitting by an open fire and eating a fresh egg. Events that are part of everyday life in temperate climates became highly anticipated.

Molly, a young Australian divorcee joined the ship at Rabaul, and I was fortunate that she agreed to come to my cabin each night. This was a bonus that was not noted in the shipping company's brochures. It was a free diversion from the usual shipboard life and I feel remiss that I didn't write to the ship's administrators thanking them. I may even have offered a small donation to the crew's Christmas fund. Molly's company did a lot to cure the boredom, which otherwise consisted of eating, sleeping and helping the captain by offering good advice on managing the ship.

CHAPTER 9

Australia, New Zealand, Canton Island, Hawaii and the U.S.

28 August 1953 -27 October 1953

INTRODUCED CHARACTERS:

VARIOUS SHIP MATES, including New Zealand couple and their teenage daughter.
TWO REPORTERS, from Australia's 'The Sun' newspaper.
MRS. SLOAN, a Registered Nurse (R.N.), and wife of Norman.
LOIS STEWART, a reporter from 'The Honolulu Advertiser' newspaper.
MRS. JEAN CHEVERTON, a fellow air traveller.
WILLIAM KAPELL, one of the world's greatest pianists at the time.
DR. NICK BILLS, the doctor in charge of the hospital on Ponapae.
DR. HOWARD, a cardiac surgeon and teacher at the University of San Francisco Medical School.
DR. BUNNEL, a world renowned orthopaedic surgeon.

A LITTLE ROMANCE MAKES TIME FLY AND IN NO time at all it seemed we had reached Brisbane, our next port. Here the wharves were crewed by typical 'wharfies'. Strongly unionised under Socialist leadership they held a very strong position in Australian society in those days. They were all shapes and sizes – uniform only in their determination to take things easy. As I had just come from Japan where they put considerable energy into unloading ships, the difference was striking.

We would be in Brisbane for 36 hours, so I sought out a trip to the mountains. I paid up quickly and went aboard the large bus, which was taking tourists into the hinterland. The driver chatted cheerfully as we passed through the usual city scenes on our way to the wide-open spaces. Once outside the city, we found ourselves in dry country with the famous Australian eucalyptus trees in all directions. My travelling companions were a cheerful crowd, including a New Zealand husband and wife who were accompanied by their teenage daughter. The mother was a good-looking blonde, and the daughter a handsome smaller edition. When I was at university, the boys used to say, "Look at the mother if you want to see what the daughter will look like in a few years." Here was a chance for a bright young fellow who needed some kind of insurance in these matters.

It was wonderful to see the miles and miles of trees stretching away to the mountains in the blue distance. I had just returned from the islands where only the ocean stretched to the horizon, and felt that if I wasn't home yet, I was almost there.

The next port of call was Sydney; I was not disappointed with my first glimpse of Sydney Harbour Bridge from the sea. Its great mass gives the impression of great strength and power, but I was surprised to learn that the tall towers at either end are window dressing. They were erected to balance the visual impression and had no part in the mechanics of the great structure.

Two reporters came aboard the ship and asked me for a short interview. A story about my experiences in Yap appeared in a very late edition of "The Sun". Many of the words were misspelled, and I think that they had sent these two young reporters to do the story for practise.

I set about obtaining a steamer passage to New Zealand, and found that it was necessary to obtain a clearance from the Australian Income Tax Department. I had only spent three days in the country so this hardly seemed necessary. In the meantime, I took a tour of Sydney, and my first stop was a historical mansion within the present city limits. There is a story that snakes on the grounds bothered the residents, so the entrepreneurial owners sent to Ireland for 200 sacks of Irish soil, which they had dug into a ditch surrounding the house. It is said that from that day on not one snake made its appearance within the magical circle of earth. The

Irish Christian Brothers at St. Kevin's in Oamaru had unfortunately missed the story, proving St. Patrick's power to repel snakes could be transferred over 12,000 miles in sacks of earth.

I arrived in Auckland, and then took the train to Wellington. Like all returning New Zealanders, I was impressed by the green countryside of my homeland. The people that I saw in the train were well dressed and cheerful, and when I stepped down at the platform in Christchurch my parents were waiting. My little Citroen car was there and after an early breakfast we set out through the rich Canterbury Plains. We had a talk feast, as there were two whole years to catch up on and I discovered that in the short time I had been away nothing had changed. The faces were the same and the things people were doing were unchanged. It was as if they had been asleep for two years. I was a little reluctant to tell Dais about any amorous adventures in the wide Pacific, though I think Arch wouldn't have raised an eye lid.

After my return, I continued to read travel books and promised myself to keep exploring the world for as long as I could. Back in Dunedin, I visited the dean of the medical school, Sir Charles Hercus, and found that he was very interested in my travels. He was kind enough to ask me to lecture the fourth year students on the epidemiology and bacterial aspects of leprosy. The students seemed interested, and I spent a half-hour afterwards answering questions.

Life at home was quiet, and I was soon writing to embassies asking for visas; it was relatively easy to get a visa for Canada.

Most of my medical school colleagues were doing their hospital jobs in various parts of New Zealand. Some had already gone to England to further their studies. The few that I visited were interested in my travels, but their conversation soon returned to their domestic interests. I didn't consider remaining in New Zealand and applying for Specialist studies. This would have been a better decision for my future but I couldn't wait to get to Canada and see what opportunities were there. This time it was necessary to fly. I had kept in touch with Norman Sloan and he suggested that I stop off at Canton Island on my way to Canada.

Dr. Slaon and Mrs Sloan waiting at the Canton Island Airport with the author.

This tiny atoll lies half way between Fiji and Honolulu, and in those days the big DC-6's that made the run between New Zealand and North America used it as a refuelling stop. It seemed sad that one of the world's most experienced leprologists would be spending his declining years on this tiny island, while the majority of the world's leprosy patients remained untreated.

Norman had grown tired of the separation from his wife and had decided to take the job of a medical officer where Mrs. Sloan, who was a registered nurse, could assist him. As there were less than one hundred people on Canton Island they must have only seen a patient every second day. It was a struggle to get a one-day stop over at Canton Island, but it was arranged and I was on my way. At the airport in Auckland, I applied for an American visa. There were all sorts of regulations, and I needed character references and had to swear that I had never been a Communist. As I had been working for the American government in the Trust Territory islands of Micronesia, I didn't feel like putting up with this and was on the point of telling the officials that I would go straight through to Canada. In the end, I stood and raised my right hand and swore I had never been a Communist. I was soon to discover that obtaining this U.S. visa would play a part in saving my life.

It was a thrill to board the DC-6 and take off on this international adventure. We were to land at Canton at 4 a.m. and Dr. Sloan was waiting on the tarmac as I stepped off the plane. We drove to the house in his Jeep and went back to bed until the sun came up.

No matter from what direction one looked from Canton Island, it was well over a thousand miles to solid land. The island sits on the coral reef and consists of an airport runway and an equivalent area of sand for the birds. There is no more; just runways, sand, sea, reef and all just a few feet above the ocean swells that roll in from Hawaii, to the north, and Polynesia to the south.

The guano deposits left by the sea birds over hundreds or thousands of years had been exploited for fertilizer in the 1800s by the U.S. and the British, who still administer this tiny speck in the Pacific. Early Polynesian voyagers must have known about this small island, as it is on the route between Hawaii and the South Pacific islands. It is not surprising that they did not colonise Canton because it has even fewer material resources than Pinelap. Now that aircraft fly nonstop between Fiji and Hawaii the airfield is only used in emergencies.

Norman's house was a quonset, typical of many structures scattered by the U.S. military throughout the Pacific. It stood on the burning white coral that formed the island. I met Mrs. Sloan for the first time that morning. She was cheerful and joined with her husband in making my stay as pleasant as possible. My days on the island were filled with a visit to the hospital, a showing of Norman's Micronesian films and Norman and I reminiscing about the Tinian Leprosarium and the Micronesian Leprosy Survey. We both agreed that its crowning achievement was establishing an effective programme and the liberation of the many patients that we had released from the Leprosarium.

While on Canton I was taken on a trip to a wrecked steamer which was being broken up, by American salvagers, for sale to the Japanese as scrap. Six men, stripped to the waist, were cutting the ship into pieces with electric torches, as the cost of bringing oxy-acetylene gas to the island would have been prohibitive. They had purchased a small yacht in the U.S. and sailed with their families to this tiny atoll in the Pacific Ocean in order to make their fortune.

They were really brown, and the fittest and toughest people I had ever seen. I was intrigued that here, just a few years after the end of WWII, young American men were cutting up a Japanese ship and selling it back to the Japanese. Not long before they could have been swapping metal shells with each other with no exchange of currency involved.

It was sad to say farewell to Norman Sloan as we had become good friends during our Micronesian Surveys and this visit had cemented the friendship. I was heartened by his confirmation that we had done much to alleviate the sad conditions on Tinian and point the way for a more humane programme for leprosy patients to be developed.

Whilst searching the internet for Leprosy information recently, I was surprised to learn that Dr. Sloan had returned to Pinelap after I visited him, to try new medications which he hoped would be more effective in treating leprosy. Norman will be long gone now so I will never know what conditions he found on the tiny island on his return visit. He could well have travelled by plane, so would have avoided a repeat of his near drowning when disembarking from the M.V. Errol on our first arrival.

Soon I was on my way to Hawaii, and as I had my U.S. visa I was taking a stop over in Honolulu. Jessie Lindsay had retired from her position on Tinian Island and had returned to her home in Hawaii. She had invited me to stay with her and had a room waiting for me in her pretty little home, which was located in the hills that surrounded the town. From the windows I looked out over Pearl Harbour and downtown Honolulu.

I slept in the next morning, but Jessie awakened me as I had a phone call. It was Lois Stewart, a senior reporter from the Honolulu Advertiser. She said that the plane which I had arrived on the day before had gone down near San Francisco, and everybody on board had been killed. I felt that a bullet had once again passed close to my head. As I mentioned previously, I had already missed a Transoceanic flight which had crashed between Guam and Honolulu five months previously. I would have been aboard this fatal crash if I had not persevered through the irritating application process in Auckland to obtain my U.S. visa which enabled my stop over in Honolulu.

Lois asked me to come down to her office for an interview. As soon as I arrived she introduced me to her colleagues, who were busily at work. The airplane crash was the news of the moment and when I was introduced to the other reporters I was regarded as a celebrity. Lois said she wanted a 'scoop' on my story, and asked that if I was approached by reporters from other papers, I shouldn't give them any information.

One of the passengers on the doomed plane was William Kapell, one of the world's greatest pianists at the time. The thirty-one year old American was on his way back to the States from a tour in Australia, and had felt that the Australian press treated him unfairly. Before departing Australia, he declared with some bitterness that "This is goodbye forever. I shall never return!" While in transit, Kapell had rung his wife from Honolulu and told her that he was tired. Although she begged him to stay over in Honolulu, he was anxious to get home to see her and his two children so elected to continue on the same plane; a fatal decision on his part.

I found the people in Honolulu to be just as friendly as they had been when I was there before. They were helpful to strangers. It is said that there is less racial prejudice in Honolulu than in any other American city, and I can believe it. The many attractive girls whom one saw on the streets and beaches seem pleased with their lot. The many successive migrations of Spanish, English, Japanese and Chinese all add to the exotic charm of the islands. While the mixture of blood seemed to make the girls more attractive than elsewhere, I didn't notice that the men were equally handsome. Perhaps I wasn't paying them the same attention.

While I enjoyed my celebrity status in Hawaii, it was fading fast. I was front-page news on the first day, but each day after that I moved to smaller columns in the back pages. I remembered the Latin phrase, "Sic transit gloria mundi" - "Thus passes the glory of this world." It was fun while it lasted, but it was also time to move on.

CONTINUED From Page 1

Two Escaped Plane Death

private practice, told friends here:

"I felt as if a bullet had just whizzed over my head when I learned of the plane crash."

Mr. Rayment told his friends he thought he was "one of the luckiest men alive" but was saddened by the loss of his flight companions. He is staying at the Moana hotel.

* * *

DR. VALENTINE has many friends in Honolulu. He is visiting Mrs. Jessie Lindsay, 2524 Waolani Ave., his former nurse on Tinian.

It was Dr. Valentine's second close brush with an air disaster. He said he had planned to fly to Honolulu last July with a friend from Guam. The friend left on a TransOcean DC-6 which crashed near Wake island, killing all aboard.

Dr. Valentine got transportation from Guam to Japan just prior to the ill-fated flight.

* * *

THREE OTHER persons arrived in Honolulu on the BCPA flight from Sydney. They were Mrs. Bepe Gauta and her two young children, Lauli and Simi, who are from Nandi, Fiji Islands.

They underwent medical check-ups at the immigration station for entry into the U. S.

* * *

THE MUSIC world might not have lost one of the foremost pianists, William Kapell, had he accepted a concert engagement in Honolulu.

Mr. and Mrs. George D. Oakley, 2110 Kakela Place, through the Artists Service of Honolulu, had asked Mr. Kapell to interrupt his trip to perform here. However, the 31-year-old pianist told Mrs. Oakley he was anxious to return home as quickly as possible.

He arrived here earlier than expected, apparently having cancelled his last scheduled concert in Australia to return to the U. S.

* * *

MR. KAPELL was regarded as an outstanding American-trained pianist. He was the youngest winner of the Town Hall Endowment series award; made his first appearance with the New York Philharmonic orchestra in the summer of 1942, and made a recital tour of the U. S. 1942-43.

He later became an outstanding interpreter in the modern school and recorded works by Shotstakovich, Katchiturian, Prokofiev and Rachmaninoff.

He was married to the former Rebecca A. R. Melson. One son, David Eugene Melson, was born to the couple.

Plane Crash Dead Listed

SAN FRANCISCO, Oct. 29 (UP) — Seven Australians, two Englishmen, one Canadian and one American made up the list of all passengers among the 19 persons killed on the British commonwealth Pacific Airliner that crashed and burned near here today.

* * *

THE AIRWAYS local office today released the following complete list of names, ages and addresses of the passenger victims:

George Eastoe, 50, an engineer, of Dereham, Norfolk, England.

Janos Feher, 39, a watchmaker, of 8 Hampden Ave., Darling Point, New South Wales, Australia.

John Feher, 7, son of Janos Feher, same address.

William Cox, 52, a shipfitter, of 42 Benbody Road, Neutral Bay, NSW, Australia.

Jack W. Butterworth, 53, No. 1 Alma Road, St. Kilda, Victoria, Aust.

Cyril G. McDonald, 60, 31 Labassa Grove, Caulfield, Victoria, A...

Capt. Paul Olsen, 39, ship's m...., ...red St., Cardiff, NSW, Australia.

Bernard R. Tischler, 31, a passenger agent, 19 Fulton St., Brighton, South Australia.

John Briscoe, 45, insurance executive, 4 Queens Ave., London, Eng.

William Kapell, 31, concert pianist, 21 E. 94th St., New York city.

Mrs. Jean Chiverton, 68, housewife, 5392 Nanaimo, Vancouver, B. C.

HOME ADDRESS of the eight crew members were not available, but BCPA said all were operating from Sydney.

They were identified as: Capt. Bruce Dickson; First Officer Frank Campbell; Purser Wallay Knight; Navigator George Murtagh; Radio Officer Vernon Walker; Flight Engineer Charles Cattanach, and hostesses June Elder and Amy Lesis.

WILLIAM KAPELL

An article from the Honolulu Advertiser reporting on the BCPA aircraft crash.

JOHN VALENTINE CHEATS DEATH SECOND TIME

It is an understatement to say that Dr. John Valentine is a lucky man.

He is alive today because, through fate or luck or what have you, he was left behind in Honolulu when a British Commonwealth Pacific Airlines' DC-6 plane crashed and burned near San Francisco Oct. 28.

It was Dr. Valentine's second close brush with disaster. He had planned to fly to Honolulu last July on a Transocean DC-6, which crashed near Wake Island. All on board were lost.

The doctor cancelled that flight when he got transportation from Guam to Japan.

Dr. Valentine would have been aboard the BCPA flight if he hadn't received a visa from U.S. Immigration authorities when he did. He received the visa in Auckland, N.Z., shortly before his plane left for Canton Island and Honolulu. The visa made possible a three-day stopover in Hawaii.

Dr. Valentine is the former physician in charge of Tinian leprosarium. When the Navy took over Tinian he was transferred by the Trust Territory to Yap. He resigned recently to enter private practice. He will make his home in Alberta, Canada.

The doctor told Honolulu reporters who interviewed him following news of the disaster that:

"I felt as if a bullet had just whizzed over my head when I learned of the plane crash."

Among the 19 persons—11 passengers and eight crewmen--who perished in the crash was William Kapell, one of the world's foremost pianists.

* * *

LOU GARDELLA IS NAMED SUPERVISING SANITARIAN

Louis Gardella, for the past two years District Sanitarian at Truk, has been named Supervising Sanitarian for the Trust Territory, it has been announced by Dr. H. L. Marshall, director of public health.

The position was established when the economy program necessitated the elimination of all American district sanitarians.

Mr. Gardella is a graduate of San Jose State College where he majored in biology. Later he studied sanitation at the University of California at Los Angeles. Before coming to the Trust Territory, he was sanitary inspector with the California State Department of Health. During a recent leave on the Mainland, Mr. Gardella studied the public health sanitation programs first-hand in southern Mexico and Central America.

In his new position, he will make regular visits to each district, confer with the district director of public health concerning sanitary conditions and program, to assist, instruct and supervise Micronesian personnel in carrying out the program decided upon. He will participate in field trips, aid in the sanitary education program and in the teaching of sanitation when possible.

An article from a Micronesian Health Department circular, reporting on the author's luck avoiding being in an aircraft crash.

Hell-Bent for Life

Articles from the Honolulu Advertiser reporting on the BCPA aircraft crash.

19 D
COA

Late News Flash

The Honolulu
97TH YEAR, NO. 33,641

Doctor and Co-
Missed Death

Two men—a doctor and a co-pilot—are alive today because, through fate or luck, they were left behind in Honolulu when a BCPA DC-6 airplane left Wednesday night for San Francisco.

The plane crashed and burned only minutes short of its goal, killing all 19 aboard, including famed pianist William Kapell.

* * *

DR. JOHN VALENTINE would have been aboard had it not been for a U.S. non-immigration visa. The former physician in charge of the Tinian leprosarium for the Pacific Trust territory got his visa in Auckland, N.Z., just a short time before his plane left for Canton Island.

The visa made possible a three-day layover in Honolulu.

* * *

ARNOLD RAYMENT, co-pilot of the four-engined plane on its flight from Sydney to Honolulu, remained behind when the DC-6 left for San Francisco.

BCPA sopkesmen said only eight crew members are carried on its flights which terminate at San Francisco. The normal complement is nine crewmen.

* * *

DR. VALENTINE, who is going to Alberta, Canada to enter
(Continued on Page 6, Col. 5)

DR. JOHN VALENTINE

Australia, New Zealand, Canton Island, Hawaii and the U.S.

E IN BCPA
ST CRASH

Advertiser
U.S.A. — To Reach All Departments Telephone 52977
TOBER 30, 1953. 24 PAGES

5¢ Red Streak Edition

Honolulu Plane Hits Mountain; Pianist Victim

SAN FRANCISCO, Oct. 29 (INS)—A transpacific luxury airliner crashed and burned in the rugged mountains 18 miles short of its destination today and all 19 persons aboard were killed.

The Coast Guard said shortly after noon that 11 bodies were recovered and there was no sign of life in the wreckage.

The British Commonwealth Pacific Airways DC-6 airliner from Sydney and Honolulu carried 11 passengers and eight crew members. One passenger and two of the crew were women.

* * *

LISTED AMONG THE passengers was Concert Pianist William Kapell.

Kapell, 31, a soloist with the New York Philharmonic orchestra, was returning home from an Australian tour. Ten of the 11 passengers aboard had flown all the way from Sydney. The other passenger, Mrs. Jean Chiverton, boarded the plane at Honolulu last night. She was bound for Canada.

Coast Guard search plane pilots reported sighting the wreckage afire in the mountains about a mile and a half from heavily traveled Skyline Blvd.

The Navy, Coast Guard and San Mateo county sheriff's office rushed ambulances out the boulevard with crew prepared to try to reach the wreckage afoot, over a mile and a half of rugged mountain terrain.

Parachute crews also were dispatched by the Air Force. Coast Guard rescue crewmen, equipped with asbestos suits to protect them from flames, set out for the wreckage by helicopter.

* * *

THE AIRPLANE LEFT Sydney Wednesday morning, Australian time, and took off for San Francisco from Honolulu last night.

Heavy weather over the Pacific delayed the flight but there was no indication of any trouble when the last radio message was received from the aircraft at 8:29 a.m. (PST) this morning.

At that time the message from the airplane said it was over Half Moon bay on proper course for the airport.

MINUTES LATER the big DC-6 airliner hit the mountains a little more than five miles east of the town of Half Moon bay.

The wreckage was spotted at an elevation of 2,000 feet in the Redwood forest area of the San Francisco peninsula. The airplane hit the mountains only 18 miles from the San Francisco International airport.

Dead Pianist Passed Up Recital Here

City Stopover Saved Plane Passenger

Two hours before he left Auckland, New Zealand, Dr. John Valentine was issued his U.S. non-immigration visa which made possible a three-day layover in Honolulu.

"I felt as if a bullet had just whizzed over my head when I learned of the plane crash," Dr. Valentine told friends here. He is a former physician in charge of the Tinian leprosarium for the Trust Territory of the Pacific and has many friends in Honolulu. Here he is visiting with Mrs. Jessie Lindsay, 2324 Waolani Ave. She was Dr. Valentine's nurse on Tinian.

DR. VALENTINE had hoped to stop in Honolulu but his non-immigration visa was not available until shortly before he left Auckland for Canton Island to visit briefly with Dr. Norman Sloan, former director at Kalaupapa, Hansen's disease settlement on Molokai. He boarded the DC-6 at Canton at 4 a.m. Wednesday. Dr. Valentine said he felt this was his second "narrow escape" as he had planned to visit Honolulu last July with a friend, but instead was able to get transportation from Guam to Japan.

The friend was lost in the crash of a Trans-Ocean plane near Wake, the plane on which Dr. Valentine would also have been a passenger.

* * *

DR. VALENTINE said he visited with members of the crew and passengers, including 6-year-old John Feher, one of the victims. The child was wearing his arm in an airplane splint as the result of a fracture. Two other children, with their Samoan mother, were on the plane but disembarked in Honolulu.

He accompanied passengers continuing on to the Mainland into Honolulu where they lunched at the Edgewater hotel. Several had not visited in the islands previously and were interested, particularly in the second hand car lots they observed, remarking that such cars would be at a premium in Australia. All seemed in a gay, holiday mood.

'Johnston 'Hopeful'

Passengers On Ill-Fated BCPA Plane

SAN FRANCISCO, Oct. 29 (INS) — Names of the eight crew members and 11 passengers aboard the ill-fated British Commonwealth Pacific Airways DC-6 that crashed below San Francisco early this morning were announced today. The crew members, all of Sydney, Australia, were:

Capt. Bruce Dickson
First Officer Frank Campbell
Purser Wally Knight
Navigator George Murtagh
Radio Officer Vernon Walker
Flight Engineer Charles Cattanach
Hostess June Elder
Hostess Amy Lewis

Among the passengers was William Kapell, world famous concert pianist.

Others listed by BCPA as passengers were:

James Feher and son, John
George Eastoe
William Cox
Jack Butterworth
Cyril McDonald
Paul Olsen
Bernard Tischler
John Brisoe
Mrs. Jean Chiverton

Home addresses were not available immediately.

City Offered Chance to Buy Sears Plant

An offer to sell Sears, Roebuck and Company's property on Beretania St. to the City-County of Honolulu was made Thursday by F. B. Carter III, the broker handling the proposed sale.

In a letter to Mayor Wilson and the Board of Supervisors, Mr. Carter said the buildings and land "may be purchased for an immediate cash consideration of $2,230,000, or over a period of 10, 20 or 30 years.

"IT WOULD EVEN be possible

Brads Studied All Morning In Dope Trial

Some small brads—they look like sawed-off nails—took up a full morning's testimony Thursday in the government's case against Sau Hong Lu, 43, charged with trying to smuggle almost $200,000 worth of dope into the U.S.

The brads were found by customs agents who searched Lee's baggage at Honolulu airport on July 24. The agent said they found five plastic green bags under false bottoms in Lee's luggage. The government claims the plastic bag contains 16 pounds of smoking opium, and that another plastic sack contains 3½ ounces of heroin was also discovered.

DR. JOHN VALENTINE

187

I said goodbye to Jessie and promised to keep in touch with her, and she came to visit me in New Zealand a few years later. She had continued to live on a small pension in Honolulu. As she remained a Mormon she did not smoke, drink or go out with bad men. She wasted very little, and if she had food over from a meal she would put it in the refrigerator and use it the next day. By practising an austere and abstemious lifestyle she was able to save enough to take a boat cruise each year. I admired her determination and resourcefulness and I wished that I was better at following her good example.

On the plane taking me from Honolulu, I thought about the others who had been aboard the ill-fated plane that had crashed a few days before. On our plane were airline officials who were going to San Francisco to investigate the cause of the disaster. As we flew through the night, I lay half awake, watching flames coming from the engine exhaust. I wondered if this was something to be concerned about and whether I should bring it to the notice of the flight stewardess; I didn't. Since then, I have flown at night many times and have often seen signs of fire and heat from aircraft engines. None of them have caught fire or exploded, and I'm still here, so it must be part of normal engine operation.

Waiting at the Los Angeles airport was Dr. Nick Bills, who was the hospital doctor from Ponapae. When we had met in Micronesia, I enjoyed his company (despite the dunking I got when he upturned his outrigger canoe!). When we parted, he had given me a warm invitation to stay with his family in San Francisco, if I passed that way on my travels. He looked well and prosperous and drove me into the city centre in his car. We went up the famous steep streets, past the Top of the Mark Hotel, and stopped in front of a small, six storied apartment building. This was where Nick's parents lived, and we were to have coffee with them.

The building's elevator took us to the top floor, and Nick took me into a luxurious, large apartment. The interior reminded me of grand rooms I'd seen in movies and were a cut above any I'd been in before. His parents made me feel welcome, and Nick's father was keen to show me his television straight away. I was very impressed by it, as we did not yet have T.V. in New Zealand. He also wanted to take me downtown and show me the sights, but we had just arrived and I didn't accept the invitation. I came to regret this as he seemed very busy and didn't offer again.

After we had coffee, Nick took me back down in the elevator and said, "Come and I'll show you where you'll be sleeping." On the next floor down there was another apartment with two bedrooms and a sitting room. I went to the window, and there the whole of San Francisco stretched out all the way to the Golden Gate Bridge. I felt I couldn't accept this if they had to pay for it, and certainly I couldn't afford it. When I told Nick this he replied, "That's OK, we own the apartment building, and this one's vacant at the moment." It seemed that Nick's forbears had been missionaries in China, and they had somehow obtained the Ford franchise for all of the country. Having gone to China to do good, they stayed and did well, and I was profiting from their generosity as well as their prosperity.

In my spare time I walked down the steep streets and followed the crowds of busy people past the buildings housing banks, insurance companies and loan companies. I learned that the New Zealand insurance company in San Francisco was one of the few which paid out in full after the cataclysmic San Francisco earthquake in 1906. This earthquake destroyed half the city and the fair treatment metered out by that insurer was still remembered in 1953, and put the company in good stead with the people of that city. The famous San Francisco waterfront lived up to its rough and tough reputation and the people who came out of the coffee shops and bars didn't look like the types you'd invite to your family Christmas party. I was able to join a group excursion across the Golden Gate Bridge, and we went into the mountains where the giant Redwoods grew. When the guide told us they were the world's tallest trees and that some were 300 feet tall, I was inclined to believe him.

Nick took me to see a heart operation at the University Hospital where they fitted me out with a mask and gown and positioned me beside the operating table. The surgeon acknowledged me, and then went about his business. The operation took an hour, as they completely stripped the covering from the patient's heart. The pericardium, (or membrane that encloses the heart) had become fibrosed and lost elasticity. This was compressing the heart and compromising its normal action. This sort of condition is unusual, but the operation outcome was often excellent , leaving the patient to lead a near normal life. I found this very exciting, as cardiac surgery was in its infancy in New Zealand.

Afterwards, I talked to the anaesthetist and congratulated him on his procedure. As the chest wall was open during these operations the patient could not breathe for himself. The anaesthetist needed to provide oxygen to the patient by manually compressing a rubber bag for the duration of the procedure. While I was talking to the anaesthesist, the surgeon came back and asked me which branch of medicine I was interested in. When I told him that I was a general practitioner he suggested it would be better to go and see Dr. Bunnel's department, as his work with the hand was very interesting and useful. Surly this could not be THE Dr. Bunnel, who had written a famous textbook on the hand. As it turned out, it was but as he was out of town for a few days his partner, Dr. Howard, was happy to see me at a clinic he was conducting and they found an intern to take me along. I was very grateful to have been treated so kindly in a country so far from home. Dr. Howard greeted me quietly, and invited me to sit in on the clinic that he was running, and I was introduced to colleagues from Finland, England and Scotland. Most of these doctors were orthopaedic specialists who were working with Dr. Bunnel. They welcomed me and treated me with no hint of patronage. Dr. Howard was friendly and while leading the discussions did not try to force his own opinions on to the group.

After the clinic, Dr. Howard invited us to get into his Jeep, and was kind enough to take us to different hospitals where he visited his post-operative patients. Can you imagine six doctors of various nationalities and backgrounds riding around San Francisco in a Jeep that was filled to capacity? For lunch, Dr. Howard took us to his club, a two-storey building on Nob Hill. Most of the other cars in the member's car-park were Cadillacs, but this did not worry Dr. Howard at all. He soon herded us past the doorman and into the richly furnished and mirrored interior. We had a drink and a fine meal, but Dr. Howard would not accept any payment.

We then went to a V.A. Hospital, where we saw returned servicemen with hand injuries. Some had lost most of their hands, but skillful surgery enabled them to make the best use of their remaining fingers. One man had only one finger but that was much better than having none at all. Dr. Howard told us that it was important to conserve as much hand tissue as possible at the first treatment.

When I returned to my room, Nick's father told me that he had some relatives coming to stay in the apartment which I was using, but he was not keen on them and would I stay on so that he could say the flat was occupied. It is not everyday that I would have the opportunity of staying in a flat on Nob Hill, but my dollars would not last forever and I had planned to start a new life in Canada. I regretfully declined his offer and prepared to fly to Vancouver.

CHAPTER 10

Canada and the Yukon
January 1954 – 18 February 1955

INTRODUCED CHARACTERS

DR. BRAMLEY-MOORE, the Registrar of the College of Physicians and Surgeons in Edmonton.
DR. FISH, a doctor in charge of a hospital in McLennan, Alberta.
DR. COLIN DAFOE, a chest surgeon from the University Hospital in Alberta.
DR. DAY, an orthopaedic specialist at the University Hospital in Alberta.
DR. LIONEL DODDS, the Head doctor at the Grand Prairie Hospital.
DR. WILSON, a Grand Prairie practitioner who died in a plane crash.
MRS. WILSON, Dr. Wilson's wife.
DR. GARTH O'CONNOR (deceased), whose practice the author took over in Grand Prairie.
DR. JOHN NELLS, an English doctor who arrived and became the author's competition.
DR. JOE STOREY, a Canadian doctor who later came and started a practice.
MISS GOW, the Nursing Superintendent at the Grand Prairie Hospital.
DR DICK MCCRUM, a colleague from an adjacent town.
MISS JANET WHITE, the author's office nurse.
AGNES COBDEN and husband CEC, a married couple who attended the author's practice as patients.
DR. AXEL CHRISTIANSEN, a fellow traveller whom the author met on the plane to Mexico.
DR. RUS BROWN, Dr. Lionel Dodd's Australian partner, who left Grand Prairie soon after the author arrived.

EARLY IN NOVEMBER, I FLEW UP THE WEST COAST of the U.S. to Vancouver, where I had to go through Canadian Customs and Immigration. I spent two hours sitting in the austere waiting room of the Immigration Department, as their doctor wasn't immediately available. As I waited, I wondered when the governments of the world would do something about their waiting rooms for immigrants. When the doctor did arrive he was apologetic about the delay. He took me in for my examination and said, "Oh, don't bother about taking off your shirt, just sit and talk to me while I fill in this rubbish." He was helpful and enthusiastic about my chances in Canada. I was not allowed to register in British Columbia unless I took a position with the Department of Health, but this did not appeal to me so I decided to move on to Alberta.

Vancouver appeared cold and bleak on this November day compared to sunshine-filled Hawaii. The occasional shoddy buildings, even on the main streets, and the many jobless men hanging about them, made me feel vaguely disillusioned about my Canadian future. I was to learn later that Vancouver had the best winter climate in all of Canada, as the North Pacific current brings warm water from the tropics. This allows the unemployed men, who migrate there during the colder months, to survive in moderate comfort. I don't know if there were unemployed women around or how they survived as I saw no sign of them. Maybe they went to sleep, as the bears did, until the weather improved. I decided to stay for a week, since it was unlikely that I would pass that way again and despite the cold I found the parks and surrounding areas beautiful.

Later in the month, I left Vancouver on the Canadian Public Rail (CPR) Express, and headed for Calgary. The trip through the Rockies was just as majestic as the travel folders had illustrated however, half the journey was at night, which was a pity, because I missed seeing the magnificent scenery for that part of the trip.

Upon arrival in Calgary, I changed trains for Edmonton, and the day after arriving in that northern city I established myself at the local YMCA. I found my way to the office of the College of Physicians and Surgeons of Alberta. The 'Registrar' was supposed to tell me if and how I could be registered to practice in Alberta, as without medical registration, I could not practice there. I found the building, climbed the rather run down stairway and presented myself with the bravest face possible to the girl at the reception desk. She greeted me cheerfully, and asked me to take a seat until the Registrar, Dr. Bramley-Moore, could see me. There was nobody else in the office, but Dr. Bramley-Moore kept me waiting for an hour. I was finally escorted into his office, but he was occupied with reading some papers on his desk. After an awkward period, during which he continued looking down at his desk and I kept standing there, he looked up. He gave me the impression that this was a pretty exclusive organisation, and not just anybody could be admitted. He suggested that it might be best to continue on to Saskatchewan, where my New Zealand qualifications would be more readily accepted, and I could be registered immediately. I did not want to give up so easily and stood my ground. After several trips to see Dr. Bramley-Moore, he at last suggested that I take a trip up north to the Peace River country, where there were a couple of vacancies for an assistant. He suggested I fly, but as I had only a modest amount of money I decided to take the bus to McLennan, where there was a vacancy.

The main street of McLennan had not seen a load of gravel for many a long day, and if you cut across the street at the wrong place you ran the real risk of losing your shoes. I found the hotel and, under the scrutiny of two old men sitting in the lobby, used the public telephone to ring my contact, Dr. Fish, who called around to pick me up a few minutes later. Dr. Fish had lost his wife the previous year, and had been drinking a great deal since. After a meal, he took me to the hospital and showed me the new wing that was under construction. Like many hospitals in Alberta at the time, it was run by Catholic nuns. The medical clinic was at the hospital, where there was also a large drug store. Because the monthly salary offered was low, it was easy to turn the position down, so I set off on the train for Grand Prairie, my next stop.

The Grand Prairie railway station was in the poorer part of the town, so my first impression was not good. When I rang Dr Lionel Dodds, my contact there, he advised me to go to the York Hotel where he would meet me in an hour. A short while later a tall and lean man who looked to be in his forties, appeared at my room and introduced himself. Lionel gave the impression of being a man of affairs who was very much in control of the situation.

He was offering a monthly salary of $800, and if I wanted to set up a practice on my own I would have his wholehearted support. He introduced me to some of the local doctors who were very pleasant, and one, a Dr. Wilson, invited me around for a meal. I returned to Edmonton on the Monday to see if any other prospects had appeared.

The day after I left Grand Prairie, Dr. Wilson was treating a man with polio and the patient was developing paralytic symptoms. The patient's wife had flown up from Edmonton and she wanted to take her husband back there for specialist attention, in the small plane she had chartered. Dr. Wilson was apprehensive about the prospect of taking a flight to Edmonton in a small plane as the weather was not good. They could have waited for a bigger plane, which would have been flown up with the Search and Rescue team from the RCAF Base in Edmonton but the patient's wife insisted that they leave immediately in her plane. The next evening I picked up the "Edmonton Journal," and saw Dr. Wilson's photo on the front page. The plane had been lost, and it was presumed everybody on board was dead. I'm sure that had I been in Grand Prairie at that time I would have volunteered to fly down with the patient, as I did not have a car, and I would have welcomed a flight back to the city. The airplane was not found that year; if a plane dived into a stand of trees the wings folded back and made it difficult to find. For four days search planes flew low over the search area looking for crows being disturbed, as they flew away from where they would have been feeding on the bodies. After four days of intense searching with no sightings, the teams were called in and the search was abandoned. It was not until many years later that two hunters stumbled onto the wreckage.

In the meantime, I had been to the University Hospital, and met Dr. Colin Dafoe. He was a chest surgeon and insisted that I stay at his home with his family.

Colin was a good looking six footer in his forties. A relaxed and charismatic man, he came from French speaking Canada, but spoke excellent English. Colin had been a doctor in the Canadian forces in WWII and told me that he respected New Zealanders because of his good experience with them in war time Italy and Yugoslavia. He had worked with a Dr. Rogers, a New Zealander, in the war and they had both been flown into the Yugoslav mountains where they acted as army surgeons to the guerillas. The guerila forces harassed the Germans in the valleys below and sustained frequent casualties. Dr. Rogers later wrote of his experiences in 'Guerilla Surgeon' and he mentions Colin in the book.

I did'nt know what to do about establishing myself in Grand Prairie, as I wanted Dr. Wilson's practice, but did not want to rush off up there looking as if I was in a hurry to fill a dead man's shoes. After careful consultation with Colin, I wrote to Mrs. Wilson suggesting that I come up to look after Dr. Wilson's practice until he was found. Mrs. Wilson replied that Dr. Dodds was taking care of her husband's patients so they did not need my services.

At this time there was a polio outbreak and the staff were having a hard time coping with the influx of polio patients at the Royal 'Alec' (short for Alexander) Hospital. Colin advised me to go there for a week to help out with the large number of respiratory patients who were fighting for their lives in 'iron lungs'. The whole ward was filled with the great groaning coffins which breathed for the patients. Specialists did most of the work, and had little spare time for socialising, but I made some good friends with the other general practitioners. Our main function was to use suction to clear the mucus from the patient's airways when they were becoming clogged. They could not do this themselves and were at risk of choking and possibly suffocating if this procedure was not done when needed.

One of the women patients, who could only speak when we used a bag to ventilate her lungs, asked me to send her a post card from the Peace River Country. During these short periods, when she could get a few words out, she would tell us what she had been thinking while lying there. She asked, "Will I be able to hold my baby, doctor?" She had two children and like most mothers, she worried that her arms would be paralysed and she would not be able to look after her children. She didn't care about the other parts of her body. After a week of helping in the ward I went back to stay with Colin Dafoe's family in Edmonton.

I bought a car and made a part of the payment in American dollars. For once the Canadian dollar was higher than the American dollar, and the car salesman rang to ask me to make up the difference. When I refused to do this, Colin Defoe was delighted and said "Oh look, he's just come to the country and is taking one of those terrible car dealers to the cleaners."

As Mrs. Wilson had said that they did not need my help at the practice in Grand Prairie, I was frustrated and not sure of my next move. After an anxious two weeks, I decided to return to Grand Prairie anyhow. It had been a month since I had been in North Alberta, and I set out on the slushy road on a cold winter's day. For the first 200 miles the trail went through a wilderness of muskeg swamp and stunted trees. As big trucks passed me going south, they splashed wet mud on to my windshield and I had to stop and clean it off each time. I had all my savings invested in the car and just enough cash to get by for a few weeks at the most. If I missed out on getting Dr. Wilson's practice I would be in deep trouble.

The snow blowing over the bonnet of the car made me even more apprehensive. After a seemingly endless journey, I drove into Grand Prairie. When I pulled up at the York Hotel the acting manager recognised me and said, "You are a fool if you don't stay now." I rang Mrs. Wilson and asked to see her. She asked if I wanted to talk about the office, and when I said yes, she said she preferred not to talk about it. If I missed out on this opportunity I really had to think about going somewhere else.

I looked for other premises but there was nothing available for rent in the town. Dr. Wilson didn't own his rooms but rented them, so I went to see the owners. It seemed that Mrs. Wilson was prepared to release the office in two weeks if Dr. Wilson had not been found. Rather than wait around town for two weeks, I decided to invest my last cash on a trip up the Alaska Highway to the Yukon. I knew that once I got started in practice I would be tied to the office so I might as well go while I had the time.

Dawson Creek, a little to the north of Grand Prairie, has the "Mile Zero" post for the Alaska Highway. Here U.S. Army

Engineers had established their southern base for their tremendous effort in building the highway during WWII. In 1942, Alaska was under threat of Japanese invasion, and in less than a year the Army engineers pushed a 1500-mile road across the bush, mountains and muskeg to get essential supplies through to Alaska, which later became the forty ninth state of the United States. Dawson Creek had been an insignificant village beside a creek until then. Now it was a prosperous little town of 5,000 people. At the crack of dawn the next day, I set out on my long journey to White Horse in the Yukon. When I looked at the map it was six hundred miles (967 kms) 'as the crow flies', but the road there is far from straight so the true distance was closer to nine hundred miles (1451 kms).

The highway starts as a broad gravel road. There was a lot of traffic for the first few miles, but once past Fort St. John, it faded out until I was passing only two or three vehicles a day. I was only doing 100 miles (about160 kms) a day and it was then that I realised I was going to have to step on it if I was to get to White Horse, all those miles further to the north. A snow plough had cleared the narrow road ahead, and it was impossible to tell where the shoulder of the road was. Great articulated trucks, whose drivers made their living on the long haul from Vancouver to White Horse, kept to the centre of the road. I do not know of anything that has terrified me quite so much as coming around a bend on this narrow road and being confronted by one of these monsters travelling south at 60 miles (100 kms) per hour. They were unable to move too far over towards the treacherous shoulders of the road, and it was horrifying to have these tons of metal hurtle past, close enough to reach out and touch.

Petrol stops were up to 50 miles apart, and you could get coffee at the attached diners. Slow speaking men or women would come from the back and after asking what you wanted, stand idly staring into space as you drank their lukewarm brew. There was beautiful mountain scenery along some stretches of my journey, but in general, it was an unending ribbon of slush through metre high snow on either side. It made for a lonesome drive on an inhospitable winter road.

The author watched this wild Canadian bear being hand fed by a tourist. He was amazed that anyone could put themselves at risk in this way.

At one of these lonely stops, a young woman with a brown left eye and a blue right eye came out to wait on me. Her condition must have been extremely rare, as I've only seen one case subsequently. It has dawned on me, at this late stage, that she may have had a glass eye which did not match her original.

The next day, I stopped at a boarding school where Catholic Brothers boarded male children of a local Indian tribe. The Indians had a traditional nomadic life and moved around a lot for their hunting, so it was better to have their children in a boarding situation so they could obtain an education. The young boys were dressed for skating, and they came out with their skates on, laughing and rolling over one another like playful puppies. I don't know what happened to these children later in life, but hope they didn't go on to welfare-dependent alcoholism like so many indigenous people in the Canadian North.

A hundred miles further north, I came upon a Jeep and trailer stuck on a hill with an entire family sitting in the station wagon trying to keep warm. The husband was a missionary taking his family to Alaska. Their Jeep was overloaded with household effects and was pulling a massive trailer. It didn't have enough traction to pull them up the steep hills, so they were forever getting stuck, with the wheels spinning, on the ice. I put the family in my car and turned the heater on, as something had happened to their vehicle's heating unit and the three children had suffered from cold during the night. I then spent two hours helping the husband get his outfit up the hill, using the Jeep's winch, which I attached to the nearest tree. I hate to think of the mess that would have resulted had one of the giant trucks hurtled around the corner and into the Jeep.

Returning from White Horse later in my trip, I ran into them once again. They were still pressing on to Alaska, but were only progressing an average of 50 miles (80 km) per day.

One of the family was an attractive sixteen-year-old daughter who kept looking at me fondly, but as her family surrounded her I was not able to reciprocate her interest.

The missionary told me that he was short of money and I lent him as much as I could afford from my meagre reserves. He asked for my forwarding address so that he could repay me when he could. I said that I didn't want the money back but would appreciate one of the soap stone carvings done by the Eskimos. We now call them by their correct name, Inuit, and their hand work was regarded as world class, even then. To this day I have not heard from the family or seen the carving or money. I gave the loan for a good cause and I am presuming the missionary believes I will be rewarded someday, but not under the terms we agreed.

Among other things, what I learned from this winter trip was that to survive in Canadian winters, it is important to have a reliable engine and an effective heater in your car. If you had to stop in 40-degrees-below-zero weather, and you left your vehicle, you would most likely be found dead on the roadside within a few kilometres. The coroner would not require a post mortem to be carried out because he would know that a healthy person would die quite quickly if exposed outside to those temperatures. When White Horse finally appeared, after the long drive from the Yukon border, it was a relief to come to a populated centre again. White

Horse is on the Yukon River, which was frozen over in winter. The town was quiet and the small riverboats had been pulled onto the shore for the season. There was little sign of the lusty dance hall days when men were men and women were no better than they ought to be.

The bard of the Yukon was Robert Service and, although he arrived late, he captured much of the emotion and events of gold mining days. Gold had been discovered in the Klondike in 1898 and thousands rushed to make their fortunes; hundreds died from the cold in the first winter, and the great majority returned to their homes sadder and penniless. Many lost their companions and others survived, losing their fingers and toes to the ruthless cold.

The cost of living in White Horse was high; most of the fruit and vegetables had to be flown in or brought in by long-haul freight on the highways. I visited a Dr. Dubois, who had invited me for a meal with his wife at their home, and they treated me hospitably. We doctors have a community of mutual interest and usually treat each other well when we meet. Perhaps it is the same with teachers, truck drivers or, dare I say it, prostitutes, pimps and politicians?

Dr. Dubois and his wife complained about the high cost of living and the fact that only 30-percent of their patients paid their accounts. The town of White Horse was virtually shut down for the winter, but I found an artist who was making a living carving Mammoth (Mastodon) ivory. When the great gold dredges work in the summer they occasionally pull up the prehistoric ivory tusks of the Hairy Mammoth. These massive relatives of the modern elephant had disappeared from Northern Canada ten thousand years ago. The first Canadians walked over the ice bridge from Russia twenty thousand years ago so they had plenty of time to get to know the hairy elephants. Mastodon skeletons have been found in the U.S. with several spear heads embedded in them, so it is likely that the primitive Alaskan natives hunted mammoths, and these remains represent the 'ones that got away'. It is amazing to imagine primitive Stone Age people attacking these hairy behemoths with only their stone tipped spears. One thing is for sure - this wouldn't have been a recreational activity. Every bit of the animal would have been used; meat and offal for food, skins for clothing , shelters and strapping, and bones and ivory carved for implements and artifacts. Any tusks found in the rivers were probably from drowned beasts, rather than those that had escaped the hunting parties.

I embarked on the long trip back to Grand Prairie, which was just as icy and dangerous as the trip North. On my arrival back in Grand Prairie, I found that I could rent Dr. Wilson's old office, starting on January 1st. Suddenly life seemed good and full of promise and I thought that I would never be poor again. However, when I went to get the things needed to start my practice, armed with my last $100, I found I was very short indeed. I went to the bank manager and suggested that I needed a loan until I was able to stand on my own feet; I said I owned my car and would not need the loan for long. He did not seem at all convinced and, after looking at his desk for some time asked, "It wouldn't be for more than two months would it?" I decided to do without the loan and all the merchants I approached let me have any credit I needed. Fortunately, the office was designed so that a single person could live in one of the larger back rooms and still leave the other rooms at the front for waiting and consultation.

The owners of the office were Dr. O'Connor's family. The Senior Dr. O'Connor was long retired but was extremely friendly and helpful, and he gave me all his old surgical instruments, which I thought I would use in my future surgical practice.

Dr. O'Connor Snr. told me that his son, Dr. Garth O'Connor, had practised from these very same rooms but had been killed while flying his private plane, only six months previously. This meant that both of my immediate predecessors who had practised from these rooms had been killed the same way, and within a relatively short period.

Dr. O'Connor Senior said his son was over six-feet tall, and being very strongly built towered over most people. Always the outdoorsman, he escaped to the bush at every opportunity in his plane, which could land on lakes in the mountains. He would stand on the top floor of the hospital and look at the horizon and say to the nurses, "In an hour I will be over those mountains."

Once, Dr. Garth was stopped from getting to the hospital because three truck drivers had blocked the road by parking their vehicles in the middle of it. They were standing around talking with no consideration for the people who needed to pass. Dr. Garth called for them to let him by, but only received a desultory verbal response and no positive action from them. Dr Garth then drove his car around the block and stopped in front of the trucks so that they could not be moved. He took his coat off, and with great enthusiasm began to fight the three men, to convince them of the error of their ways. The impasse ended when he had subdued them all, and then Dr. Garth took them to the hospital for needed repairs. One of them had a broken jaw, so would have been feeding through a straw for many weeks, as his jaw was wired shut. I guess that ensured he wouldn't be giving anyone else cheek and had learned a valuable lesson; "Don't talk back to the doctor".

Dr. Garth did not mince words with his patients, and if they did not play the game according to his rules he told them to move along. On occasions he threw people out of his office and told them not to come back. While most patients were frightened of him, women had a peculiar fascination for him and the legends of his paramours were abundant (and probably true). I was sure there was no way that I would fill this virile doctor's boots but I loved hearing stories of his, and others lives in this rough, last frontier.

Since I was single, I began to get dinner invitations which was useful as in this cool climate I developed a hearty appetite. I loved these meals so freely offered. I was also introduced to many single women, but after a few dry runs the matchmakers gave up on me as being unworthy of their efforts.

I was an unskilled cook as Dais had neglected my training in this area, so everyday meals were a problem for me. The local restaurant meals were just terrible; they presented plates loaded with fat, no matter what one ordered. This was probably because the fare was designed to satisfy the requirements of outdoor workers who

LEPROSY IN THE U.S. PACIFIC ISLANDS
JOHN VALENTINE, M.D., Ch.B. (N.Z.), L.M.C.C., M.Int.Leprosy, Assn.
Grande Prairie, Alberta

Introduction

There are thought to be seven million cases of leprosy in the world today. Less than one million cases are getting treatment although the very effective modern treatment cost four cents a day. The treatment of the six million will play a large part in anti-communist activity in Asia and Africa.

A skin "snip" referred to below is made by nicking the skin at the edge of a lesion with a sharp blade. A small amount of tissue fluid is put on a slide and fired and stained for acid fast bacilli. If bacilli are seen the "snip" is positive.

Etiology

Leprosy or Hansen's disease is associated with a gram positive and acid fast bacilli called Hensen's bacillis. The bacillus is not found in all cases of the disease It has not yet been cultured and it does not cause the disease when injected into humans or laboratory animals.

Leprosy in general is associated with unhygenic living conditions. As the standard of living rises in a population so the incidence of leprosy falls off.

Children are most succeptible to leprosy and must never be left in contact with an infectious case. It is mainly for the protection of children the infectious cases are segregated in leprosaria.

Again in general, it requires close bodily contact of a succeptible person with an infectious case in order that the disease be handed on. These conditions are fulfilled when a child shares a bed with an old person who has infectious leprosy.

Some people consider that when an infectious person has started treatment with sulphones he is less infectious though the number of bacilli in his skin remain the same. The bacilli in the skin of a person undergoing treatment may be long dead. Dead acid fast bacilli injected into the skin of a rat still show up after one year when the skin is biopsied or snips are made.

Types of the Disease.

There are two basic types: (a) Tuberculoid and (b) Lepromatous. Tuberculoid leprosy is the commonest type of leprosy seen in Yap. It is my impression that 90% of the cases here are of this type. This is the reverse of the distribution in most other parts of the world where only about 10% are tuberculoid.

Tuberculoid Leprosy

This is the old neural type. The lesion is typically depigmented with a red raised border sharply demarcated from the normal skin. Generally there are one or more spots on the skin with perhaps some enlargement of the nerves. Apart from this the patient is essentially physically intact. Snips are negative but may be positive in a reaction.
Biopsy specimens show the epitheloid cells typical of tuberculoid leprosy. There are no organisms reported or just an occasional organism.

Lepromatous Leprosy.

This is a more generalized form and the whole body may be involved. The skin lesion or macule is depigmented and fades off imperceptibly into

An article written by the author that appeared in the Alberta Medical Bulletin (Volume 20 Number 1 February 1955).

normal skin. There is no charp edge to this lesion. The ear lobes are enlarged early. In the later stages nodules appear on the back and face. The skin of the face is thickened especially on the cheeks and between the eyes. The testes atrophy and the nasal septum is frequently perforated. The cartiloginous part of the nose collapses but here the cartiloginous part of the nose also collapses in Yaws.

The snips are usually positive. They should be taken from a depigmented macule or a nodule may be found on the elbow. If in doubt, a snip from the ear is always worth taking.

Biopsy reports show lebromatous infiltrations with many small round cells. Typically there are many organisms perhaps 50-100 per high power field.

Indeterminate type (Intermediate type).

As expected this has something of the characteristics of both lepromatous and tuberculoid leprosy. It is an in-between station for all types not falling definitely into lepromatous or tuberculoid. It is well to wait for the biopsy report before attempting to classify an atypical case.

Approximate criteria for treatment and isolation
Treatment

All lesions which are reddened and look active should be treated. If the biopsy report shows active leprosy and there are organisms present, treatment should be started.

Isolation

Theoretically all persons showing positive snips should be isolated. It is better to wait for the biopsy report and if it says that there are more than one or two organisms per high power field, the patient is probably infectious and should be isolated.

In general all legromatous cases will show positive snips and 30-40 organisms per high power field on biopsy. They should be isolated in all cases.

Recognition

In Yap the patients usually know what is leprosy, what is fungus and what is yaws. If the doctor has their confidence they will often point out a spot of leprosy, which is mixed up with tinea versicolor, which the doctor would usually overlook.

Treatment.

DDS* is now the drug used in the Trust Territory. It can be started as 100 mgs. twice weekly and build up to 200 mg. each month, till the patient is receiving 300 mg. twice weekly.

Children of course should receive only a fraction of the above adult dosage according to their body weight.

Toxicity

A mild anemia which is usually transient often develops when DDS is started. It should be observed and if necessary treated with iron and liver. Headaches and nausea may be toxic symptoms and indicate stopping or recuding the dosage of the drug.

The Yapese people are gentle, courteous and kind. The chiefs are extremely co-operative and helpful at all times.

---

* Di-amino-di-phenyl-slphone.

needed high caloric intake to keep them alive and warm. In winter the outside temperatures were often twenty-degrees below zero, even during the day. People working outside require much more food than a person leading an indoor and sedentary lifestyle.

When I chose to walk to the hospital I needed to dress like an Antarctic explorer, or more appropriately, an Arctic explorer as I was in the Northern Hemisphere. I had to don the minimum woollen underwear, hat, gloves, overcoat and fur lined over-boots to venture outside. Even with all this gear on I had to be aware that my nose could freeze. I didn't hear of anyone losing their nose, so people were pretty careful to cover any extremities enough to preserve them.

I didn't have a garage for my car, so it was necessary to run an electric line from the house and put a heater under the bonnet to warm the engine block. I ran the heater overnight and in the morning, the car would start reluctantly, as the battery acid was semi frozen. When I drove off I could hear the engine parts rubbing together as the lubricating oil was semi solid. When the wheels moved they bumped as you drove along the frozen road, because the tyres were frozen solid, and had a flat spot where they had rested during the night. In a few minutes the warm air from the car heater and engine made the inside temperature rise, and as the tyres thawed the ride became more comfortable.

One morning I woke to find the temperature in my room well below zero, and was horrified to find that the furnace had gone out and there was eighteen inches of water in the basement. I called the plumber and told him the problem, and he said, "What's the time, 7.30? Well I'll come over as soon as I get to work at nine." The building was getting colder by the minute and I knew that if the building began to freeze any water filled pipes would break. A pipe had broken in the coal-fired heater in the basement and this had flooded the fire, and water had run over the floor during the night. The plumber eventually came, pumped the water out of the basement and replaced the broken pipe so that I could get on with my business for the day.

The Grand Prairie Hospital.

My practice was building satisfactorily when a new doctor arrived in town. Dr. John Nells had been working for His Majesty's Colonial Service in Africa, but had now resigned and had decided to try his luck in Canada. He was ten years older than me and, having been born and educated in England, spoke with a 'posh' accent. I felt that he looked down on Colonials but he did not actually say this, it was just the impression I got. Maybe my assumption was a reflection of a prejudice I held about those with upper-crust accents, rather than it really being the fact of the matter. Despite this, we were both poor and made protestations of undying friendship and solidarity.

The hospital was poorly equipped and not overly clean, but the infusion of our fresh blood and enthusiasm would alter that. Although the hospital was not up to standard, it was better than the ones I had worked at in Micronesia. It stood just outside the town and was a two storied brick building. From the outside it looked in good shape. Inside the paint was grubby and the eighty beds

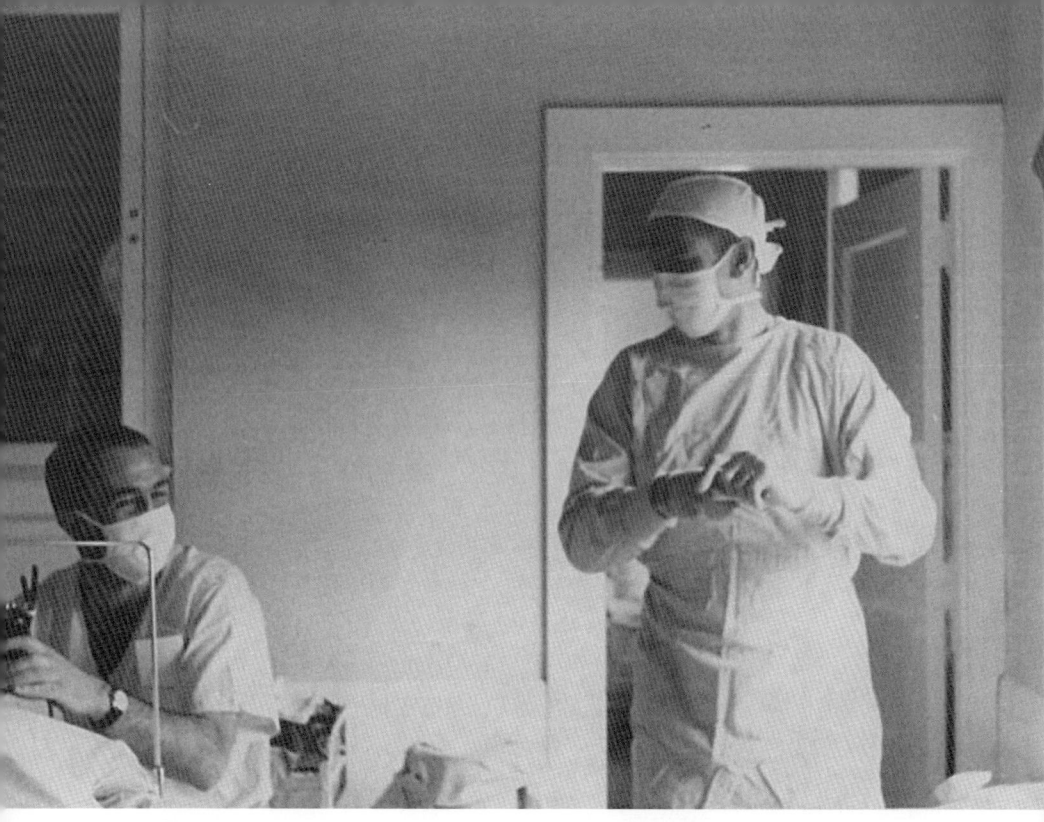

The author giving an ether anaesthetic to one of Lionel Dodd's patients in Grand Prairie.

were in long, old fashioned wards. In contrast to most of the other hospitals in the area, it was not run by Catholic Nuns. There were no medical specialists and the local general practitioners did all the medical work, including the surgery and anaesthetics.

Dr. Lionel Dodds, who had met me when I first arrived, was the senior doctor and had the biggest surgical practice in town. His partner was Dr. Russ Brown, a robust and friendly single Australian who welcomed me to the medical scene in Grand Prairie. He explained that he was about to leave town and when he heard of my trip to the Yukon said that had he known I was planning a journey up the Alaskan Highway, he would have come with me.

At long last I was asked to give my first anaesthetic, while Doctors Brown and Dodds removed an infected fallopian tube from a middle-aged woman, I decided to give ethyl chloride induction and ether afterwards. My patient was under the anaesthetic by the time the surgeons were scrubbed and gowned. When I asked for the suction machine the nurse told me that it was away being fixed and it would not be ready that morning. It is forbidden to give an anaesthetic if a suction machine is not available, in case the patient vomits or has excess mucus in their airway. The operation was not an easy one and lasted for two and a half hours. Although a little blue from lack of oxygen, the patient survived the lack of suction and my inexperience. Later, in the doctors' room, they paid me $30 for the anaesthetic. I had half expected not to be paid, and here I was getting more money than I had ever earned in such a short period of time. It was enough to pay my office expenses for the day.

A Dr. Cec Cobden, one of the local dentists, and his wife Agnes, were very kind to me and introduced me around. Everybody seemed pleased to meet me, and quite a few people asked me to be their new doctor. There had been trouble amongst the local medical people in the past, and on one occasion two of the older practitioners had had a fist fight in the middle of the street. On more than one occasion, Dr. O'Connor had sent a patient on his way for suggesting that a colleague's fees were lower, saying "If you want two-bit medicine, go and get it from a two-bit doctor." I was assured that the hostility within the local medical community was now past history.

I found that my office nurse, Janet White, was a real friend. She was a sociable, softly spoken woman in her early forties. Janet had lived in the town for sixteen years, and having been a dental nurse as well, knew just about everyone. My work kept increasing and I welcomed every consultation, because I was $400 in debt from my necessary set-up purchases, and did not want to go back to the bank again. Each consultation was $3, and I used to sit and listen as the patient went out. If the outside door banged soon after they left my office that meant there had been no pause before leaving, and therefore I knew the patient had left without paying. However, if they stopped to talk to Janet, oh what a glorious moment! I knew that in all probability payment was being made. If I was fortunate enough to have patients waiting in the waiting room, and they saw the first patient pay, in general they followed suit. We would then have a good afternoon with some cash in the cash box. If the first client sped on his way without a thought about paying the $3, it was likely that only a few of the rest would pay.

Dr. Russ Brown finally left, Lionel asked John Nells to give an anaesthetic for him and I waited for my turn. John's anaesthetic had gone off well and Lionel had asked him to give another the next morning, but John referred Lionel to me for this one. Unfortunately my anaesthetic was not good and the patient was coughing and spluttering long after the induction. This meant his muscles remained tense because the coughing kept him from entering into a totally relaxed state.

Lionel had a habit of looking down at the patient, when he came into the theatre after scrubbing to put on his gloves, and asking, "Is he breathing?" or some other unhelpful remark. Shallow breathing at the beginning of an ether anaesthetic does happen occasionally, even in competent hands. I was by no means skilled at that point in my medical career, and this and other complications were common. Sometimes the patient would be breathing too lightly and gagging, or not breathing and going blue from lack of oxygen. By then we had bottled oxygen available and I gradually got to grips with the induction process.

As the weeks rolled by more and more people made their appearance at the office, and I got to know them by their first names and soon made many new friends.

I found it necessary to learn about the lives of the people before giving advice about their ailments. It was little use to tell a man with a painful back to keep warm if his work meant that he was outside all day where the temperature hardly ever rose above twenty-degrees below zero. In those days social services weren't generous and it was important that the men kept on working to keep the family income flowing in.

One young married woman, who lived in a log house out of town, had just had her second baby. A dog bit her little boy, and her husband wasn't working because of a back injury. She was under considerable strain because she had to carry water into the house and stoke the wood fire every four hours, even at night. She was only twenty years old, but could easily have been mistaken for thirty. This woman, like many others had their hard lives reflected in their prematurely aged faces. The conditions in Grand Prairie were harsh enough without the added complication of poverty.

As I was hoping to build up a surgical practice, my first operation was of great importance. A man walked in to the office one day and asked that I remove a cyst from his forehead. I arranged for him to come to hospital the next week so that I could do it under local anaesthetic. It was important that it did not become infected. He was a large, handsome man and the operation went off without a hitch. He felt weak afterwards, as a local has this effect on some people, so I took him home in my car. The next few days were anxious ones for me, but all was well and the forehead healed perfectly. His entire family became patients.

One morning I had been to the hospital and ruptured membranes to bring a woman into labour. Unfortunately the baby's umbilical cord had prolapsed past its head, and the baby was in danger of asphyxiating. While still in the mother's abdomen the baby's only source of oxygen comes from the placenta via the cord. When the mother has contractions the pressure compresses the prolapsed cord, and in the worst case the baby is born dead or brain damaged. I called my colleagues Lionel and John, and with Lionel's assistance I did a caesarean and both mother and baby survived. I later learned that I should not have ruptured the membranes until the baby's head was engaged in the mother's pelvis.

The new mother was mildly mentally retarded and she always greeted me in the friendliest manner. She had been told to bring the baby to my practice rooms every week for weight checks after she left the hospital, and when she did, she also brought her other five children. The older children would sit out in the office and carry on an animated, if one sided conversation with whoever happened to be in the waiting room. One of her little boys was incontinent of urine so for my own, and the carpet's protection, I told her that the baby had been weighed enough now, and she need only to come for his scheduled injections. Slowly but surely my practice was building.

That first winter I was struck by the poor sanitation in many houses and the high incidence of nose and throat infections. There was often no piped water into the log cabins then, and water was carried from nearby wells. All the windows were tightly closed and shuttered against the 40 below outside temperature, and when you walked into a cabin you could smell the indoor chemical toilet. The children could not go outside to play and were constantly underfoot. Usually the floors were without covering and the only source of heat was a large wood or coal furnace in the corner of the central room.

The summers were only three months long and the winter seemed to last forever, with only very short daylight hours. As soon as the last frost left the ground, the farmers had to plant their wheat as it was a race to get it ripened and harvested before the frosts returned in ninety to one hundred days later.

As the scientists developed wheat that would mature quickly, the farmers could try planting it further to the north. Unlike New Zealand, where it gets colder as you go south, in Canada the further you go north, the colder it is.

People living that far north get moderately depressed during the long winter months and they call the condition "Cabin fever." If they could afford it, they took holidays in Hawaii, Mexico and the West Indies, looking for the sunshine that eluded them at home. While it was difficult for working people to make it through the Canadian winter, I was happy because my income was much higher than I could have expected in New Zealand; also the taxes were lower and I could further my surgical experience in provincial Canadian hospitals. In New Zealand my involvement with surgical work would be minimal unless I first obtained a post-graduate surgical qualification.

Just as I was becoming confident that I could fit into this small community, a dark cloud appeared on the horizon. Well, not a big dark cloud, just a smudge on the horizon as big as a man's hand. Later on it was to develop into a full blown storm.

Dr. Joe Story, a young Canadian with an East European background, came to visit. Joe was of medium height and build with a dark complexion and a chatty manner. He had been at medical school with Lionel Dodds and had come to visit him. During the visit Lionel asked him to give an anaesthetic for an adult while Lionel did a tonsillectomy. Joe did an intubation. This procedure meant passing a tube through the nose into the patient's windpipe so that they did not gag on the abundant blood lost during the tonsillectomy.

At that time, in Alberta, it was recommended intubation be used during all tonsillectomies in adults. Neither Dr. John Nells nor I had learned how to do intubations so this put us under some pressure, and unless we learnt this technique our income from anaesthetics was at risk.

When Lionel introduced me to Dr. Joe Storey, it became obvious that he was trying to impress Lionel with his wide knowledge of the general practice of medicine. Fortunately, Joe did not stay long this time, and was gone the next day. John Nells and I continued to give anaesthetics and sometimes I was asked to assist Lionel with a major operation. Most operations in Grand Prairie were done without an assistant, but in other centres they insisted on two doctors at the operating table.

During the winter, I had the opportunity to visit two oil rigs in the remote north of the country. It was only possible to get to the drill sites when the ground was frozen. Roads had been bulldozed over the frozen muskeg swamps that were an inaccessible, wet morass in summer. They were pushing the search for oil as deep as 13,000 feet in those days. At these rig sites, six or eight men slept in a small caboose in two tier bunks. They worked twelve-hour days, seven days a week, with seldom any breaks until the job was over. It was little wonder that some of the men became accident-prone. They were always coming in with cuts and crush injuries, and would spend time in hospital or on compensation at home. This gave them an honourable way of getting a break from the hard grind.

Without warning one day, Dr. Joe Storey reappeared and informed all the people whom he came across that he had come to work with Dr. Lionel Dodds. Joe had brought his car, children and his pretty blonde wife with him. He did not secure the desired partnership with Dr. Lionel Dodds, so he came to me and suggested that I give up my living space at the back of my office, so that he could use it as his office. This did not appeal to me, as I disliked his pushy personality. I told Joe there was no room in my premises but if he decided to start a practice I would help him. Both Dr. John Nells and I began to feel uneasy and we soon found out that we had every reason to be worried. We wondered if Lionel would decide to give Joe most of his anaesthetic work. For some time Lionel had been prodding us to use Pentothal as an intravenous anaesthetic. This is much pleasanter for the patient but at that time was thought to be less safe than ether in non-expert hands. Dr. John Nells and I made no claim to be expert anaesthetists. Having Joe Storey on the scene now put us under pressure to learn to administer Pentothal anaesthetics, as well as to perform the intubations.

It became obvious that Joe used unconventional methods to attract patients. We heard one story where a patient said that their previous doctor had given them the wrong treatment for many years, and it was fortunate that he had gone to Dr. Storey, since he had now been put on the right path. Mrs. Storey joined in and told the patients that they were well advised to go to her husband. This added to my tension, but there was no real alternative but to battle on and see what the future would bring.

One morning Dr. John Nells asked me to assist at an operation that he was doing. He had asked Joe to do the anaesthetic and we were all set for the removal of a large mass from a woman's abdomen. A tumour had been growing on her uterus for years until it made her look as if she was pregnant. As soon as the operation was underway John informed the small audience, and me in particular, that he had done many of these operations in

Africa. The main reason that he had asked me to assist was to support the large weight when it was lifted out of the abdomen. I kept my eyes open and my mouth shut with some difficulty. It was soon apparent that the operation was not going well. There was considerable blood loss and this would soon cause the patient to go into shock. When the massive tumour came out of the abdominal cavity it would accentuate the shock.

John began to sweat a little as the time passed, and it was proving to be extremely difficult to remove the mass. It had buried itself in the posterior abdominal wall and was not as easily freed as he had expected. The anaesthetic had been going smoothly, but now Joe said that the patient's condition was deteriorating and it would be as well to hurry. John then asked Joe if he thought it best to put in an intravenous drip to administer fluids. This is a routine procedure for the anaesthetist in most cases, but Joe said he would not do it, as we would soon finish the operation.

Another half hour went by and we were still struggling to separate the tumour from the posterior abdominal wall. The patient's condition was beginning to deteriorate further and John asked Joe again for a drip to be set up. Joe tried to put a needle in an arm vein but was unsuccessful, and told us that the patient's blood pressure was so low, as a result of shock, that he was unable to find a vein. The patient could not stand this for much longer without her life being in danger, and it was imperative that she get intravenous fluids as quickly as possible.

While John's statement at the beginning of the operation that I was there to help lift the tumour mass still rankled with me, I did my very best to help. Neither of us could leave the table, as we were working as hard as we could to finish up as quickly as possible. Joe went down to the other end of the table and began lifting the drapes. If a suitable vein cannot be found in the arm, for insertion of a large needle , a vein at the ankle or in the leg is the usual next option. He tried to put a drip in her leg, but after a few minutes, he said that he could not get a drip in there either, as the veins had collapsed. This is a situation where the body's blood fluid volume has dropped so low that the veins are no longer full of blood, and

Hell-Bent for Life

are more difficult to find. Most anaesthetists would have ordered a cutting down set at this point. This enables a procedure where the skin is cut through to locate the vein easily, and you can then actually see where to insert the needle. Such a procedure requires a little time, but an experienced doctor could do it in ten minutes. Joe, however, was not prepared to take any more steps to save the patient, and retired to the top of the table and told John that the patient had lost so much blood the pulse was imperceptible.

It seemed that Joe didn't care whether the patient lived or died. We pressed on with the last part of the operation while Joe said that he was not giving any more anaesthetic and as soon as the patient was back in the ward it was the surgeon's responsibility to put up the drip. John was conducting himself with admirable restraint and seemed to have the situation under control. I, however, was as tense as a bowstring. At last we tied the last ligature, stitched up the abdominal wall and put on the dressings so that the patient could go to the ward.

We quickly transferred her to the trolley and hurried along the corridor. She was hardly breathing and the elevator seemed to take a week to arrive. We got her into a bed and asked for the transfusion apparatus. She was breathing even more slowly now. Joe then said that he had another case with Dr. Dodds downstairs and had to leave right away. When John tried to put the needle into the vein his hands were shaking like a leaf. After getting John's permission, I asked the nurse to get me the instruments for cutting down on the vein. When at last I had found a vein John appeared and took the needle out of my hand and began to try and insert it. His hands were still shaking so much that it was impossible for him to do it, so I once again took the needle and was able to insert it and tie it in. The intravenous fluids began to flow rapidly in to the vein and within a few minutes the patient's condition began to improve. Ten minutes later I told John she was out of danger and would be fine, and walked away.

I was amazed that a doctor would apparently not care what was happening to his patient under an anaesthetic. While sitting in the doctor's room after the surgery, John entered in a humble mood. He thanked me for my help, but made no adverse comment about Joe's dereliction of duty. Nevertheless I could tell that he was extremely upset about Joe's conduct. In turn, I resolved that I would never trust Joe or put myself in a position where I was completely dependent on him. If Joe had refused to put in a drip line while I was operating, I would have been devastated. I admired John's restraint, but I could not understand it. I tried to make excuses for Joe, such as, "Perhaps he didn't know it was his responsibility to put up the drip", but even so, he still should have waited in the ward until the patient was out of danger.

No matter what I thought of Joe's behaviour, if I was to have a good income I needed to maintain a presence in the surgical theatre. While we received $3 for a consultation and $5 for a consultation with laboratory tests, it took quite an expenditure of time and mental energy to earn this money, and my office expenses were $30 per day. If the patient needed an appendectomy the consultation took five or ten minutes, and the operation another twenty minutes. In the end, we were able to present the patient with a bill for $100, and it was surprising that while people complained about being billed $50 for a long stay in hospital for a condition like heart failure, nobody was bothered about a larger bill for a relatively simple operation. When I first arrived in town, people asked if I did surgery, and although I was now operating every week, people still asked the same question. I suspected that somebody was putting the word out that I was not interested in surgery.

As we had very few daylight hours during the cold Grand Prairie winter, I spent most evenings at the movies or skating rink. While I was in Edmonton, I had purchased a pair of topnotch ice skates - the type that were used by professional hockey players. At the beginning of the season the youngsters around the arena were on the lookout for any new ice hockey players to boost the local team. Early in the season, I was sitting in the dressing room putting on my skates and unknown to me several young men were watching me with some interest. Doubtless, seeing the high quality skates I was putting on, they were expecting me to jump on the ice and race around the arena. But instead, I stood up and just about collapsed onto the boards of the dressing room floor. It must have been an anti-climax for the youngsters as I made my wobbly way to the door displaying that incomparable technique that beginners develop when first walking on skates. By season's end I was getting pretty good on the ice. The girls who had laughed at my clumsiness at the beginning of the season now screamed (with fear or delight) as we skated together, at high speed, around the corners.

Walking to the hospital on most mornings, and ice skating at nights and on weekends, were my only exercise during winter. In the summer evenings I would often go out to the golf course with Janet, my office receptionist, but the longer days quickly passed into autumn and it was back to the shorter days of snow and ice.

It was expensive to keep an office going during the winter months, as I had the extra costs of coal and electricity. By about the end of January, I began to look forward to the better weather and the relief brought by the 'Chinooks'. These were warm winds which quickly melted the snow, giving the impression that spring had arrived. This was only an illusion as a cycle of fortnightly snowfalls from the mountains, followed by more Chinooks, was the usual pattern. Most of the streets were poorly paved and the melted snow produced mud, which tracked into cars, through doorways and across rooms, and high overshoes were the order of the day.

Agnes Cobden had been visiting friends one evening and had walked out into the street where she stepped into the mud in the dark, and had lost her shoes. Her main complaint was that her $22-shoes had disappeared in the mud, and although Cec did his best to find them, he had no success. When they told me the story, I began to laugh and Agnes never forgave me for my insensitivity.

A few months after my arrival, I decided to sit the examination that would qualify me for practice throughout Canada. The exam was held in Edmonton and was called the Licensed Member of the Canada Council examination (L.M.C.C.). Most young Canadian doctors sat it soon after graduation, having the benefit of their final medical exam information still fresh in their minds. I, on the other hand, was a bit uneasy as I had not studied intensively or sat an examination for four years. It would cost me several hundred dollars and a trip to Edmonton to sit the exam, taking income from my practice and I might not pass. I had read some pathology in the islands and decided to make this area my main reading for the exam. The other subjects were medicine, surgery, obstetrics, gynaecology and public health. It was impossible to revise all of these subjects thoroughly, since I was running a practice and also had to keep up with Canadian drug combinations.

I wrote a cheque for $200 and sent it in with my application. Most people who failed the exam did so in public health, because the Canadians had different problems and different regulations to other countries, so it was necessary to try and learn these. I went to the local health inspector and got information on rural latrines and devices to make water safe. I also needed information on obstetrics because I had not done any of this work in the Islands.

At last the time came for the exam, so I flew down to Edmonton from Grand Prairie. I found accommodation at the YMCA, because my bank account was not healthy; It would be in worse shape if I failed. I sat the exam with doctors from Canada, England and Europe. Some had postgraduate degrees, but examinations are great levellers and no one taking the exam thought himself superior to anybody else. I thought that I had probably passed in the 'writtens' but was apprehensive about the orals. I still suffered a degree of nervousness when faced with verbal questioning in an exam. This was a lingering symptom of the psychological damage suffered after being beaten senseless by Big Dig, when I didn't answer his question satisfactorily, at St. Kevin's.

Most of the oral examiners were specialists from Alberta, and when they found that I had been in the Islands, they asked me about medical conditions there, which made the exam all the more interesting. However, having heard that the pathology examiners were tough, I went in apprehensively. I was careful to agree with everything my examiner said, and as he felt that I was interested in pathology he talked for the whole time about his theories and impressions, rather than ask me any questions about my knowledge of the subject. Then he looked at his watch and said, "Well, we can go on for another five minutes." But again, instead of asking me any questions, he went on about observations on cancer of the breast and I continued to be an appreciative audience, and when I stood up to go he asked me what mark I wanted. I assumed that fifty may have been the pass mark, so replied "Sixty" He said, "You want sixty? Alright, I'll give you sixty!"

The only oral part of the exam that I found a little sticky was in the area of public health. By the time it was over, I felt that I'd done my best and flew back to Grand Prairie to wait for the results, which were to be available in about six weeks.

The first week back at work was relaxed, as it wasn't busy at the hospital and Joe was helping Lionel most of the time. In the morning John and I would sit together in the doctor's room drinking coffee, since neither of us had much else to do. At about that time I began to wonder how long I could continue to tolerate the medical situation in Grand Prairie. John had adopted a difficult, superior and patronising manner. He was forever saying that there should be more specialisation in the town. He said that he was mainly interested in medical problems as he had a post graduate medical degree from Britain. He suggested that we refer most of our surgery to Lionel so that he could gain more experience. I was certainly happy to refer any of my more complicated patients to somebody else with more experience, but it would be economic suicide to pass on my minor or intermediate surgery cases.

This presented a difficult diplomatic dilemma; I had explained to John that I hoped to do more surgery as time went along, but realised I had to keep on John's good side to do this. I agreed to help Lionel gain experience by passing on my major surgical cases, because if I refused this request from John, I was at risk of losing his co-operation with giving anaesthetics to my surgery patients. That would leave me relying on Joe Storey for anaesthetics while I operated, and I had resolved not to put myself in this position.

In the meantime I was starting to do quite well from the

combination of surgery, general medicine and anaesthetics. I was giving anaesthetics for three doctors, and at the end of each month was getting small cheques from each of them. Things seemed to be rolling along quite smoothly, but an event was just around the corner which was to become one of the worst medical experiences of my career.

One of my maternity patients was the wife of a bank manager. During her previous pregnancy she had developed toxaemia. Because of this she had had convulsions and become temporarily blind and the baby had died. She had eventually recovered her sight, but was fearful of a reccurrence this time. She knew these complications in pregnancy were due to toxaemia which is accompanied by high blood pressure, but thought to be largely preventable. By restricting fluids and salt in the latter stages of pregnancy and ensuring she had plenty of rest, the toxaemia could usually be managed until the baby was born. The patient had trained as a nurse before her marriage, and was not easily convinced of this as they had taken every precaution the time before, and she had still suffered convulsions.

In her last month of pregnancy, I noticed that her weight and blood pressure were gradually climbing and I gave her strict instructions about restricting fluids and prescribed some sedatives. I also told her that if her condition did not improve by the next visit I would put her in hospital and induce labour. I felt that the child would have a better chance of survival being brought into the world a little early, rather than being left in the womb to be poisoned by the toxins in the mother's blood.

At the next visit her appearance was terrible; her face was swollen and blood pressure sky-high. I explained that she should go to hospital, and if her blood pressure did not settle it would be necessary to bring on labour, as it seemed obvious that her life and that of the baby was in danger.

I spent a very uncomfortable afternoon at the office and dashed up to the hospital as soon as I could. Her blood pressure was much the same when I next saw her, and I decided to do an induction right away. This involved breaking the sac holding the amniotic fluid.

This procedure allowed most of the amniotic fluid that cushions the baby to run out and trigger normal labour. The labour pains would usually start within a few hours and, hopefully, a normal delivery and healthy baby would result.

I rang the husband and explained what I intended to do. Later, when I returned to the hospital I found that Miss Gow, the nursing superintendent, was standing by the maternity ward desk. She said she was unsure that an induction was the correct procedure at this stage and she asked about a Caesarean section. I told her that I was also concerned, but considered an induction the best course of action, and would take responsibility. Miss Gow then said that she was still apprehensive and that I should get another doctor in for a consultation. As she was legally in charge of the hospital she was able to ask me to do this. I was mortified! As Lionel was away on holiday, I would have to get John's opinion. When I rang John, he was very cooperative and he came to the hospital immediately. We went together to see the patient, and John gave her a very thorough examination and we went down to the laboratory to do some tests on the patient's urine. When the preliminaries were over, John told me that he agreed with Miss Gow, and that despite her high blood pressure and appearance, there should be no medical intervention and we should wait to see what happened.

I could not have been more shocked if he had hit me with his hand. I told the nurses that I would not be doing the induction that evening, and that John and I would see the patient in the morning.

I found that sleep did not come easily that night. It was one of the most anxious nights I have ever had over concern for a patient's welfare. What if the baby should die? She had only one little boy, and was getting too old for further pregnancies. What if she should go into convulsions, become blind again or in the worst circumstance, die?

The next morning I could hardly wait to go along with John and see her. We found that her blood pressure and condition were much the same. Perhaps now I could do the induction, but no, John would not move - he would not authorise the procedure. We would leave it until the next day. The next morning the patient's condition and John's opinion were yet the same and I became desperate.

Eventually I decided to ring Dr. Dick Mc Crum, who lived in an adjacent town, but sometimes visited our hospital. I explained the patient's condition and what I wanted to do. "Yes, certainly," he said. "Go ahead." He would sign a consultation sheet without even seeing the patient. He always did an induction in these cases, and as a result of the consultation I went ahead and performed this simple operation, which could be done without an anaesthetic. One hour later the mother gave birth to a tiny infant that squawked lustily. The mother was delighted, and when Miss Gow put her head into the room I felt triumphant. The baby had a good colour and suckled normally. The mother's blood pressure returned quickly to normal.

After this event, I was annoyed with John and developed a distrust of his medical skills, and this lack of faith in his judgement persisted while I remained in Grand Prairie. My relationship with Miss Gow had not been good to begin with, and now it was worse. She did not apologise for delaying the procedure or acknowledge the good result I achieved in the end. Our relationship remained formal and decidedly unenthusiastic. There was a chill in the air in the hospital, and it had nothing to do with the season.

At this time, I was having difficulty sleeping because I was concerned that a death could happen while a patient was under my anaesthetic. Anaesthetic deaths are rare, but I was giving a lot of them, which increased the chances of a death occuring while I was in charge. Joe Storey had been appointed the coroner for the town and district, and to appear in front of him would be difficult and embarrassing. The tense inter-personal dynamics caused stress in the hospital and made life difficult to the point of being almost intolerable. The nursing staff were not highly competent, and the poor doctor-to-doctor relationships did not help the work situation. To add to these difficulties, the nurses had little respect for Miss Gow. If nursing orders were not carried out to my satisfaction, and I made a complaint to Miss Gow, the nurses took little notice of her. My position was becoming increasingly difficult, so when an unexpected opportunity for respite from the situation appeared, I reached out and grasped it with both hands.

The Canadian civil defence people wanted doctors to go to a civil defence course in Ontario. The Government would pay all expenses, and we would stay for a week at the Civil Defence School, where specialists would lecture us on the various aspects of atomic, bacterial and chemical warfare. The chance of an all-expenses-paid break in the east intrigued me. I found that by adding an extra $100 to the airfare, I could fly to Ontario via Mexico City. This was a thrilling possibility that really needed looking into. It was soon arranged and I flew from Edmonton to Mexico via Vancouver.

We left Alberta, which was enjoying the usual cold and slush, and as we were about to land in Vancouver, I looked down and saw men in whites playing cricket on the grass. No wonder half of Canada wants to retire there, to enjoy a mild climate warmed by the Ocean currents coming up the coast from California.

In Vancouver I boarded a DC-6 for the next leg of my trip and found myself sitting next to a Dr. Axel Christiansen, who had just returned from a two-year tour of duty with the Eskimos in Aklavik. He was sixty-plus, thinning on the top and a little overweight, but retained a youthful vigour and alertness. We got along well from the beginning, and he offered to take me with him into Mexico City. He knew some Spanish, and had been in Mexico before, so this was indeed kind of him.

I was all set to enjoy a change from the cool professional and climactic conditions in Grand Prairie, and Axel's warmth boded well for things to come.

CHAPTER 11

Mexico and Canada

19 February 1955 – 27 February 1955

INTRODUCED CHARACTERS

DR. FERNANDO LATAPI, Professor of Dermatology at the University of Mexico, Head of the Dermatological Institute and President of the Mexican Leprosy Association.
MARIA LISBON, Assistant Professor of Dermatology at the University Medical School.
SENOR CARDOZA, Maria Lisbon's father.
GEORGE BELL, a patient at the Grand Prairie Hospital.
MARY, who provided a temporary distraction for the author in Grand Prairie.

IN MEXICO CITY THE LARGE STEEL AND GLASS air terminal contrasted strangely with the grinding poverty of the small houses around the airport. There were few airport formalities and we were soon in a cab on our way to Axel's choice of accommodation. He had chosen a small, older hotel in a side street, where we were greeted by a Spanish speaking man at the slightly tired reception desk. Axel surprised me with the speed and vigour of his Spanish and he negotiated a twin room. He also explained to me that the hotel adopted the American system where the ground floor is called the first floor, in contrast to the British scheme, where the first floor is the one immediately above the ground floor.

Axel seemed satisfied and I had no reason to question his judgement on the hotel or anything else in Mexico City.

The author at the Mexico City Museum.

There was a tiny two man elevator which clanked its way hesitantly to the third floor, where we found our room which was clean and well aired and had its own bathroom; this was to cost us each US$1.50 per day. The view from the window was bright and clear. There were six million people living in the huge urban sprawl around the city. By 2008 the population had grown to over forty million, and Mexico City now has one of the worst environmental pollution problems in the world.

Axel had fractured the calcaneal bone in his left heel and, as frequently happens, it had not healed properly. However, it did not stop him going down to the front office and arranging for tickets for the Plaza Mexico bullfight. He came back triumphantly with the tickets and we set off for the plaza. It had 50,000 seats and was the biggest bullfight arena in the world. When we got inside I looked down the steep steps into the arena and I felt dizzy. There were a few North Americans around us, but the great majority of patrons were Spanish-Americans of both sexes. Most of the dark-skinned girls were very attractive and wore lace or silk scarves around their heads and shoulders.

At exactly four in the afternoon, the Toreadors paraded into the centre of the arena with their attendants. It was all very exciting and colourful, and it was obvious how much the fight meant to the enthusiasts around me. However, I could not respond fully to their excitement and their "olès!" I felt that I should be down in the arena with a pair of artery forceps to stop the blood that was soon flowing freely from the black bulls. When the sword had at last been plunged into the bull's neck up to its hilt, I felt relief that it was all over. The drag mules came in and pulled the carcass away, and two men came in and spread sand over the blood the dead bull had left behind.

The toreadors were very skilled and very brave, as each time the bull's horns swept past their abdomens their life was on the line. On one occasion, the bullfighter was given the honour of keeping one of the bull's ears. On another occasion, after a very good performance, he was given both of the bull's ears, which had been detached from the dead animal's head. For the best performance, the tail is given as well. The most skilled toreadors must have problems storing all of these trophies. Perhaps they keep them in the refrigerator and just bring them out for significant occasions like Saint's days and at Christmas. When the last of the five bullfights was finished and the drag mules had done their job I was glad to leave the arena. Axel said that the meat from the sacrificed bulls was given to the poor in the area. I am sure that the penurious locals did not mind that some of the bull's peripheral parts had been removed before they were given their meat for the week.

When we got back to the hotel, we put through a rather complicated phone call to a Dr. Fernando Latapi. He was the professor of Dermatology at the University of Mexico and President of the Mexican Leprosy Association. He invited me to come out to his leprosy clinic in the poorer part of Mexico City, the next morning. He said that his own car would call for me.

A young man who spoke very little English came to the hotel at 8 a.m., and we drove to the older part of the city where the streets had exotic names like 'Paseo de la Reforma'. We arrived at a hospital, which was a large sprawling group of buildings, and then continued to the Dermatological Institute which was a rundown two storied building. Dr. Latapi was very friendly, but a little apprehensive of his English, which turned out to be pretty good I thought. He showed me around his two-storey clinic and explained that almost all of the leprosy patients had to be treated as outpatients. He said that once under treatment the infectious cases rapidly became non-infectious and this meant the patients could return to live with their families.

At that time up to 5% of the general population in Mexico City had leprosy, so it was a tremendous health problem. Surprisingly, 90% of the leprosy cases were the serious infectious lepromatous type, with only 10% intermediate and the minimally infectious, tuberculoid. This distribution is the inverse of that in Micronesia, and I don't know the reason for this. Dr. Latapi and his colleagues conducted massive outpatient clinics. As many people as possible were persuaded to come for examination and treatment. In other countries, where most leprosy patients are confined to leprosaria, the authorities find it difficult to get the people to come for diagnosis and treatment. They are not willing to be shut away from their families, and so postpone their treatment until it is too late. In the worst cases the disease has ravaged their bodies, leaving permanent deformity, and little can be done.

Leprosy is not a very contagious disease, and it is passed along after prolonged skin contact. When an infectious grandparent, for example, sleeps with a child for several years the disease may be passed along. Married couples are also liable to pass the disease to each other for obvious reasons. I was happy to agree with Dr. Latapi when he said that when patients were treated, they then become less infectious. The Mexican doctors were doing a very good job under difficult conditions and seemed completely devoted to their work. When I asked about funding I realised how financially pressed they were.

The institution was supported by private contributions, by the patient's fees and partly by the government. Most of the patients weren't able to pay anything towards their treatment, and in fact many were helped financially by limited clinic funding. I asked Dr. Latapi if the Government should shoulder a bigger part of the financial load. Surprisingly he said that more government aid would mean more control, and that he would prefer to get along as he was, without increased interference. The doctors were on very small salaries, and I was impressed that these men and women were prepared to carry on without complaint. They did the best work possible under the conditions, and with the patient's welfare always the priority.

The work that they were doing was of world standard, and Dr. Latapi and his associates were always having papers published in International Journals. These selfless people were regenerating my faith in the kindness and dedication of the medical profession.

The next day I was invited to see a presentation dealing with skin diseases at a general hospital, and I went in with Dr. Latapi and his staff. There were already doctors waiting in the conference room, and he introduced us around: "This is Dr. Krukendorf from Berlin; this is Dr. Bennington-Brown from London; this is Dr. Valentine from Grand Prairie" etc. After the introductions, and once the conference got underway, I found that it was standing-room-only, but I had been given a priority seat in the front row. It seemed only a short time before that Miss Gow, in Grand Prairie, had tried to stop me from doing a simple procedure. Now here I was, viewing 'cutting edge' surgery from a prime position. I'd enjoy it while it lasted, as I'd be back in Grand Praire soon enough.

The demonstration was of very high quality. A young Mexican surgeon demonstrated his 'tube-graft technique', explaining in Spanish as he worked. This was a procedure for replacing noses, which have been eaten away by one of the tropical infections or by a malignancy. He showed slides and colour photographs of patients progressing through different stages of the operation. If the condition was cancerous the patients had to be given enough radiation therapy to stop the growth of the tumour and it was then necessary to clean up the odiferous and ulcerating cavity that was left behind. Once the area had been cleaned the surgeons elevated a flap of skin from the arm. Leaving one end of the flap still attached to the arm they made a tube out of the rest and stitched the end of the tube to the nasal area. The patient was left in this uncomfortable position, with his arm attached to his nasal area by a living bridge of flesh, for several weeks. The living tube of skin was getting its main blood supply from the arm, but new blood vessels began to bridge the small gap between the previously ulcerated nasal cavity and the free end of the skin tube.

Over the weeks, these new blood vessels grew bigger and were eventually able to take over the blood supply to the skin tube. The surgeons were then able to cut the tube free from the arm. The patient now had a flap of living skin where his nose had once been. It was then possible to shape this flap into something resembling a nose, while leaving a space through which the patient could breathe. Sometimes cartilage from an ear, or bone from the hip had to be transplanted, to hold up the skin which replaced the nose. At the end of the presentation, Dr. Latapi brought some of the patients who had been successfully operated on into the room. Most were poor peasant folk and the end results were excellent. It must have

CORRESPONDENCE

MEDICINE IN MEXICO

To the Editor:

While on a short visit to Mexico last month, I was fortunate enough to see something of the work being done by the medical men in that turbulent metropolis, Mexico City.

Before leaving Canada I wrote to Dr. Fernando Latapi, because his name was on the list of members of the International Leprosy Association. He was kind enough to reply promptly; but unfortunately in Spanish. However, in the plane which was to deposit me in Mexico, I was fortunate enough to sit beside Dr. Axel Christensen who knew enough Spanish to confuse the taxi drivers. When we settled into a Spanish hotel, we rang Dr. Latapi and found that his wife spoke very good English. From then on the going was relatively smooth. Dr. Latapi is Professor of Dermatology in the University of Mexico and President of the Mexican Leprosy Association. We were invited to his clinic, which is in a poor part of the city because most of the patients are from the poor.

The clinic deals mainly with leprosy cases on an outpatient basis. They estimated that up to 5% of the population of Mexico City have leprosy in one of its many forms. This startling fact makes it impossible for them to hospitalize even a small proportion of the total. They feel that by treating virtually everybody as a home patient they can encourage almost everybody to come for treatment. In the old days when patients were sent away from their families and confined in leprosaria, people frequently concealed their disease until it was too late. Leprosy is not a very contagious disease, and nobody has ever proved that isolation in leprosaria has done the least good.

Most of the patients cannot pay, and the clinic is supported by sparse government grants and private gifts. The many doctors get very little payment for their services and seem devoted to their work.

I asked Dr. Latapi if he would not like more government support, but he replied that that would involve more government control and it was better the way it is.

The next day I was taken to the General Hospital, where they were having a skin cancer clinic. The proceedings were in Spanish, but there were plenty of English speakers to translate. Most patients were unfortunate people who had lost their whole nose with a malignancy. The young surgeon showed by Kodachrome slides how he had given these people very presentable noses. The tube graft technique was used, and the end results that we saw were very good. When he spoke to me later, I asked how many times a week he operated. He told me that he averaged six operations a day, and he operated six days a week!

The buildings are old, but the work is of the highest calibre. I saw only one other small hospital and again was impressed with the doctors' courtesy and the good standards they maintained under suboptimal conditions.

If there is a moral to this story, it is that there is a rich field for clinical material here almost at our back door. Canadian physicians will find the Mexican doctors interested, interesting and extremely cooperative.

JOHN VALENTINE, M.B., Ch.B., L.M.C.C.

Grande Prairie,
Alberta,
June 4, 1955.

A letter written by the author about his time in Mexico with Dr. Fernando Latapi (Professor of Dermitology at the University of Mexico).

been a great source of satisfaction for the surgeons when they saw these unfortunate people return to relatively normal lives without the stigma of an unsightly cavity where the nose had been.

Once the demonstration was over the young surgeon threw the meeting open for questions. He was able to answer all of them quickly. I asked the surgeon how often he operated, and he told me six times a day, six days a week. He also told me that he was training young men to take some of the burden off his shoulders. He had given his presentation in Spanish, and apologised that he did not have time to repeat it in English.

When it was time for Dr. Latapi to leave, he asked me if I wanted to stay and be shown around the dermatology wards by his assistant. Earlier I had been introduced to a rather good-looking young woman who had stood at the back of the room during the demonstration; She said that she also was staying behind to go to the wards and that was an added incentive to accept Dr. Latapi's invitation. The patients were friendly and cooperative, and the young doctor showing me around was pleasant and helpful. She said that her name was Dr. Maria Lisbon and she came to the Dermatology wards every morning. When I asked Maria about beriberi she pulled a textbook on dermatology down from a shelf and asked me to look at some of the illustrations that demonstrated some aspects of the disease. I soon found that she was only twenty-nine-years-old, but was one of the three authors of this text book. She was an assistant professor of Dermatology at the University Medical School.

Well! Here I was, in the presence of a very intelligent and exceptionally good-looking young woman. After about thirty minutes, I had exhausted all the interest I had in dermatology, but was still interested in the girl. We began the long walk to the gate of the hospital, and I wondered how I could retain her company for a longer while. I asked what she was doing that afternoon and she told me that her father did not let her work for money, and as she only worked mornings at the hospital for charity, she was free in the afternoon. It was obvious that there was a small high-class group of Spanish-speaking people in Mexican society, and a much larger, poorer class. Some of the higher-class people had used their education to become qualified and were prepared to do medical work for little or no payment.

I took my courage in both hands and asked Maria to show me around the new University. She seemed quite agreeable to this, but said she must first ring her father for permission. While I waited for her to come back I allowed one of the young bootblacks to clean my shoes. He was still at it when Maria came out and said that she could go with me. She told me that I should not let bootblacks clean my shoes as they used this occupation as an excuse to avoid real work.

She took me to the campus of the University of Mexico, where Diego Rivera had decorated many of the buildings with colourful, mosaic murals. Most of his designs showed Mexico's struggle for independence from Spain, and later from France. The new forms of architecture showed imagination and courage out of the ordinary. The glass and ferroconcrete had been skillfully used, allowing for much more window space. Some of the buildings were raised on pillars, allowing the students to walk freely underneath. They were imposing buildings and I was impressed that the authorities of this very poor country had gone the extra mile to embellish their buildings.

During our visit an old man approached and held out his hand for money. I put my hand in my pocket to give him a few cents and Maria protested, saying, "That man does not work; you must not give him money." As she did not work for money herself, I was startled to hear these strong opinions from her. When I suggested that we take a taxi for further sightseeing, she again protested. I was only able to persuade her to agree, because a bus would have involved a change and a long wait. This was going to be a most economical outing. If in the future I had extravagant girlfriends, I thought I might tell them about Maria's Spartan austerity; but then again, perhaps not.

Maria had never seen a bullfight, and thought that they were for people who had nothing better to do with their time. I wondered if other educated people were as uninterested in bullfighting as

Maria Lisbon, in front of a mural at the University of Mexico.

Maria. At midday I suggested that we have a meal at the University Student's Cafeteria, but also wondered if it was time for a traditional siesta, and asked about it. I soon regretted asking that question, as she said, "We do not have the siesta now. Everyone in the new Mexico has to work hard."

I had no response to that, but was left with the understanding that Maria was waving the flag for a new and energetic Mexico. Okay, the siesta had no place in their modern society, and indolent people did not build the buildings I had seen.

We had our meal in a bright and airy cafeteria with students and a sprinkling of teaching staff. Maria had a good grasp of world events and it was a strain to keep up with her reasoning. Even though she had never been beyond the borders of Mexico, she knew more about the world than most people I had met.

The outside walls of the University library showed scenes of the history of the country. Maria told me that Diego Rivera had done most of the designs, but this time he had allowed the Catholic

Church to be let off lightly, and there was only the occasional reference to bloated plutocrats.

By the end of our visit, there were plenty of buses to take Maria and me back to town, and she insisted on using one this time. The seats were hard, and as we bumped along it was time for my next move. Maria's good figure had come into focus and when I reached out for her hand, she did not object at all. She was sweet, and above all she was interesting; dare I ask her for a date? The bus ride would be at an end soon, so I made my move.

"Maria, could I take you out this evening?" I asked.

"Where?"

"We could go to dinner at a good restaurant and then take in a movie."

"But my English is not very good," she replied.

"I can easily understand you," I said.

Then she said, "My Father speaks very good English, I think it would be better if he came along."

This was an unexpected complication. Did Maria really think that the evening would be more enjoyable if her Father came along too? I knew that old Spanish customs required chaperones, but perhaps Maria was just trying to explain that she could not go out at night un-chaperoned with a young man. She was a medical graduate and went off to the hospital each day, so why should she not be able to go out with me at night?

I tried again but I could see that although Maria may have wanted to go out with me, there was something holding her back. We seemed to be at a blind end when she suggested, "You come out to dinner with my family when you get back from your short trip to the silver city of Taxco."

The opportunity of visiting a Mexican home was too good to miss. She told me that I was to come to her home at 194 Pesito Street at 7 p.m. in the evening, when I returned to Mexico City. We walked to the bus stop on Reforma Avenue, and after a gentle squeeze of my hand, Maria joined the crowd getting onto the bus.

When I returned to my hotel room, Axel was waiting. He had been out all day making arrangements to join an archaeologist friend who was working on some previously untouched excavations in the south. Axel had met him in the Canadian Arctic when he was looking for pre-Eskimo relics. Now Axel was looking forward to spending a month in remote rural Mexico as a voluntary helper on a dig.

He was enthusiastic when I told him about Maria. "Ah! When I was your age I never thought that I had the feel of a country until I had slept with one of the women," he said.

I hated myself for taking the Cook's tour to Taxco, but had just two days to see this old city. It was important that I get back to Mexico City on time, and if I went by myself I couldn't be sure of getting the correct bus connections. The tour was by taxi and included hotels and meals. I had not told the three people in the back seat that I was a doctor. They were a Canadian doctor and his wife, and a middle-aged American businessman. Like tourists worldwide, they set about telling each other all about themselves, their jobs, their lives, their pets and most importantly, their children. They were agreeable people but were much more interested in telling me about their own homes than discussing the poor shacks the peasants lived in, on either side of the road. Just fifty yards from this fine two lane highway people were living in houses whose walls were made of light mats, plaited from flaxes. A few donkeys and goats wandered around on grassless land.

We travelled over a mountain range and after a few hours drive arrived at Cuernavaca. This town had been the country-seat of the rich people from Mexico City for hundreds of years. The Spaniards had discovered that this mountain retreat had an ideal climate - just the place to come to when summer heat caused the mosquitoes to rise from the swamps around Mexico City. The guide assured us that throughout the year it was always warm enough during the day to go about in shirt sleeves, and in the evenings it was always cool enough to wear a jacket.

There were many fine old Spanish houses in Cuernavaca, and Emperor Maximilian, who had been supported by French troops, had a palace here during his tragic reign. When the U.S. Civil War ended in 1865 the U.S. population demanded that the French troops were withdrawn. With the troops gone the Emperor was defenceless and he was executed in 1867.

While the others were being shown around the mansion and palaces, I asked to be let off at the market place. They would pick me up there afterwards. The market was typical of what one might find in a third-world country, with stallholders selling all the daily necessities of life. The women stallholders had brought along their young children and housewives had on their brightest clothes for the morning's shopping. Everywhere, they were diligently turning over the produce and bargaining for fruit, vegetables and meat. The butcher shops did not have refrigeration, so most of the meat was kept in fly-screened boxes. A three-year-old girl was wandering in and out of the fruit stalls, making ten-yard forays, before returning to her mother who worked on one of the stalls. She was a sweet child and her red frock made a good colour shot with the multi-coloured fruit as a background.

As I had her in my camera's focus, I heard a woman's shout. I released the shutter quickly as I wondered if it was directed towards me. A large lady left her stall and waddled towards me. "Don't take pictures here in the poorest part of the town. If you want to take pictures, go to the palaces," she said. I replied, "This is a free country and I can take pictures here." After their troubled history the Mexicans were free at last. While I thought this I was re-evaluating the situation as the lady was still coming towards me. "I will report you to the American Embassy. I will tell the police," she said. "Tell the American Embassy, if you like, but I'm not an American" I replied.

The rest of the stallholders and shoppers were beginning to take an interest in the proceedings. Most of them didn't understand English, and I didn't understand Spanish, so when the lady was speaking to her friends in Spanish, I had no way of knowing what she was telling them. There were no policemen about, but as the crowd was beginning to be a little too interested in me, I thought it would be a good time to explore other sections of the market. I was relieved to find that my antagonist did not follow me, probably because she didn't want to leave her stall, but the further I retreated, the louder her accusations became. I was soon out of range of her voice, but retained an admiration for her pride.

The rest of the trip, through the mountains to Taxco, was thankfully uneventful, and we reached our hotel which was an old Spanish mansion. The Aztecs had known about the mineral wealth in the hills around Taxco and had been mining the silver when Columbus rediscovered the New World in 1492. I don't know if Aztec technology could extract the copper, zinc and lead mined in the area today. When the Spanish saw the silver mining they compelled the local peasants to work in the mines, but the Mexicans had little resistance to measles, mumps and influenza. Over half of the nation was dead within a few months of the Spanish arrival, from the diseases they brought with them. In this case the virus was mightier than the sword. As most of the local people had been killed or disabled by disease there were few of them left to be enslaved.

In the Colonial period the silver mines produced great wealth and some of the profits were spent on high quality architecture in the town. The church in the plaza was partly faced with gold leaf. The castle now being used as our hotel had been the mine manager's home.

The walls of the hotel were four-feet thick, bathrooms had been cleverly inserted in the corners of the large rooms, and each room had a balcony with a view. The town was in rolling countryside, and small houses, previously occupied by the silver miners, were scattered over the hills. The stone walls and tile roofs had weathered uniformly over the years.

As the silver mines became depleted, the fortunes of Taxco declined. A road that was later built over the mountains from Mexico City, by-passed the town and Taxco went to sleep for two hundred years. The people kept living in the houses and the donkeys kept going up and down the cobbled streets. There were no new buildings built and the old ones were not altered. When the road was later brought back through the town they found that it looked just as it had done two hundred years before. The city fathers were fortunately aware that they had a precious historic village, and forbade anyone to erect modern-style structures. All plans for new construction or renovation had to be submitted for approval to the town council, to ensure that the town's historical flavour was preserved.

Later that evening, as soon as dinner was over, I left the other tourists to their drinks besides the swimming pool while I set off down the hill. Soon I was amongst the narrow, cobbled streets where there were few street lights, and only the light shining from open doors and windows to show me the way. When a child came along driving a donkey over the cobbles, it was not hard to believe that it had been much the same 300 years ago.

After walking for ten minutes, I found myself in Taxco's central plaza. Some of the older people were scattered on seats beneath the trees. A few shops were open, the church was in darkness, and a few people were still sitting on the church steps. The town would soon be asleep again. Having only recently opened up to holidaymakers it must have been hard on the local people to see their lovely town invaded after 200 years' slumber.

When I returned to the hotel, most of the guests had gone to their rooms and only four bridge players remained on the lighted terrace, with a solitary waiter remaining behind the bar, in case any guest needed an emergency gin and tonic.

On the following morning at nine, the cars arrived to take the hotel guests down into the town. We had to crawl through the streets at five miles an hour, and when we met a car coming the other way, we had to back up until a place wide enough to pass could be found.

The ancient craft of fine silver hand work was revived by William Spratling, an American living in Taxco, in the 1930s. Taxco then became the outstanding centre for silverwork in the Western Hemisphere. The silver shops were open for business. The pretty girls behind the counters were bright-eyed and friendly and the silver work that they were selling was attractive and well displayed. Silver rosaries, which must have taken a day or more to make, changed hands for fifty cents. Heavy jade and silver bracelets cost as much as five dollars, but the thinner silver ones could be had for $2.50 each. Two of the prettiest shop girls came out of their workplaces into the sunlight of the Plaza to pose for me. They were as bright as buttons and gave old world smiles for the camera. As they were leaving, the eldest one inquired, "Did you use Kodachrome? I will give you my address if you will send me a copy when you get home." Taxco might look the same as in ancient times but it was catching up with the modern world in leaps and bounds. The girls seemed to be uniformly pretty and helpful. I assumed that if a sales job was advertised, the qualifications were most important, but I wondered if the girl's looks were considered. I can think of other instances where this happens.

Before the day was over, a minor disaster had befallen one of my purchases. The handle on the basket that held the giant bottle of rum which I had purchased for less than $2.50, started to unwind. I couldn't find the boy who had sold me the basket, so I asked the nearest policeman where I could get the handle repaired. He did not speak much English, but signalled for me to follow him into a room on the ground floor of one of the old buildings in the plaza. He handed my now empty basket to an old man who then took it towards a heavy, barred, wooden gate. He started shouting, "Antonio! Antonio!" There was no immediate reply from the dark interior, but in a couple of minutes Antonio came to the perforated gate. The old man then opened the large padlock that kept the gate closed and handed my basket in. Antonio then absented himself into the darkness from whence he came. This was the prison, which had been built when the town was founded four hundred years ago, and was still in use. I was signalled to sit down in a room where a middle-aged woman was using an electric iron, and a younger woman was feeding her baby at the breast. I could hear men talking but could see nothing through the gate's bars.

A few minutes later two women entered the room and, after nodding to the warder, walked to the gate. Their men must have been expecting them, because they came directly to the other side of the wooden bars. After a preliminary kiss, through the bars, they started into a quiet conversation. I was embarrassed to be watching this but the others in the room did not take one bit of notice. The women had baskets of food and they handed them through the bars. After ten minutes they took leave of the men as if they had just taken ten minutes talking to friends in the street, rather than visiting imprisoned relatives.

I was beginning to get a little anxious, as the cars were due to leave in twenty minutes, and Antonio showed no signs of returning with my basket. Another ten minutes passed. The lady went on ironing, and the baby continued to suckle.

Finally I said, "Can I get my basket? my car leaves in ten minutes" Blank faces turned towards me, they did not understand English, and so I tried sign language. They evidently thought that the gringo was trying to amuse them. I must have looked a bit odd waving my hands about, and a couple of prisoners even came to the gate to watch the show. It was really late now and I went into the street asking anyone I met, "Do you speak English?" Still no takers, and when the policeman who had taken me down to the prison in the first place arrived, he was a welcome sight. "Please ask the jailer when my basket will be ready." The policeman and jailer had a quick conversation and the jailer went to the gate and began shouting again "Antonio! A-N-T-O-N-I-O!" There was some shuffling in the darkness, and another conversation in rapid Spanish. There was some talking between the policeman and the jailer, and then Antonio's verdict. "Your basket will be ready at twelve O'clock." "Oh no!" I said, with considerable anguish " Please! My car is due to leave in five minutes!"

I knew that they would be unlikely to leave without me, but the other passengers would be none too pleased with a prolonged wait. If I could get hold of the basket, I would be happy to take it back with the handle undone. Then at least I would not have to carry the big bottle of Bacardi around naked. The policeman was speaking again, "Just sit and wait, they will try and have it ready soon." With that, the policeman went outside, and my only real contact with my basket disappeared. At last Antonio brought the basket back to the gate. The large rusty lock creaked and the basket emerged. It had been fixed, and the handle was as solid as it could be. When I offered to pay, the jailer took a few pesos and I dashed out of the door and across the plaza to where the cars were waiting. One of the passengers was still away doing last minute shopping and the drivers were beginning to show impatience. I had the basket, I had the rum and I was happy not to be the final reason for the hold up.

The passengers in the back seat had a discussion on the dangers of travelling in a foreign country. The wife was the most anxious and said, "Our friends told us that we must not eat any raw vegetables at all. We are not to drink the water as there is dysentery and even typhoid here." All this was for my benefit as her husband was a doctor, so she could speak with authority. The other passenger had been given the information the previous evening. All had been chewing little white tablets before each meal. "Our time is too precious to be laid up in bed through sickness. These tablets will prevent infection you know. My husband and I just eat the hot freshly cooked meat and vegetables and we drink only black coffee." she said.

When I turned down the sulfaguanidine tablets, and instead ordered papaya and salad, there was the silence of impending demise. In fact, most of the hotels here had much better food than you would get in a similar place in Canada. The vegetables were always washed in permanganate and the water was reasonably safe. The management did not want their guests to be sick and complaining in this life, or sending bad vibes back from the next.

At the next meal, there was a repetition of the evening before. White tablets went down the hatch with obvious effort. It would have been easier with half a glass of water but who would know what 'nasties' lurked there? While they drank their black coffee and ate the hot meat and vegetables, I risked a fate worse than death by eating the Mexican dishes and subtropical salads. The doctor's wife had not given up the fight, but was getting rather annoyed at my persistence. It was their first trip outside of Canada and the States, and her husband had taken the precaution of reading some old army handbooks on tropical diseases, and had armed himself with a good supply of sulfur drugs from the hospital dispensary.

As we drove down from the mountains, and Mexico City spread out below us, the doctor's wife softened her attitude a little. "Will you be in Toronto for long?" she asked. "Just seven days, I think," I replied. "If we can be of any help to you, just give us a ring. My husband is attached to the Toronto General Hospital, and he knows a lot of people. This is our card," she offered.

"Thank you. It's good to know somebody in a big city. You may be rung up to bail me out sometime," I said.

"What do you do for a living?" she finally asked, as I had not been part of the general sharing of personal details earlier, and I answered, "I'm a medical doctor."

"Oh." was her short reply as our taxi brought us to our stop in Mexico City.

Axel was still at the hotel when I arrived back, so we set about exploring the city and its surrounds. While going along the street we saw two drunken men leaning against a wall. To our surprise they lurched towards us and began hitting us on our backs. They then lurched off down the street. Axel felt for his wallet in his top pocket. Surprise, surprise; the wallet was gone and the two drunks, now surprisingly coordinated, were running off down the street. Axel took off after them and in spite of his un-healed fractured calcaneus, caught one and brought him down with a flying tackle. The miscreant soon yielded up the wallet and Axel was prepared to let him go. A large man appeared from the crowd and insisted upon taking us all to the local police station. The thief kept looking at us with pleading eyes, and it was obvious that the large man was a detective. The drunk man had recovered his senses so we left him in police custody to re-examine his technique or increase his fitness. We got to the station and made the usual statement, which we signed.

We decided to take a taxi home, and Axel told the taxi driver what had happened. The driver then told us that all the old police had been fired and we asked why. "Oh, they were corrupt and took bribes" he said. "So the new police are not corrupt?" Axel asked. The reply was, "Oh yes, they are still corrupt, but we only have to give them smaller bribes now."

Axel decided we should go and see the Great Pyramid of the Sun, and the Pyramid of the Moon, so we took a bus ride for half an hour out into the country.

The biggest pyramid has a greater volume than the largest pyramid in Egypt, but the pyramid of Cheops, is higher. Both Mexican pyramids had been the centre of a large city built of stone, with good housing for all of the inhabitants. Construction had started about the time of Christ and the town had thrived for almost 1,000 years but the end came and the inhabitants vanished. We do not even know their names and we only know their art from the wonderful stone carvings that were left. There was no sign of wooden buildings as they were destroyed by fire. Like the Egyptians, these vanished people must have been superb engineers.

The Pyramid of the Sun had only lately been completely excavated. The Spanish had lived in Mexico City for hundreds of years, ignorant of this large stone city with its pyramids. All had been covered with earth and vegetation, and when I was there the Pyramid of the Moon was still covered with earth and trees.

It was quite a climb to the top of the Pyramid of the Sun. All around the base there were people selling silver jewellery, imitation pottery relics and wooden carvings. As we mounted the tiers of steps the vendors grew fewer and fewer, but right at the top, an old man and his young son were open for business - imitation pottery was their speciality.

The view from the top was excellent. Vast green plains stretched across to the mountains, and we could see Mexico City in the distance. The tour guide had been reluctant to accompany us to the top, but now seemed resigned to his fate. He told us that there was a room in the centre of the pyramid with a shaft leading down from above. The sun struck down into the room twice a year, at the equinox. The small museum at the base of the pyramid contained many of the carved artefacts found during evacuation of the pyramid. All the complex carvings in this building had been made by people without the use of iron and steel. They must have had superb social control. If fear of the Gods wasn't enough to keep the workers in line I'm sure that they would have been told "We have other methods to ensure your compliance! Now back to work!"

Later in the day Axel took me to the Mexico City Museum. Here were miniature models of the reconstructions of the pre-Spanish city. It consisted of pyramids and stone buildings, set up on islands in the Texcoco lake.

The Spanish, led by Hernan Cortez arrived in 1519. They then set about rebuilding the city in a ruthless manner. They pulled down the original buildings and used the stones to build their own structures.

As Mexico City had been built on land reclaimed from a lake, many of the old Spanish buildings were sinking. The cathedral was built on the site of the former Aztec central temple. Instead of walking up steps to the cathedral we now had to actually step down eighteen inches to enter, such was the extent of the inexorable subsidence. In order to keep the cathedral in one piece, workmen were continually at work pulling the walls together with metal struts to prevent great cracks tearing it apart.

When work was being done below the cathedral's main altar they came upon a great carved stone, weighing over 25 tons, in the rubble. It was circular in outline and had numerous designs worked in circles within its twelve-foot diameter. It was a calendar stone that must have formed the centre of the ancient temple that was destroyed to provide some of the building material for the cathedral. The experts tell us that it was more accurate than the calendars used by Julius Caesar, and is 100 years older than the Gregorian calendar created by Pope Gregory the Thirteenth in 1582. It is estimated that the stone took twenty years of labour to make, again, without the use of iron tools. This calendar tells us that the Aztec year was divided up into seasons, and the months were shorter than ours.

It hard to believe that Cortez, with just a few hundred soldiers, was able to pull down this high and ancient civilization. He was able to exploit divisions within the Aztec community, but the diseases he brought from Europe were his strongest weapon. Here they told us the story of the Aztec priests' human sacrifices. It was said that the priests stood over the bound victim and at the moment the sun rose they slashed the abdomen open with a stone knife. They then cut the diaphragm from the chest wall and reached up to the heart. They cut the great vessels to free the base of the heart and held the still beating heart up to the sun - I didn't think so! Even with a super sharp steel scalpel, this would be difficult, as in my estimation the heart would have stopped beating due to massive blood loss long before it could be pulled from the chest. But "STOP PRESS!!" I asked a cardiologist colleague about this, and he feels that while the heart would not beat effectively, it would fibrillate for two or three minutes after separating from the body, so it is possible that there could still be movement in a heart pulled from the chest cavity.

It was hot in the city, and I hinted to Axel that it might be a good time for a siesta. However, we were near the National Palace, and Axel thought it would be a pity to pass it by. The large building was used for government offices and the government had once again commissioned the famous muralist Diego Rivera to do plaques depicting the history of Mexico. We were told that Rivera also had been commissioned to do murals in the Rockefeller Centre in New York, where he depicted Mr. Rockefeller as a bloated plutocrat, taking money away from the workers. That was using too much artistic license for the Rockefellers, and Rivera was sent home before completing the commission. I hope that he was paid for the work that he had finished.

Rivera was a communist, but was given free license to design the murals in Mexico City. There were two plaques depicting Cortez the conqueror; the first shows Father Bartholome protecting the Indians from Cortez's cruelty. In the background the soldiers are beating the natives and forcing them to labour in the silver mines. After the picture had been completed, Cortez's skeleton was exhumed and evidence of advanced syphilis was found. Diego's next assignment shows Cortez landing at Veracruz in 1590. In contrast to the first plaque Cortez is now given the grossly swollen knees of advanced syphilis. His eyes are sunken with dissipation, gummatous swellings cover his skull and the lower jaw is shrunken and receded with the syphilitic process. He is shown touching the cross while a hard-faced monk looks on. In the background, a native was strung up by the feet. The Mexican Government paid for the murals, and while Diego's representations offended many of the people, the authorities wisely allowed him to do as he pleased. I'm glad they did, because the murals are powerful and striking.

That evening Axel took me to the luxurious, but still comparatively cheap, restaurant at the hotel Reforma. It was a magnificent new building, with a modern interior. I hope that they put this new building's foundations down deep enough to stop it sinking.

At last, the time came for me to go for the evening meal with Maria's family. It was only two days since I had seen her, but it seemed like a week. She had asked me to come at 7 p.m., and it was ten past six when I started heading down Reforma Avenue. I had no idea how to get there by bus, and thought that it would be best to take a taxi. As it happened the bullfight crowd also wanted taxis, and whenever an empty taxi pulled up a dozen people began trying to get in. Some were climbing in one side as another group was climbing in the other. When I showed the driver the slip of paper on which Maria had written her address he did not seem to be very impressed; however, away we went at great speed. It was the same old story with much tooting and sudden braking. After ten minutes of this the driver pulled up at a poorer part of the town. It did not look like a good residential suburb, and there were mostly small shops in the street. The numbers did not seem to run in order. It seemed to be Pesito Street, and that was the address I had been given.

I went into the best looking shop but the owner did not speak English and did not show any signs of recognition when I showed him the piece of paper with the address on it. I noticed that he had a telephone in the shop, and I asked in sign language if I could use it. I had Maria's number and if I could speak to her father he would tell the taxi driver how to get there. The damn telephone seemed to need someone with a degree in engineering to operate it. I showed the number to the shopkeeper, and by signs that he should ring the number. When a man's voice was heard I thought that it must be

247

Maria's father. She had said that her father spoke good English. "Hullo, hullo, is that Mr. Lisbon?" I asked.

"No, you must have the wrong number," was the answer, that was followed by a click as he hung up.

I was in a difficult situation. I liked Maria, but it looked as if I was not going to see her that evening. What about the meal she had prepared? I was in Pesito Street, but for all I knew there might be twenty streets of that name in Mexico City. The plane for Canada was due to leave early in the morning and I would not be able to contact Maria at the hospital before I left.

I decided to give it one more try on the phone. "Hello, I am inquiring for Maria Cardoza Lisbon," I said. "Is that you Dr. Valentine? We have been expecting you. Where are you now?" came Maria's welcome voice. "I don't know," I said, "but would you please speak to the driver and tell him how to get to your house? I am badly lost."

Finally we were underway, and in a few minutes the taxi was pulling up in front of a house with high boundary walls. A middle-aged man was standing in front of the high ironwork gate. He introduced himself as Maria's father. He was pleasant and spoke good English. He opened a small door in the iron gate and asked me to step through, and then closed the door and put a chain around it before locking it with a large padlock. "Doctor Valentine, I think you had a lot of trouble in finding us because you were asking for the house of Mr. Lisbon" he said.

"Yes, that is correct," I replied. "Well, I am Maria's father, but in Mexico the girls take their mother's name as their surname. The father's name they take as the middle name, so you see that my name is Cardoza." "Yes, I'd been asking for Mr. Lisbon and that explains why I haven't been able to contact you on the phone. Please accept my apologies for being so late". "Forget about that. Mexico City or 'Mexico D.F.' as we call it, is a big city." We were now entering the large sitting room. "Please come in, Maria will be here in a moment."

On the wall facing the door was a large circular reproduction of one of Michelangelo's Madonnas, but there were two rough holes in the centre. "I notice that you are looking at our Madonna, Doctor. We are Catholics you know and in one of the revolutions some of the militia came into the house and shot holes through the picture. We were lucky to escape the same fate. Some day I will get it repaired. I have been meaning to do so for years." "No, don't do that, I think that it is much more interesting the way that it is now" I offered.

Now Maria entered the room; she was dressed in black, and had the mantilla on her head, her dress showed up her slim figure and the mantilla set off her fine features. She was startlingly beautiful.

I knew that Maria was an exceptional girl, with a good mind and fine figure. All this was alarmingly obvious now. If only 'Popa' had not been about! But now the family had come in to be introduced. Senor Cardoza had lost his wife a year previously, and Maria was now foster mother to her five younger brothers and sisters. They all tried out their school-English on me, and we shook hands formally. They were a pleasant group of children, but everyone in the room seamed to be very conscious of their father's presence. Maria also deferred to him. It seemed strange to me that this intelligent and self-reliant girl should be so dependent on her father. He held the key to the gate and it seemed certain that Maria had to ask permission to go out. I was surprised that she had been able to ask me for a meal. I thought she must be completely dependent on her father for money, as he did not allow her to earn an income.

The family had already eaten, but Maria and her father kept me company as I ate the Mexican meal that she had prepared. The father did most of the talking, but I found it difficult to keep attention on the conversation while Maria looked so glamorous sitting at the other side of the table under the chandelier, and my replies to Mr. Cardoza's questions were getting a little stereotyped.

"Yes Mr. Cardoza."

"No, Mr. Cardoza."

"I certainly think so, Mr. Cardoza."

He spoke four different languages and had a good grasp of world affairs, but I was not as interested in him as I was in Maria. I felt like saying, "Mr. Cardoza, isn't it past your bedtime? Don't feel you need to sit around entertaining me; just run along to bed. Maria and I can entertain ourselves". When I caught Maria's eye, I thought that the same thoughts must be running through her mind. In her position, it would be a hundred years before she could even hint to her father that he should take off.

When the clock showed ten thirty I decided it was time to make a move. "Well Mr. Cardoza, it is 10.30, and I shall have to go now. Maria has to be up early in the morning." Maria was alert now. "You do not have to go so soon, however I can ring for a taxi if you insist" said her father. "No, please, I can walk down to the nearest taxi stand with Maria and bring her back in the taxi." "No, please sit down, Maria, go to the telephone and call a taxi."

Oh my God, not this! Not even a few moments alone together before I left tomorrow! Perhaps a higher consciousness could have found a way to be alone with Maria, but I couldn't find one. Only a miracle could save me now. Miracles don't happen on these occasions. As Senor Cardoza walked down the short path to unlock the gate, I gave a gentle pressure on Maria's hand. She squeezed in return, and I left. What an intelligent lovely lady gone in the mists of time forever.

There was a long wait at the airport the next morning while the tickets were processed with both customs and immigration looking at my passport. I hadn't had the chance to even peck Maria on the cheek before leaving. She had promised to write but that was of little consolation.

As we flew north to Toronto, there was the awful thought that Grand Prairie would be waiting for me. I wondered what the other doctors had said to Joe Storey when he asked them to assist him? I also wondered how many of my patients he had persuaded to use his services. Perhaps we could develop a little of the selfless devotion that Mexican doctors had towards their patients. They were doing a better job and under much worse conditions than we had in Grand Prairie.

We were flying first-class, but the hostesses must have had a hectic night in Mexico City, because they were not wearing the charming smiles seen so often in the airline's advertising material, and when I asked for a magazine, I was ignored.

The airliner touched down in Florida for re-fuelling, and U.S. authorities made sure that we were not going to bring in 'drugs' or subvert their existence. The aircrews walked past the line of passengers, and were let through at once, but the passengers were put through the hoops. Within a few hours we were heading into Toronto and we could see snow on the ground. It was like another world and Mexico was far to the south.

The customs people were as good as they could be. We were soon aboard the airport bus on our way into the city where the Hospital's convention had already booked me into a first class hotel. The convention people arrived to take me under their wing and I was soon surrounded with programmes and literature on hospital administration. The week had been well planned and passed quickly. I enjoyed the talks and discussions, but always my thoughts drifted back to Grand Prairie.

Some times the things most dreaded are found to be easily dealt with, or turn out to be non-existent in reality. Possibly Dr. Joe Storey would be gone by now. There would not be long to wait to find out, as in two days I would be back.

The flight over the broad wheat prairies was uninteresting, just miles and miles of open plains. Even the towns were stereotyped. There were tall buildings of the business centre in the middle, then the suburban housing and suddenly surrounding wheat lands with tall circular grain silos.

The airport at Grand Prairie hadn't a shadow of cloud as we circled to come in. I anticipated plenty of difficulties ahead. I hated the stress caused by the doctors' arguments but I had to hold my temper and hope that Dr. Storey would move out of town. Before going out onto the football field or into the boxing ring I'd been afraid, but at the same time the danger and the unknown had acted as a stimulant and I would begin to feel excited. This was a different game; there was no physical danger and the play took place at dinner parties, in operating theatres and in consulting rooms. There were no goal posts and no referees to appeal to.

I despaired at the shoddy medical ethics, and the continual vying for surgery and patients. Now that I was back perhaps the situation had changed for the better; was I hoping for too much? The airport was the same, with a few people waiting to take the plane out. A couple of farmers greeted me and the young man behind the counter was anxious to hear how my air bookings had gone. "I hope you did not have a problem in Vancouver over the Mexican visa."

"No, the consulate people came out to the airport on Saturday to give it to me. They were very agreeable for a suitable fee, but I guess you have to expect that when you are travelling" was my reply.

When I got to my consulting rooms my receptionist, Janet, was waiting. She treated me like a brother and took a friendly interest in everything I had done while I was away. Janet asked me if I had met any pretty Senoritas when I was in Mexico, and I told her "There were lots of lovely looking girls there, but as I do not speak Spanish, it was all too difficult and they weren't interested in me". She replied that it was good to have me back, as it had been dull while I was away, and I said "well, it's good to know that someone missed me." I was pretty sure that some of my colleagues wouldn't have.

Now that the greetings were over I was bursting to know about Dr Storey, and asked Janet what the situation was. "He seems to be a little quieter lately. It's said he is not in good favour up at the hospital" she replied. This meant that Joe was still in town and getting the big picture would have to wait until the next day. I needed a good night's sleep before facing the hospital in the morning, and as long as the others did not know I was back, then I would not be called out to give an anaesthetic after midnight.

As I walked up to the hospital the next morning, I noticed that my muscles were tense and I had a mild tremor when I held my hands out. I had to acknowledge that I was generally stressed. This was not the feeling that one should have when returning from a fortnight away with a week in sunny Mexico.

There were lots of questions that I wanted to ask; what had happened to Dr. Joe Storey? What did the others do about him? He must have had to ask some of them for help in the last two weeks. Did they refuse as they said they would? The hospital looked the same. The nurses were pleased to see me, and greeted me cheerfully.

The organisation was going on as usual. Dr. Joe was in the hospital as his car was in the usual place. The other doctors were doing rounds in the hospital, as their white coats were not on the coat rack. It was not long before they started to drift in for morning coffee.

They asked about the trip to Mexico, but as soon as I had started to tell them the conversation soon drifted back to patients, x-rays and fees again. Joe was the last one to enter the room and he greeted me cordially, "Glad to see you back in the fold," he said.

I forced myself to reply, "It's good to be back."

Dr. Lionel Dodds saw that there was no cup for Joe. He got up and washed his own and handed it to Joe and struck up a conversation.

"Joe, I had a look at that woman with the mass in her abdomen."

"What did you think of her Lionel?" Joe asked.

"That mass certainly has to be investigated, but I think that it would be better done in the city."

"We could manage it here," said Joe. "Her old man has plenty of what it takes you know".

"I'm not worrying about that side of it Joe. It seems to me that we should not operate on that type of case here. There are more experienced men in the city to do it."

Joe seemed to contemplate this for a moment, then said "As you say, Lionel, I thought I'd give you the chance to see her though, because we should do as much surgery as we can here to stop so much going out to other places." I heard Lionel answer that he agreed wholeheartedly. To me, Joe's comment about the patient having plenty of money reinforced what I thought of his medical motivation and was probably the reason he didn't want surgeries referred elsewhere. I was grateful that Lionel at least put the patient's welfare before economic considerations.

Soon after, the other doctors had drifted out, and Lionel had a chance to talk to me privately. As soon as Joe was out of hearing, Lionel wrinkled his nose and shrugged his shoulders saying, "I could have done that case, but I'm not putting myself out for that bastard. He has been putting it around that I operate too much. That'll show him that I don't put the knife into every abdomen that I see. Since you've been away I have been avoiding him as much as possible. I've not asked him for any anaesthetics. If I've seen that he is in the hospital I've just done my work and left."

I was getting ready to go back to town and Lionel offered me a ride in his big, new Buick. The large machine was the pride of his life now. It had all the power in the world and could cruise at 70 m.p.h. It rode beautifully. More important than the car's performance was the ambience of success that it provided. Lionel's life was devoted to showing how successful he was, how good his operations were and how financial solidarity followed as the night follows day. Despite his success, Lionel was still tense and nervous although he appeared relaxed and in control to his patients. Inside, however, he was not a happy man. He told me that his systolic blood pressure was 200. This was thirty percent higher than it should be, and was in the danger zone. In those days the effective anti-hypertensive medications were being developed but had not arrived in Grand Prairie.

Couldn't Lionel see that the money he had spent on his car would have been better used on a vacation? If he didn't work so hard he could spend more time at home with his teenage children. Perhaps I'm being optimistic that associating with teenagers would bring his blood pressure down.

I would have loved to tell Lionel to work less, but if he was offended he might take away my anaesthetics. He may even give them to Joe, and that would be worse, just adding insult to injury.

Before I went away I had been the only one to stand up to Joe and tell him I would not work with him by choice. Despite assurances from the other doctors that they would also censure him, they hadn't. It now looked as if Joe was going to be able to continue in Grand Prairie indefinitely. The other doctors disliked him intensely, but there was not one amongst them who would go to Joe and tell him that he would not assist him. There was always some way of getting out of it without offending Joe too much. They would beg off on the excuse that they had other work on that morning, or that their wives wanted them to take the children to the river, but never a direct refusal. They were afraid to lay themselves open to criticism from the public if it were known that they had refused to assist Joe.

There was a sick feeling in my stomach as I realised that it was up to me to make a stand against Joe. A confrontation was looming. Dr. John Nells was going to a medical conference in the south, so there were only going to be three doctors running the hospital. John had left by the Thursday afternoon, and I noticed that Dr. Joe Storey had booked in three children from one family for tonsillectomy on the following Saturday morning. He could not do the children's operations under local anaesthetic, and so Joe would be obliged to ask either Lionel or me to help, as we were the only doctors available who could give general anaesthetics.

When I went into the hospital on Friday morning the children were still on the operating list. I got through my work as quickly as I could, hoping to avoid Joe Storey. After gulping down a cup of coffee I pulled on my coat and headed for the door, but I was not quick enough; Dr. Joe was in the doorway. A nervous smile, a couple of quick coughs and he said, "John, I have three tonsillectomies in the morning. All the others are away so I will have to ask you to give the anaesthetics".

"Oh.....please get me out of this, let me be anywhere else but here" I thought. I could so easily fail myself and say yes, but I would despise myself forever. I had to refuse. I replied clearly and firmly "I'm sorry Joe, but I do not want to work with you. Get someone else to do it."

Joe was red and as tense as a bowstring and said "I have to get someone to give the anaesthetics; they have been booked in for three weeks and they come from out of town".

"Get another doctor," I answered.

"Why won't you do it?" he asked.

This was the opportunity I'd been waiting for. Should I burst forth with the accumulated grievances of the last month? Would it do any good? Instead I opted for the short version;

"There is no one reason Joe, other than I do not like working with you," I said.

Joe's eyes were blazing with anger, but I did not wait for his reaction. I had said what was necessary, and now it was time to escape into the fresh air outside. I couldn't help thinking that Joe's wife would really have something to talk about now. I had insulted her husband so I knew the telephone wires would be running hot, vibrating with my name.

I could hardly wait to get back to the office to tell Janet what I'd done. As I had expected, she was right on my side and told me that I should have done it months ago. I did not feel sorry that I had waited, and also felt that I had given Joe every chance. Now I was finished with him for good. It was a great temptation to ring up Lionel Dodds and find out if he'd been approached to do the anaesthetics, because Lionel had told me earlier that I should stop assisting Joe, so I assumed that he too would not assist him.

I remained tempted to ring Lionel on several occasions but resisted the urge, and tried to concentrate on a book. I was awake at six the next morning, and only began to feel like sleeping when the clock showed it was time to get up and start preparing breakfast.

It was almost ten o'clock when I walked into the hospital again as nonchalantly as possible. I went into the matron's office and glanced at the operating sheet. The tonsillectomies had not been scratched off and as they were due to start at nine they must be underway. I walked slowly along to the doctor's room and glanced towards the operating theatre. Doctor Joe Storey was pulling a trolley out of the doorway. A child was coughing blood; there could be only one person at the other end of the trolley. In spite of everything he had said and promised, Lionel had been giving the anaesthetics!

My rounds that morning were done with little concentration on the patients' problems. I asked the usual questions and received the usual replies, but I was distracted from the business at hand as I kept thinking about the operations that were going on down below. Lionel had affirmed repeatedly that he would not assist Joe. This was an opportunity to show Joe that his presence was not wanted in the town. Lionel had not been true to his word, and I was devastated by his betrayal.

I had a good practice, and a moderate amount of money was coming in. Eighteen months before, this situation would have seemed too good to be true. I had a lot of patients who liked and respected me, but was it worthwhile putting up with this distressing professional situation?

It was sickening and frustrating to think of Lionel down there, pouring ether while Joe did the tonsillectomies. Lionel hated to give anaesthetics, and his work in this area was not the best. As a result there would be plenty of coughing and choking when the patient was under the anaesthetic. Joe was sure to have blood coughed all over him which was just the right situation for a full-blown row to blow up between them. I found that a cheering thought, as I doubted that Lionel could be counted on to show much backbone and tell Joe his true feelings, unless something else triggered him to do so.

I felt like confronting Lionel about why he had given into Joe by saying, "Don't you realise that Joe could not have done these operations if you refused to give the anaesthetics?" It sounded good, but I knew that I didn't have the guts to throw away everything I had been working for, just because I was annoyed with Lionel. Although I was disgusted, I knew that I would have to get over this major disappointment and make the best of it.

I was alone in the doctor's room when Lionel walked in. "Hello John, I'm afraid that I was trapped into giving these anaesthetics this morning," he said. I wasn't having any of it and said, "But you didn't have to give them Lionel."

"Oh well, yes, but Joe had the patients in hospital and they come from forty-miles out of town. It would have been too far to send them home. They have to be done some time anyhow" was his excuse.

"All that's Joe's problem. He didn't think of us when he damn near let that patient die last month," I said, holding my ground.

"You're right John. I wish that I had not done the anaesthetics in a way, but they would be in again in a week or so, cluttering up the list. It would be as well to get them over with" was his lame reply.

Perhaps this was the time to tell Lionel to go to hell. His rationalisations sounded so good, he just didn't have the guts to say no to Joe. Surely Lionel did not believe all this tripe he was saying. Suddenly I wanted to be out of there before I said something I would regret.

On the long walk back to my office, I kept thinking, "I cannot work without Lionel, and I cannot work with him." There seemed to be only one honourable solution to the problem...GET OUT!! This would mean giving up the security of a good practice in Alberta. It would be difficult shattering Janet's loyalty with the blunt statement, "I am leaving Grand Prairie." She did not deserve that after all her months of good service and friendship. And what of all the families who had come to accept me as their family doctor? They had continually asked me at the beginning if I was happy to stay in Grand Prairie. They had trusted me with their children's tonsillectomies and had come to regard me as essential to their own health care. They had had many doctors, and would feel let down again if I left. Was it fair to accept their trust and then throw it away because of my discomfort with the medical scene? There must be hundreds of other medical practitioners carrying on under similar burdens who were still contributing to their community in a useful manner, so why not me?

Regardless, I knew that I was on my way; I had had enough. Joe would go on telling his patients that he was the best doctor in the province, and continue poaching patients. Lionel would go on mismanaging his affairs and his own health until he blew the top off the blood pressure machine. The situation was bad, but there was nothing in this world that I could do about it.

Meanwhile, George Bell had been sitting in his bed in the middle of the men's ward for ten days now. He was not my patient, but I could not but notice that his jaundice was getting worse. Each day his skin was a deeper shade of yellow and he was scratching more.

Jaundice causes a severe itching and the creams that he was forever rubbing on his skin did little to relieve his discomfort. For the last two days George had not been alert when I passed the end of his bed. Even from a distance, it was obvious that he was slipping badly. Then one morning, Lionel stopped me in the corridor and asked, "John, have you noticed the man with jaundice half way up the ward?"

I answered, "It is getting a bit hard not to notice him."

"I want to operate on him tomorrow morning. Will you assist me?" Lionel asked.

"Certainly, but what's the story?" I enquired.

"Joe Storey has had him in the ward for two weeks treating him for infectious hepatitis. He's not getting better so we suspect that there may be a malignancy," Lionel replied.

"I suppose the relatives are pretty anxious," I said, knowing that it would be obvious to them that his condition was deteriorating.

"Yes, they have had Joe call me into consultation. We have decided that surgery might relieve the obstruction and give him some comfort."

I agreed with this, commenting further, "He looks pretty sick."

Lionel agreed and added, "He is sick, John, but he must have an obstruction there and his only hope of life is surgery. I don't think that we should be afraid to go in if we can save his life. If he dies it will be hard on us, but he will have had his chance."

I asked what the patient's condition was now, and Lionel said, "He is pretty sick, but Joe has volunteered to give the anaesthetic and let me operate. I think that all the surgery we are capable of should be done here, besides he is too ill to fly out now."

I was caught between the devil and the deep blue sea. I was asked to help with a very dangerous operation on a moribund patient. Lionel had taken responsibility for the case and had asked me to assist him. I was happy to help Lionel, but Joe would be there, looking over the screens, and that made me uncomfortable. I resigned myself to assisting and having said I would, asked what time we were to start.

Lionel was very pleased and said, "Good! I've asked for the

operating room at 8.30 in the morning." So that was that.

When they wheeled George Bell in the next morning, it did not take a trained eye to see that he was moribund. His tearful wife looked through the half-open door with fear in her eyes. She knew how sick he was and suspected that he might not come out alive. The nurse gently shut the door. Lionel was in good form, but the fear of a bad outcome was just under the surface. He'd arrived a little before time and had spent twenty minutes talking to Mrs. Bell - hopefully trying to instill some confidence in her that he didn't feel himself.

Dr. Joe Storey had come in early too. He had been talking to Mrs. Bell with Lionel and then had come into the operating room to get the local anaesthetic ready. It had been decided to try and do as much of the operation as possible under local and so save his already weakened system from additional stress. When we got down to the peritoneum it would be necessary to use some inhalant anaesthetic to prevent pain and restlessness.

The operation got underway when the skin had been scrubbed and painted with iodine. If the suspense had not been so great it would have been fascinating to give more attention to the yellow abdomen skin changing to brown, as the iodine spread over it. The yellow of the skin and ruddy brown of the iodine mixed produced a random, streaked effect. It was reminiscent of a modern abstract painting and not something seen often in the operating theatre.

At the first skin incision we saw that the fat was yellow with bile. It was relatively easy to get through the several layers necessary to expose the operative area. There was nothing blocking the common bile duct and no cancer of the head of the pancreas.

Then Lionel ran a probe down inside the common duct, but there was no opening into the small intestine at all. It must have been one of those rare cases of stenosis, or stricture of the lower end of the duct. There were beads of sweat on Lionel's forehead as he realised that he was in for a long and demanding operation on a very sick patient. He would have to join the end of the gall bladder to the small bowel, so that the bile could by-pass the common duct and the jaundice be relieved.

I knew that I was speaking out of turn, but felt compelled to say, "Lionel, wouldn't it be enough to take the gallbladder out to the skin and let the bile escape that way?"

"Now that we have started I don't want to do things by half. He'll be better off with an internal drainage." was Lionel's reply.

"But he won't stand a prolonged operation," I suggested.

"Well, I think that his condition is alright now. What do you say, Joe?" asked Lionel.

Joe Storey was pleased to join in to this conversation, and said, "Well yes Lionel, you just do whatever you want. I will tell you if his condition is deteriorating."

I had been now put firmly into place, and resolved to act as an assistant and not offer advice. It was difficult to stand by and assist in an unnecessarily prolonged operation. I knew that Lionel didn't want the patient to go to the city to have the job completed, but at the same time I felt that it would be preferable to have a technically incomplete operation rather than a dead patient.

Lionel went ahead with the operation, and did even more than join the gall bladder to the small bowel. The small bowel looked kinked, he thought, and he spent another three quarters of an hour correcting the problem.

There was nothing wrong with the surgery, but I felt it all a waste of time. The patient could only survive if he had a supreme constitution. Lionel was not leaving himself open for the relatives to say "Dr. Dodds found the job too big for him. He had to send George away to have the operation completed."

It was four and a half hours later when we wheeled George Bell up to his bed. He was very weak, but was still alive. Mrs. Bell spent the rest of the next week beside her husband's bed, but at the end of the week he died. When Lionel did the post mortem there was no break in the operative area. It was firm but there was not the slightest sign of healing. The operation was a success but the patient was dead.

If there had been a choice before, there was none now. I knew that I had to leave this town. Every doctor makes mistakes, but the more enlightened ones admitted them. They did not say, as Lionel did on this occasion, "We did everything in our power. He was beyond medical help." Nothing that Lionel said to me mattered now. Even when he suggested that he and I should enter into a closer relationship, and eventually a partnership, I was not tempted. It would mean a lot more money, but I could not live with myself working in this sort of medical and hospital environment.

Even though I had decided to leave Grand Prairie there was no slackening in my practice. I was busy in the hospital each morning, and in the afternoons I could hear Janet telling people that all the appointments were taken for that day. It was going to be hard to leave my old friends and the children who ran into the consulting room and looked in the top drawer for a sweet. Would they be able to understand my leaving?

I had also grown fond of Janet. She did her work cheerfully during the day and in the evenings she took home the books so that the bills would be out in good time at the end of the month. Whenever I left a shirt lying around in my room, I would find it washed and hung up to dry. What sort of fool would give up this service?

I was not sleeping well and it was well past the time that I should have told Janet of my plans. On a previous occasion when her employer had left, she had been without work for two months, so I felt it was important she have reasonable notice of my impending move.

Janet had been offered another job in the city so I felt she should be the first to be told that I was going, although if she decided to take the city job immediately I would be stranded. She knew far more about the accounts and banking than I did.

Janet was not surprised to see me when I called at her room that Sunday morning. She thought I had just come to see if she wanted to go out to golf in the afternoon and told me to take a seat. My words had to be forced out. "Janet, I am going to leave."

Her face was pale and it was a few seconds before she spoke. "I know that you aren't very happy at the moment, but I didn't think it was as bad as that."

"I'm sorry Janet, but I thought it was only fair to tell you first."

"Well, if it must be, thank you for telling me. I will keep it to myself of course until it is definite."

It was a bit lame rewarding her loyalty with, "I'll do my best to see that the next employer gets a good report about your skills and efficiency" but I said it anyway. That was soon followed with an embarrassing burst which was a true reflection of my inner turmoil "I want to do some more travelling Janet. If I don't go now, I'll never be able to get away." Janet responded like a real friend saying "If that's what you want, then you should do it. Don't worry about me; I'll make out."

I did not feel good, or brave or adventurous. I only thought that I was letting a good friend down. "Thank you for your kindness Janet. I'll do everything I can to ensure you're taken care of and can stay on with the next doctor if you want." It was all very unsatisfactory and depressing, and I never did get over the feeling that I was not being fair to her. Even when I had secured her a position with the incoming doctor I felt badly.

The worst was over now. It was just a matter of writing to the Registrar of the College of Physicians to advise him that I was leaving. There would be no difficulty in finding someone to take over.

I didn't have a current intimate relationship, so there was not much to tidy up in that department. Grand Prairie was a small community and it was strictly taboo to get involved with any of the young women in my practice, so I never considered that as an option.

When I first arrived I met a young woman named Mary who was agreeable company and pleasing to the eye. Her parents were East European but she had attended a Convent in Edmonton before returning to Grand Prairie and getting a job. I took her out to a movie and on the way home I made an advance to her for a little horizontal recreation. She wouldn't have a button of this, so I was able to take her home unsullied and untainted. However Janet soon told me that Mary had told all those who would listen that I had tried to seduce her, so that put me on the back foot for a while, as in all small towns news travels fast, and a local doctor didn't need a reputation as a 'womaniser'.

When I went to Edmonton, I had been introduced to another young lady and when I returned there a few times a year, she kindly invited me to stay at her flat. She told me once that my small testicles bouncing on her bottom were a delight to her, so I repeated the dose as often as possible. Then one evening, after four enjoyable congresses, I told her that we should have a rest that night. She replied "What! Is it rationed now?" Just as well my visits were occasional and these were not frequent trysts, as I may have risked a serious case of exhaustion.

On the local scene, one of the technicians accepted my invitation for an evening out and we parked out of town by the golf club. We were sitting in the back seat, and I was doing the usual preliminaries for intercourse. She said to me, "You don't know what you're doing," and the next moment she went into a convulsion, and I thought, "My God, has she had an epileptic attack!" I was apprehensive that she might stop breathing and I would be stuck with taking a body back to the hospital. However, she was having an orgasm and she had two or three of these before we got around to having intercourse. Once I got used to her responsiveness, it was quite enjoyable, and I got over my initial impression that something terrible was happening to her. We got along quite nicely for a while, and then she became quite bossy. I thought it better to fade out of that scene, before I became entrenched in a relationship of life long disputes and subservience.

The last few weeks before leaving were busy. There was all my gear to be packed and stored and arrangements made for it to be sent on later. I felt like the dance hall girls of the 1890s, who had taken themselves off to the Yukon gold rush. They had arrived with two suitcases, but when they left six months later they had ten.

I did not feel good when loyal patients came to say goodbye. The nurses put on a party for me and they invited all of the doctors and their wives. It seemed that I was more popular than I had thought. Again, I wondered if I should be leaving. When the last trunk had been stored in the basement and the car was loaded with the rest, I knew my time at Grand Prairie was at an end. On Sunday morning, as I drove out of town, I knew that I was on my way at last, and that I wouldn't be back. It was sad to leave, having had twelve months of interacting with this community, but I was hopeful that life would be better somewhere else.

I set off in my car to go to the east coast of Canada, where I would depart for England, and then go on to South Africa. I had decided to travel through the United States, as I was told they had better highways. I was taken by the town of Cody in Wyoming, the hometown of the famous Buffalo Bill, who took a troop of Cowboys and Indians, with their horses, to Europe from 1883 till 1916. His entertainers were lauded by all and crowned heads did not hesitate to entertain them as celebrities. One member of the troupe was Annie Oakley, who could shoot the eye out of a needle at fifty paces. That was her reputation, but the truth was that even if the eye-of-a-needle claim was just 'spin', she was an amazing shot anyway. She could shoot holes in playing cards that were thrown up into the air, from a considerable distance. She was certainly not a girl to fool around with, if you expected to hand on your genetic material to future generations.

In the centre of Cody, there was a statue of Buffalo Bill and the whole atmosphere had something of Central Otago in New Zealand. It was a 'Wild West' town, but there were few buffalos, as Buffalo Bill had shot most of them. The buffalo is a pretty versatile animal and nowadays they are being bred on specialised ranches, and are no longer threatened with extinction.

I contacted one of the local doctors who kindly invited me for a meal with his family. We got along well and he suggested that I might join their medical group in Wyoming. I said that I was interested in surgery which was his field of interest too. The opening they had was for a person interested in medical work so I decided not to apply for the position and move on. In retrospect it would have been very interesting to have returned and do the medical work there. It was a place that I would have felt most comfortable in, as it reminded me of familiar country towns in Otago. This was another turning point in my life and I probably made the wrong decision once again.

I would have liked to have stayed, but since I had arranged to meet my parents in London, I continued on as planned.

CHAPTER 12

London and South Africa
29 September 1955

LIST OF CHARACTERS

DR. L. SLEE, A medical practitioner in Southend who employed the author to locum.
MISS JOHN, Dr. Slee's receptionist.
MY 'CORONATION STREET' LANDLADY in Southend (where the author boarded).
MRS. MARIA VAN STROM, a hotel receptionist.
WILHELM BOHLER, the husband of the author's Auntie Queen (Dais' sister)
DAVID and DANIEL, Queen and Wilhelm's two sons,
OLD BILL, a middle aged Zulu who was a 'Bohler' servant.

I EVENTUALLY GOT TO THE EAST COAST OF CANADA, put my car into storage and flew to London to meet my parents, who were part way through their world tour. Arch and Dais met me at the airport and I joined them at their lodgings. Once settled I went to a locum agency to see what employment opportunities were available; the meeting went well, and I was offered an interview for a two week placement as a GP locum in Southend, (a coastal holiday resort 30 miles from London). While I stayed to do the locum, Arch and Dais were to continue on their way through the British Isles, and we would meet again in South Africa.

I had no difficulty getting a rental car and set off for the appointment with Dr. Slee at his rooms at 10 a.m. the next day. The traffic was heavy on the London Circular road and I began day dreaming, lost my way, and was late for the interview.

John and Arch entertaining the pigeons in Trafalgar Square, London.

The doctors' offices were called surgeries in England, and I pulled up in front of a converted wooden dwelling on one of the side streets of the little town. There was a plate on the gate that read, "Dr. L. Slee. Hours 9 - 11 & 5 - 7." It was the right place, but there was little time to take stock of the surroundings. I was late already and he might be fed up and tell me that I didn't have the job. I straightened my tie and sailed up to the front door. A little old lady was waiting inside the door and looked at me appraisingly. "You the new doctor?" she asked.

Well, that was something; I must have looked like a medical man, or perhaps she knew all the patients. "Yes, I've come down to do a locum for Dr. Slee," I replied. She took me in and introduced me to my prospective employer. Dr. Leslie Slee was in his late fifties, was tall, dark and overweight. He wore a day's growth of beard and his suit had some stains down the front. When I stumbled out my apologies for being late, he replied in a reserved manner, "I thought you may have some trouble with the traffic on the way down. Don't worry."

Well, that was over and he now went on, "I thought we might go over a few of the patients whom you still need to visit while I'm away."

"Surely this wasn't his consulting room!" I thought to myself.

The desk faced the door and being of the old-fashioned roller top type, anybody entering the room couldn't see if there was anyone sitting behind it. But that wasn't all - on top of the desk was piled all the junk in the world; old medical journals, advertising material from the drug firms, free samples and lots of empty and half empty bottles. It was a mess.

A small gas fire supplied modest heat for the room and Dr. Slee signalled me to sit on the wooden chair by the fire, while he retreated behind the huge desk. The shelf above his head was heavily loaded with many years of unopened copies of the British Medical Journal. There they were, lying virgin and inviolate in their original wrappers, waiting for the day of intense mental activity when Dr. Slee would devour them in one gigantic session. The Medical Journal was wrapped very tightly and it was well known that many doctors used them to spank their young children. This taught them the way the world was managed; the person with the power is the boss. All these things were running through my mind as the good doctor went on. He did not seem in the least embarrassed about the condition of his premises and went on telling me about his patients. My appraisal by the time I left this locum position was that it was not only not a great practice, but it could have been one of the worst in the country and to this day it remains the worst that I've seen anywhere.

It was teatime now. He got out of the chair and going to the door put his head out and shouted into the dark spaces at the back of the house, "Miss John! Miss John! Let's have some tea!"

He then looked at me and said, "Just do that when you're ready for tea. While it's coming I'll show you where things are."

That was simple enough, as there was next to nothing to be shown. He had a stethoscope, a blood pressure machine and a Bunsen burner and test tubes for testing urines for glucose. However, there was no solution for the testing and the tablets were blue and outdated. What of all the shiny instruments in the glass fronted cases? There just weren't any, but there were forms - books of them. They seemed to be much more important than anything else and he went on to explain their intricacies. He said, "These ones are filled in when you send a patient to the hospital outpatients department. These are for sending to specialist consultation clinics, and the little yellow ones are given to the patient when he needs his eyes tested. Copies of these and the forms for writing prescriptions need to be carried while on all house visits of course."

By this time we'd heard the front door bang shut a couple of times. The patients just walked into the waiting room and were called into the doctor's room by an electric bell with its push button located on the left hand side of his desk. When the patients entered, the doctor walked over and took them by the wrist to take their pulse. He talked to them for a minute and then sat down and wrote out the prescription. This seemed to be a hangover from the old panel days when they came for their six-penny bottle of medicine. The patients were never disappointed in their quest for the bottle of medicine. It may contain nothing but a few minerals but it represented something accomplished. They had been to the doctor and had received something in a bottle to see them through till the next consultation.

Dr. Slee said that he seldom examined a patient; indeed he warned me that with a large number of people coming to renew prescriptions, or to get another piece of paper for a sickness benefit, there wasn't much time or need for them to take their clothes off. When there were no more patients Dr. Slee took me to the pharmacist, who had his dispensary next door. This pleasant little man was immersed in a tangle of bottles and paper at the back of his shop. In those days the pharmacists were still expected to make up and dispense the prescriptions. There were lots of bottles labelled ipecacuanha, digitalis pulverata, magnesium sulphate, and even sodium chloride.

Everything seemed to be in the greatest confusion. Old prescriptions were scattered around in odd boxes and overflowed onto the benches where the balance scales and stock medicines were kept. The pharmacist was cheerful, and promised to be helpful and see me through any problems (like finding out the names of the doctor's favourite mixtures) if there were no records in the patient's sheets. I was soon to find out that there was seldom any record of

Daisy and Arch Valentine in Ireland, during their World tour.

any medications given out. It was also a surprise to learn that I was not to spend the nights at the doctor's house, but was to board in 'digs'.

The doctor led off in his car and pulled up at the other side of the town in front of a rather run down house. All the homes were two storey brick houses with shared walls, so popular at the turn of the century.

After prolonged ringing of the doorbell, an old dark woman appeared at the door. She stopped a severe bout of coughing to explain that she had been at the back of the house. "I thought that you were coming at 11 0'clock. Anyway, come on in," was her welcome.

We entered a narrow hall and went up the steep stairs. My room contained three beds and when Dr. Slee commented on this, the landlady explained, "Yes, I take children in," talking through a serious bout of coughing, and then added "I have to go for a chest x-ray on Thursday." I hoped that she didn't have tuberculosis, as I would be having meals in the house. Dr. Slee asked where the phone was, and did not seem perturbed to find that it was on the lower floor, in the kitchen. It was a long way from my bedroom. Dr. Slee said, "You will have to leave the doors open at night." As he retreated down the stairs, he assured me "You will have no trouble with the practice; they don't call you much at night." From then I was on my own. I was to be in charge of a panel practice in England's welfare state for two weeks.

The next day, my first patient was an older woman who stated her problem and then asked "Do you examine, Doctor?" I assured her that I did, and she seemed pleased that I was a 'hands on' doctor.

On the first weekend I was on-call for several practices. I didn't have any night calls, but on Monday morning a very irate colleague rang me. It seemed that one of his patients had been trying to ring me at the boarding house number, but I didn't hear the phone ring. This patient was understandably annoyed, and requested that their family records be transferred to another doctor. The doctor was furious that he had lost this family, as the government paid a certain amount each year on behalf of each patient enrolled with him. I survived those two weeks, and when Dr. Slee returned he didn't complain. As he paid me he told me that he couldn't pay me more than the fixed rate, and we parted on good terms.

I went back to London, handed in the rental car, and made arrangements to fly to South Africa. My parents, who were on a world tour, had gone ahead as planned, and would be waiting in Durban for me. We were to stay with Queen and her family and while there, attend the wedding of her oldest son, David. I was tense and excited, but felt exhilarated and I loved it! The world was rolling along under my feet at long last.

The great bird that was flying me south roared through the night, over the African continent. I wondered about the golden eggs in its belly. I was tempted to ask the air hostess, but she would have had to ask the Captain, and he might have said "There are passengers with gold in their teeth, women with gold wedding rings and jewellery, but no golden eggs as far as we know". I would just have to wait until I got to Zululand to find those mythological golden eggs. In a short while I would be touching down at the Jan Smuts Airport in Johannesburg. Since leaving New Zealand I had known that I would be travelling to South Africa, and my time in the Pacific and in Canada had been in anticipation of this moment.

When I graduated from medical school Queen had invited, or rather insisted, that I visit her in South Africa. She said that the opportunities would be great, and I would have the assistance of her husband's considerable wealth. An added plus was that my cousins wanted to take me around and introduce me to their friends and show me the various game parks.

You will remember that Queen had refused to return to Kurow to enable Dais to go away and do her nurse's training. Instead, Queen had gone back to Coker's Hotel and worked and saved for her overseas trip. When Queen had eventually left for her big 'O.E.', twenty-eight years before, she had stopped off in South Africa on her way to England. It was a 'working holiday' and Queen had taken a nursing job in a Natal Hospital. One of her male patients, Wilhelm Bohler, had severe malaria but soon recovered enough to appreciate Queen's attractive face and generous figure. He fell in love with her, and after a short engagement, they were married. Queen would have impressed him as a vivacious, intelligent and good-looking woman, and these were the desirable characteristics a large landholder wanted in a wife. For a moment I almost said 'a land holder's large wife' but I caught myself. In New Zealand, Dais had warned me that there was tension in Queen's marriage, but that warning didn't mean much to me until I had lived with the Bohler family for a while.

Wilhelm was of German stock, but had been born in South Africa. Most of the Germans had close relations with the Afrikaners and spoke their language fluently. Afrikaans is a form of the Dutch language, developed in South Africa and easily learned by those who speak German. Rather than having an Afrikaan accent, Uncle Wilhelm had chosen to adopt the influence of the English in his speech, and spoke with an English accent. The rest of Wilhelm's family spoke German at home and associated with Afrikaans speakers and had a mixed accent.

Queen admitted that she would have liked one of her sons to have done medicine, but they weren't interested - both David and Daniel worked on their large sugar farm with their father. They had both been at agricultural school and did the office work connected with the farm and helped supervise the workers. The schools they attended were English speaking, and their English was excellent. They had both been good rugby footballers at school, and still played in a local team. Rugby is a religion amongst the white South Africans, and every young man's ambition is to become a member of the National team called "The Springboks." The boys were interested in my career, and also had assured me in their letters that they would like to show me around the country in their cars. The chance to come to David's wedding and see something of the cities and wildlife parks was too tempting for me to miss.

When I arrived at Johannesburg I passed through customs with no trouble and went to the hotel as I had a one night wait before flying on to Durban the next day. At the hotel reception desk the young woman was attractive; as I turned to go to my room she invited me to call on her if there was anything I needed.

My room had a bathroom with a window view of a busy street below. I watched a crowd of about fifty native men surging down the pavement. Most were walking quickly, but others were jogging and I felt their pulsating energy. While they were roughly dressed it was obvious that they were fit and muscular. I thought that it might be a riot, but there was some sort of order in the crowd because when they came to an intersection one of their leaders stopped them until it was safe to cross. They then poured on across the street and down towards the railway station. I soon learnt that these men were mine labourers on their way to work. Their movement was a normal feature of Johannesburg life, and I was quite likely the only bystander making any observations about the crowd of men. Even from the hotel window this mass of regimented Zulus, Swazis and

Basutos sent a shudder through me. The physical strength and fitness of these people was obvious; there was real power there. Watching them, I had the sense of something really different from what I had previously known, and felt I was in Africa at last.

In the morning I saw the great heaps of slag that had come up out of the mines and formed the flat hills which made the skyline of this 'City of Gold'. The rock had been brought up from thousands of feet below the surface. Some of these greenstone lava samples are four thousand million years old, which makes them some of the oldest rocks discovered. The earth temperature rises 2.5 degrees Celsius with every 100 meters of descent, and it would have been impossible to work in the mines 2,800 meters below sea level, without having cooling systems in place. Even so, it was only possible to mine these great depths because of the relatively cheap labour, recruited from African tribes, who tolerated the conditions despite the excessive heat.

The phone rang, and I found that it was the hotel office calling. There was no mistaking the voice that asked after my comfort and inquired what time I'd like breakfast in the morning. She spoke for five minutes, but I did not have the courage to ask her out, although I thought there might be the chance of friendship here. I was relieved when the phone rang again, and it was the same voice. I was told that I had to pay for breakfast that evening: "You can pay me and then if anyone asks again you can say that you have paid Mrs. Van Strom." "Mrs. Van Strom?" I queried? "Yes, but I am divorced." Was the reply. Well! That detail was dealt with; now the old plan could go ahead! "Look, I'm to meet my relatives tomorrow, and my mother told me that I must be well dressed. My suit looks like nothing on earth. How can I get it pressed?"

"All the girls are off duty at this hour, but there's an ironing room at the end of your corridor."

"That doesn't help one little bit as I'm not good at ironing." I continued "Could you press my coat for me after you finish work?"

Hell-Bent for Life

She took a deep breath, a long pause, and then replied "Why don't you come over to my flat after I get home? You can bring your coat and I'll press it then." This was too good to be true!! These things just didn't happen to me everyday!

"Just give me time to write your address down. Will I need to bring anything to drink?" I asked.

"No," she responded. "I have everything at home. The important thing is not to tell anyone from the hotel that you are coming, as I don't want to lose my job."

"I'll be there in an hour," I managed to say. My hands were trembling now, and despite me thinking myself a man of the world, I was as nervous as a kitten. Perhaps she was leading me into trouble. I had read about people getting into problems with this sort of thing, but I didn't want to turn this chance down. I knew that if I didn't go I would regret it for the rest of my life. I'd been sorry for my sins in the past, but it would be worse to have regret at not accepting the opportunity to sin when it was offered.

As I went down the stairs I noticed that my heart was beating wildly, and if I stood still I could hear it against my eardrums.

The streets were well lit in this part of town, which was filled with large blocks of flats. It wasn't difficult to find the block she lived in. There was a native doorman, but he only saluted as I went past. I got to the third floor and Maria Van Strom answered the door at once and asked me to come in. She looked even more attractive in the shaded lights of the sitting room. She walked over to the tiny bar in the corner of the room and said "I'll let you fix some drinks while I start pressing your coat."

This little sitting room was just perfect - Maria had good taste. The light shades were pink and cast a flattering glow about the room. Against the wall, there was a radio phonograph playing soft music. On the other wall, there was a glass door leading out to a small balcony and I could see city lights winking through the glass. Maria was back again. "My friend who is staying here tonight will do that pressing before she goes to bed. She's much better at that sort of thing than I am." she said.

Well, that took a little of the icing off the cake, knowing we weren't alone, but her friend was going to bed. That was something. Maria explained that her friend stayed with her when she worked late, as she did not want to go the long distance to her own home after dark. It suited Maria, as she did not like sleeping alone in the flat.

This made me smile, because my immediate thought was that I'd be happy to ensure Maria wasn't lonely if her friend wasn't available.

"We don't like to be alone when there are native people around. Just two weeks ago, two men tried to break into the flat while we were here," she added

"But you could call the police," I said.

"Yes, but these are new flats, and the phone isn't connected."

"What about the neighbours?"

"The other flats on this floor aren't rented yet."

By then, Maria's friend had finished pressing the coat, and when I suggested that she join us for a drink, Maria shooed her off to have a bath. I was hers and she was going to look after me by herself.

Maria wanted softer music, and went over to the phonograph to change the record. Her hips moved provocatively in this rose light; or was it the good Scotch whisky taking effect? Life was good and Maria was just the girl to relax with. She was pretty and petite, and she had her flat to herself most of the time. When I put my arm along the back of the couch she laid her head on my arm in the gentlest manner. When she turned her face towards me she yielded ever so gently. The outside world ceased to exist and there were only we two people floating in space.

"John," she murmured, "I want you so much, but don't do that, my friend can walk in any minute and that would be embarrassing."

It was 2 a.m. before I got back to the hotel with a firm invitation from Maria to return to Johannesburg.

The Durban plane left early, and the next morning at 6.30 a.m., I was waiting for the elevator at the hotel. Standing there were two African housemaids, looking rather shy. One had a tray with ten cups and saucers resting on her head. Both her hands were by her sides and she did not even put a hand up to support the tray when the elevator started. "Don't you drop those things?" I asked.

A big smile spread across her face, and she replied quietly, "No Master, we never drop them, we are used to carrying things like this."

It was the first time in my life that anybody had called me "Master," and I wasn't sure that I liked it. I didn't have much time to think about the incident before I was aboard the smaller plane heading for Durban. The stewardess gave instructions in English and Afrikaans, ending up with "Danke." Well, that was one Afrikaans word I wouldn't have to learn. "Thank you" was the same in German.

There was quite a reception for me at Durban. Arch and Dais were there, and after family greetings, Dais turned to introduce me to the rest of my relatives. Uncle Wilhelm stepped forward and with a firm grasp said, "Welcome to South Africa, John, we have been expecting you for a long time." Wilhelm was a medium sized man with a modest tummy, a full head of hair and a small, thin mustache. He seemed genuinely happy to welcome me to his home and country and I was pleased to be there.

My cousins David and Daniel were a little younger than me, and were cheerful, good-looking boys who were both about six feet tall. They wore blue blazers and grey slacks, which were uniform for young European men at that time in South Africa. They had several cars, but Uncle Wilhelm insisted that I go in his new American Ford, which was a large two-tone job. It had plenty of power, and we were soon in the centre of Durban.

We went to the Grand Hotel, where all the waiters were Indians and the potted palms on the open verandah reminded me of the Grand Pacific Hotel in Fiji. I found it difficult to pay attention to the conversation, as I was distracted by an exotic procession of people passing on the street. There were many Africans in European clothing. The European women were well dressed, and many of the young men wore shorts. Finding that shorts were acceptable dress was a relief for me, because they make tropical living much more comfortable. Some of the Indian women were in their saris, many of the Sikh men wore turbans, and the scene was rounded off with the gaily-feathered rickshaw boys going past on the lookout for fares. When they saw a likely customer, they would stop and attract attention by prancing, shaking the rattles that they had around their ankles and rolling their eyes. The occasional young African woman had her hair cropped short and wore a well-cut cotton dress, which showed her figures to best advantage.

I was happy to be with my mother and father in this exciting country. I hoped that we would get along with Wilhelm. Up to now, he had done everything for us and he told us that we were all going back to their farm that evening. He said that he was occupied with extending the landing strip and hanger for his large plane, and my cousins' smaller plane. Once that was accomplished he would be taking us for the trip of our lives.

I noticed that my cousins deferred to their father for every decision. Wilhelm Bohler had built up his farm from nothing. At the age of sixteen, he bought 2,000 acres of rough, un-cleared land. Now he had a rural financial empire, which was admired by all. His word was law on all farm and family matters, so he had the whole package. When it was time to move along from the hotel Wilhelm organized the exodus.

The trip to the farm in Zululand would take two hours. It took only a few minutes to pass through the Indian area of Durban and get onto the narrow road north that headed to Zululand. We were rapidly passing into Shaka territory, where the famous African leader had welded the Zulus into one of the world's greatest fighting forces. The grass was unbelievably green, and the Australian gums trees carried a bloom that I hadn't seen in their native country. Australian koala bears would have enjoyed the conditions in Zululand, except that leopards climb trees to eat their kill (to avoid being disturbed by other predators). In the past this may have been a threat to visiting koalas, but leopards are now rare and only found in National Parks in South Africa.

Sugar cane fields, that covered most of the countryside, began to appear on both sides of the road as we approached the Bohler farm. Wilhelm told me that all of the physical work on the farms was done by Africans. There were some African supervisors and Indians and part-Europeans drove the tractors and did the maintenance work as they were thought to be more suited to working with machinery. The African men traditionally did the heavy work of cutting and stacking the cane, but women were now joining them to do the harder work. Wilhelm volunteered that this was because it was becoming increasingly difficult to get men for the cane cutting, in spite of the high wages being paid.

When we reached the farm, Queen was at the door to meet us, as she had recovered from a migraine she had suffered the previous day. She had been a charming woman in her youth, but her lined face and stressed appearance showed her at a disadvantage beside Dais, whose happy face had not altered in fifteen years. Queen made us welcome in their two storied mansion and settled us down in the sitting room, while she organised the kitchen staff to bring in the tea.

It was not long before a barefoot native boy, 'Old Bill' brought in a silver tea service, and a small Indian girl followed with cups and saucers. Bill was a middle-aged Zulu man, with a family of his own on the reservation, but he would always be referred to as "a boy", while he worked for Europeans. He was deferential, and shook a little as he put the tea service down. When this was done, he lost no time in fleeing to the kitchen. The small Indian girl looked to be ten-years-old, and was dressed in a simple white frock, with her hair in long, neat braids with a small white maid's cap on top. I would have liked to have caught her eye, but she kept looking downwards and scampered off to the kitchen as soon as she had put the cups down.

The room was comfortable, and filled with high quality furniture. Facing me was a portrait of the Duke of Edinburgh, and a bust of Winston Churchill. Even if Wilhelm had feared that he might be taken into custody during WWII, because of his German background, there was no room for doubt about the loyalty of the family now. It was suggested that South Africa was going to become a republic, so the symbols of Empire might yet disappear.

After the first animated discussions about family matters, there was a lull. David and Daniel took me out to the swimming pool, which was set in the large garden and was approached through a framework of climbing roses. A few leaves were floating on the blue water. This upset my cousins, and in the Zulu language they called for the garden boy. He had been standing in the background but now he came trotting forward and picked up the wire netting scoop to take the leaves off the water. He had been there for fifteen years, and having seen the boys grow up he must have known what they were going to say before they even thought it. He lived with his family in a little hut that could be seen poking through the greenery at the bottom of the garden.

The water looked cool and refreshing, and I looked forward to using it while I was on the farm. Past the pool there was a tennis court where I could play with my cousins, whenever they were free. They were both good players, and I looked forward to many grim struggles. Life promised to be good in Zululand, in this grand house with a swimming pool, tennis court and hot and cold running servants.

All the men were up at 4.15 the next morning. Uncle Wilhelm was always up first, and made the tea. I came down next, and the two boys drifted down in various stages of wakefulness after me. They had set me up with a shirt and shorts, and this morning I was to see how the farm operated. Uncle Wilhelm went off alone to the aircraft hangar that he was having built, and my cousins visibly relaxed as he went out of the door. They explained that the work-boys would have been wakened by the estate policeman, and be waiting outside for their task for the day. Each of my cousins would have to go out with separate groups and see them begin their work. There would not be horses for all of us, but David said that I could have his and he would get around in the light truck.

Waiting at the front gate were two large boxer dogs, which bounced up to me and cavorted around my feet. They belonged to David and Daniel, and had been tied at the front gate as watchdogs.

I had not had time to appreciate the beautiful rose garden the previous evening. There were masses of roses of all colours and descriptions, and the whole thing seemed to cover half an acre. Already, at 5 a.m., a garden boy was on his knees, hard at work weeding under the tall standard roses.

A crowd of fifty or sixty natives was waiting for us. I noticed, with a start, that there were women and children mixed in with the group. I had been told that the women cut cane but it had not really registered. Many of the children seemed to be no more than six or seven-years-old. Some of them only wore a jute sack which had holes cut for the neck and arms, and some of the women were wearing clothes that were little better than the sacks worn by the children. None of them made eye contact and all cast their eyes to the ground whenever I looked at them.

With the help of the head boy, the Africans were being divided up into groups to go out to the fields. The children carried hoes for the weeding and the men and women carried cane slashers or hoes. Most of the adult men and older women were cane cutters. They went out in two groups to the fields, where the mature cane was to be cut and stacked in heaps. The children and younger women were weeders, and it was their job to do a certain amount of weeding in the young cane. They put their hoes on their shoulders, and were sent off to their tasks at the other end of the estate.

As we went to get the horses, we passed the shed that housed the tractors. Several Indians and 'Coloureds,' were getting some of the dozen tractors started up for the day's work. Coloureds, was the name given to people who were part European and part black. Both the Indians and Coloured people had a little more education than the blacks so the Europeans gave them more responsibility. With this responsibility came a higher wage so they were suspended between the elite Europeans and the Black people in South African apartheid society. The Black people worked very hard in poor conditions for low wages. The Indians and Coloureds were not as regimented as the Africans and were mostly allowed to carry on with their work independently.

The horses were standing ready and saddled, each with an

African groomsman at their head. The horses were in good condition, as everything here was the best that money could buy. My cousins took great pleasure in showing me their vast acreage. There was 1,500 acres under cultivation, but it seemed even bigger than that. Most of the land was under sugarcane, and the rest sown with grass, to provide pasture for the working bullocks and cows.

The strings of working oxen were especially useful for dragging heavily laden cane wagons out of swampy ground, where tractors could not get a firm grip. The oxen were the South African type, which have the hump above their shoulders, a characteristic seen in cattle from the north. Their great chests and wide horns gave them a noble appearance, as they plodded patiently along in their yokes.

By now we had caught up with the first group of Africans, who were standing waiting in a cane field. The cane plants had been sown in rows three feet apart, and it was the job of the weeders to hoe the weeds from between the rows. If this was not done the weeds hindered the growth of the young cane plants. Each woman and child was given a length of row to clear of weeds. That would be their task for the day. My two cousins went up and down the rows giving each worker a task. They seemed to know most of their labourers by name and when they called, the person stepped forward and came to stand by his row.

It was sad to see the little ones come forward to have their rows allotted. The hoes were heavy and it was going to be hot under the summer sun while they worked away for six or seven hours. A jute sack can't be the coolest thing to work in under the harsh African sun. An adult African man was left in charge of the group, and we rode on over a small hill where the cutters were already hard at work. The cutters worked in two groups. Each member of the first group had a quota of cane to cut before they went home for the day. If a man or woman did their quota in four hours, they went off home. The second group consisted entirely of adult men and they worked on a different system. The whole group had a quota, and they worked until it was cut. It seemed to me that the first system of individual quotas was the fairest, but my cousins assured me that the natives preferred the group quota system. Although it obviously put the slacker at an advantage over his more conscientious work mates, they still preferred to work as a team.

It was hard work cutting the cane. The mature stalk is two inches thick at the tough fibrous base, and is slashed through with a stroke of the heavy razor-sharp cane machetes. The ten-foot stalk is then turned upside down while the leaves at the top are cut away with another stroke. A few more cuts with the knife and the tough stalk of cane is stripped bare and ready to be thrown on a neat heap behind the workers. It was heavy labour and soon the sweat was beginning to pour down the black backs of the well-muscled men.

One of the boys had a brass plate on an armband with, "Wilhelm Bohler and Sons," marked in large letters on it. He was the boss boy for the whole farm, and his was a strictly supervisory job. The bicycle lying at the back was his, and marked him out as a man of rank among the Africans. He looked to be a wise old man, and my cousins told me that he'd been their 'nurse boy' when they were young. He had seen them through their teething troubles and tantrums, and had kept them from falling into the swimming pool. Now, twenty years later he was still their servant and called "boy".

Most of the harvesting of the sugarcane in South Africa was done by hand, while in some other countries machines did it. When I asked my cousins about this, they said that in other countries the cane was burned off to remove the leaves, and then machines cut the stalks. However on their plantation, the leaves that were cut off were left to lie one foot deep over the soil. This hindered the weed growth and then rotted to make a valuable fertilizer. Despite this strategy, the estate expense for chemical fertilizers was more than the entire cost of labour.

The countryside we rode through on our way back to the house for breakfast was beautiful. As we passed the front gate, we picked up the morning paper, which had been left in the mailbox. Wilhelm was waiting for us in the sitting room.

"Well John, how did you like your first visit to an African farm?" he asked.

"I liked it very much. I think you have a good farm and a good life here."

"We do have a good farm. It is probably the best in the district, and we don't want for much."

Wilhelm had to go back to the aircraft hanger, and left me with Daniel.

"But tell me about the labour; how much do you pay the weeders?" I asked him.

"Well John, they don't work by the hour and they get free board and lodging you know."

"Do the young ones live with their parents?"

"No. In most cases their mother is living on the reserve while the father is out working. He may have a job in town where he gets a higher wage and has to keep himself, or he can work for a farmer, where his wage is not so high but he gets free bed and board."

"But how much do you pay the little ones?"

"The children are called umphans. As I said, they get food and shelter but they have to complete thirty days labour before they get paid. With Sundays off, and the odd wet day when they do not work, this takes them between five and six weeks."

"And what do they receive then?" I asked.

"The umphans only get three dollars a month. Sometimes their mothers come along and pick up their pay and don't give them anything at all."

"Three dollars doesn't seem much."

"No, it doesn't seem much to you, but it means a lot to a native."

"What about the older men and women?"

"We have just raised their wages again. You know they're getting so spoilt with the big wages being offered in the factories that they won't come to work on the farms anymore. We have just put their wages up to fourteen dollars a month, and still we can't get enough workers. We are employing women in the cane cutting this year as you can see, but I doubt that we will get in all the cane that is ready to be cut."

"What will happen to all the cane that is not cut then?"

"It will be alright. We just leave it until next year."

"So raising the wages didn't help?"

"Last year they only got eleven dollars a month and the year previously, only eight dollars, but money means nothing to a native. As soon as he has enough to live on for six months he goes back to the kraal, and sits around and drinks native beer in the sun. The women do all the work there you know."

David had been listening to Daniel and now joined in and supported his brother's perspective. "I used to feel sorry for them when I first returned from college but now I have come around to my father's point of view. There is no gratitude in a native. The harder you are on them the more they respect you."

David was good looking and charming, and it was obvious he believed the things he was saying. However, more important matters distracted him.

"Well, I am starving, and I see that Old Bill has just put out our breakfast."

Old Bill was dressed in his best white uniform in my honour, and he kept padding around in his bare feet, bringing in course after course. These young South Africans ate a large breakfast, and after three hours in the saddle I found no difficulty in doing the same, easily demolishing the cereal, bacon and eggs and toast and jam. If at any time there was an interruption in the flow of food one of the lads had only to shout, "Bill! Bill," and Old Bill would come pattering in with a scared look on his face. A few rapid words in Zulu and the missing supplies appeared. Bill had been with the family for ten years, and he had just come back after four months at the kraal. If they did not return to their family on the reservation they lost their rights to live there and would have nowhere to go in their old age.

My cousins assured me that Old Bill was a rich man now. He had several cattle on the reserve, and last year he had asked their father to look after thirty dollars for him. It was very important to my cousins that Bill had enough confidence in their father to entrust his money to him. David had to go off and do some office work, but before he left he said to me, "Take my racket and go on down to the court. One of the lads will give you a game. You can have a plunge in the swimming pool when you're finished."

This was the life that I had been assured would be mine when I came to South Africa; a beautiful climate and tennis court with partners on-tap was luxury indeed.

All through school, my mother had told me about the good life of our millionaire relatives in South Africa, and we were here at last! Arch and Dais would be coming down for breakfast soon and I would find out if they had made any plans for the day. I knew that I was lucky to be here, but I was vaguely uneasy about the whole set up. Perhaps this feeling would pass when I had time to settle in and got to know my cousins better.

Arch and Dais were having breakfast on the shady terrace when my cousins came in from their morning swim. Queen was the gracious hostess, and was more relaxed now that Uncle Wilhelm was away working on his new airplane hangar. Dais called out, "Come on lads, have a cup of tea with us now." And one of them replied, "We will if we can join in the food. Swimming in the morning makes us hungry."

Thirty years previously, Dais and Queen would never have thought that life could be like this. Back then it had been a matter of existing on my grandfather's modest wages. This sort of affluent world, where there was a pool at the backdoor and a half-acre of rose gardens at the front, would have been beyond their wildest dreams. Queen must have anticipated a good way of life with the prospect of marrying Wilhelm, with his large farm and affluence. I have told you about their life in Kurow and this marriage would have been her big chance to move up the social ladder and enjoy a high standard of living. I don't know if Queen had fallen in love with Wilhelm or not. My guess is that she knew that many happy marriages were based on understanding and tact, and hers could be too. If it seemed too good to be true, Queen was soon to find out that it was. Queen hadn't been aware of Wilhelm's dominating and mean nature, as he had wisely kept it hidden during their engagement. Wilhelm had to be the leader in everything. Wilhelm needed to control the farm and all it contained and as the natives were submissive to Europeans it was easy to dominate them. In his quest for overall power, Wilhelm gave loans to his family and acquaintances as soon as he had enough capital to do so. He wanted more than the interest though; he wanted power over the debtor.

One of Wilhelm's brothers had paid his debt in full fifteen years previously, and still disliked him so much he refused to talk to him.

Queen was a bright girl, and in the early marital years found her subjugation intolerable. Queen told Dais that she knew in the first year of her marriage that she had made a mistake. She had miscarried twins, and when referring to this sad time said, "I should have left him then Dais."

Later on Queen had David and then Daniel. While Queen could have almost any material thing that she wanted, she was never allowed to have any money in her handbag. On the many occasions she thought of leaving, she didn't have money for her return fare to New Zealand. I'm sure Wilhelm kept her without money so she could not escape from the farm with her sons. Even her engagement ring was part of his estate. At first she stood up for a few things but gradually, and irrevocably, Wilhelm wore down her resistance and her spirit. His financial situation was impregnable, and Queen had no chance of independence or equality. Wilhelm had the farm, he was in his own country and knew Afrikaans, English, German and Zulu. Even when she wanted to take her sons to New Zealand, she knew it was impossible. I suppose that the boys did not have passports and if they did, Wilhelm would have them and ensure that they didn't get out of the country without his approval. Queen was well dressed and materially well off but was in a prison without bars. She must have looked back at the Kurow desert with nostalgia. There life was not so comfortable but it must have been better than this.

Queen, despite her unhappiness, remained tall, slim and good looking, and was a valuable social asset to her husband. He used Queen as his entry into the English side of the Zululand social scene, and over time lost his Afrikaans accent and adopted an English one.

In New Zealand, Queen had been tops in the final nursing

examination, so she must have been in the upper 5% for intelligence. When she decided to quit Kurow, she said, "You stay at home, Dais, and look after the family and the house. I can make enough money for both of us." Dais was stuck with living in Kurow to look after Pampa Joe and her brother Jack. Later on, when Queen had married into this affluence she never did send money back to support those remaining in Kurow. It was now obvious to Dais the reason why Queen never sent any back, despite living amongst great wealth. Even when they had a cup of tea in town, Queen would say "You can pay Dais" as she never had money in her purse or had her own bank account.

What is the good of a bright mind and a beautiful body if you are basically selfish and desert your family when they need you?

Money had not brought Queen happiness or good health. Dais, the less advantaged of the two, had found reasonable happiness in Kurow. Although she was seriously overweight, her face was relaxed and she was forever telling jokes and could see the bright side of life. Queen, in comparison, was thinner but strained, with increasing hypertension, asthma, anxiety and depression. She had escaped the poverty and desolation of Kurow, and ended up in a place that should have been Eden. Queen must have had a thousand regrets about deserting Dais in Kurow.

If Queen and Dais were sitting talking while Wilhelm was away building, Queen was moderately relaxed. As soon as she heard Wilhelm's car that would change, and she felt obliged to jump up and pretend to be busy. There seemed to be plenty of servants around so it must have been hard for her to find the little jobs that she needed to show how busy she was. Perhaps there was some chance for change now, as Queen had some members of her family around her for the first time in her married life. She assured Dais that she would make a stand against Wilhelm's domination. Her spontaneity and joy for living was gone and her health was plagued by bouts of migraine and asthma. I was sure that Queen's headaches were caused by the unhappiness in her life, but I doubted that her sons recognised this. Wilhelm's crushing dominance of her often caused her to retire to bed with a migraine. Then Wilhelm and my cousins would move into a solicitous mode; anything that Queen wanted, in the way of food and medicine, were obtained quickly from the town. Her meals were attractively arranged and taken to her by a servant, with one of her sons in attendance. While everyone awaited her recovery, Queen was given her rightful place at the centre of the family.

We kept waiting for Queen to take a stand against Wilhelm. As the days went on it was obvious that nothing was going to happen, so we had to make the best of life on the farm while we waited for a vehicle to manifest.

At lunchtime on the next day, the atmosphere was grim. It seemed that Old Bill had been on the booze. He had taken his weekly ration of Kaffir beer, and instead of drinking the partly fermented cereal right away; he had added sugar and let it re-ferment. This treatment increased the alcoholic content and really gave it some hitting power. Old Bill was so pie-eyed in the morning that he started the day by chasing one of the young Indian girls around the kitchen with obvious amorous intent. When he was out of breath from this exercise, he knocked over one of the Doulton serving dishes, and it had smashed into a hundred little pieces on the floor.

Wilhelm picked this minute to walk into the kitchen. With one sweep of his eyes he had taken in the panting girl, the broken dish and Old Bill's fumbling movements. It was too bad for Old Bill. My cousins had not taken the sjambok so it was still hanging on the wall in the kitchen. In a few strides Wilhelm had the sjambok and soon it was biting into Old Bill's back. Bill did not try to do anything to defend himself, as he well knew that the police were not at all lenient on a native who hit a European. It amazed me that an adult man could take to another with a sjambok like that, but it did not seem to surprise or concern my cousins. If their father chose to beat a black servant that was accepted as being in the natural order of things. After all, Old Bill had broken the rules; he'd got himself drunk and chased the Indian girl, so what would you expect?

Just three weeks previously, Daniel had been downtown, and after drinking for a couple of hours at the hotel had run his car into the side of the garage. Like Old Bill he could not do his work properly the next morning. It was fortunate that he avoided getting the sjambok across his back. Wilhelm would not want the local people to know that he had beaten Daniel because it would sully the family reputation. As Daniel was two inches taller than his father he might have resisted a beating at this age, but being so dominated by Wilhelm that wouldn't be a sure bet.

On one of the early morning rides, David repeated his views on the natives to me. "When I first returned from school I used to feel sorry for the natives, but I've got over that. They are dirty and ungrateful you know."

"How do you mean ungrateful?"

"Well for example, we give them an extra ration of food and beer at Christmas time. They usually get a ration of sugar, 'mealies' or Kaffir corn, and meat each week. This time we doubled their ration and gave each worker a present of cloth."

"They were pleased?"

"Not only did not one of them thank us, but several of them actually came back to ask for more food!"

He was getting wound up now.

"The more one gives them, the more they expect. You should go and see how they live in their kraals. They have a hut on a dry hillside and nothing else yet when they come to work for us they want the world."

"But why don't they stay on the reservation and make their living from farming?"

"Some do, but the great majority can't stay on the land because it is worked out. They overstocked it with useless cattle for generations, and now the light soil will not support them. The soil has given up the unequal struggle and is washing down into the rivers every time there is a fair-sized rainfall."

"Can't the government do something about the over stocking?"

"Yes, they try but the native is unwilling to kill one of his animals even for what little food it will give him. You see, his wealth is counted by the number of beasts that he owns. The quality of the stock is not important and he keeps as many weedy animals as possible."

"Why do they place such a high value on the number of animals?"

"I suppose the main reason is the labola or bride price. You know that when a young man wishes to marry, he must present six to ten oxen to his prospective father-in-law. He will then be allowed to get married."

"It must pay to have plenty of daughters then?"

"Perhaps. But the obligation is not finished there. The labola acts as a sort of balance, and even insurance."

"I'm afraid I'm not with you any more,"

"Well, if the bride leaves and goes back to her family, her father is under an obligation to return the labola to the husband."

"So this means the daughters are encouraged to return to their husbands so the father can retain the labola?"

"Yes, but if the husband dies then the widow can return to her father's kraal with her children. The father will then support her and if she has sons, will help them with their labola when their time comes to marry."

"So they had this form of social insurance before the Europeans began restricting them to reserves?"

"Yes, a government commission sat on the subject, and recommended strongly that the custom of giving and taking labola be continued."

"I suppose that many of the young men working here are getting enough money for their labola?"

"True enough, but as soon as they get enough they disappear for a while."

"Do they return after that?"

"Well, of course they have to. The soil on their reservations won't support them. I'm afraid that if the reservations could support the people then we wouldn't get many labourers. The men are fundamentally lazy and would rather sit in the door of the hut, drink beer and let their wives till the land."

I knew that at one time the Zulus ruled Natal and north to Rhodesia, so had unlimited fertile land, so commented, "It must have been different in the old days when the Zulus overran this whole area."

"The men have always been the warriors, and most of the hard work on the farms has been left to the women and girls. In the time of Shaka, the great Zulu warrior King, the men were organised into battalions and did no agricultural work. They spent their time drilling behind their magnificent ox hide shields and practicing that iron discipline that made them practically invincible in the wars of the time."

"I suppose that the rifles beat them in the end."

"Yes, but even then they were worthy opponents. Just a short way from here Colonel Durnford's central column was attacked by 10,000 Zulus, and virtually wiped out. That was in 1879, and as late as 1907, a military force had to be sent into Zululand to stop the murder of Europeans and put down the unrest."

"Aren't you afraid that they will rise again?"

"There is always that possibility, we have to admit, but with the present government in power it's unlikely. They are under a hard hold."

"I understand that the South African Government can use machine guns and bomber planes if the time comes. Do you think that would stop the natives?"

"I am sure that nothing would stop them if they organised. Our main strength is the fact that they find it difficult to unite. Most of the tribes dislike and distrust each other more than they dislike the Europeans. In fact, they would be at each other's throats if it were not for our police. Even now you will read in the paper of factional fights with loss of life before the police arrive."

"Will they organise?"

"I can't see them organising themselves, but they may be organised from outside. For example, in the Mau Mau areas of East Africa, the natives there were being supplied with guns by the Indians."

"Do you think it will come in your lifetime?"

"I don't know, but we have certain safeguards against this, which you'll learn about later. Why don't you go into the house and tell Old Bill to organise some tea? I'll be back in ten minutes when I've checked on some of the boys working on a tractor." With that, another of my many fact-finding conversations ended. I was still trying to get my mind around the situation in South Africa. I felt the potential pulsing power of the black people and wondered how long the police could keep it suppressed.

Wilhelm was being good to us. His sons could not remember when he had shown such generosity to previous visitors. Of course, there had not been many visitors before because Wilhelm was not the most popular person in the area. My cousins said that while we were visiting the quality of the food on the table had improved. Wilhelm took us out in the car whenever he had time, which was a mixed blessing as he was a fast driver but not a good one. He had almost run down a native on the road on more than one occasion. He seemed to hate the natives who dared to walk on the public highway. If a European ran down and killed a native child there wasn't too much fuss. Perhaps a ten-pound fine would finish the matter. I'm finding that I am using dollars and pounds interchangeably, so wonder if they were near par with each other in those days.

Wilhelm had told us that when he had finished his new airplane hangar, he would be free to drive us around the National Parks. My father had heard of Wilhelm's driving marathons, and having already experienced his driving on several occasions was not thrilled with the impending prospect of accompanying him on a race with death. We knew that it would put a strain on family relations if we refused, so were not too concerned about him making good with his invitation.

The Bohler family had been to New Zealand when my cousins were infants, and Arch had lent him our single seater Essex. With Pampa Joe accompanying Wilhelm as his passenger and guide, they had left Kurow and taken off through the Central South Island. The roads were rough in those days, and when Pampa Joe returned he said that the car had been airborne half of the time. Our family car never seemed to recover from the treatment it received on that trip, and after Wilhelm returned, it coughed and spluttered its way to an early grave.

We had been told we would have the use of a car when the

invitation to visit South Africa was given, but it became obvious that Wilhelm was not prepared to reciprocate and lend us one of his bigger cars. We thought we could perhaps go off in Daniel's car on our own, but unfortunately it was in the garage having something mysterious done to the engine, so wasn't available. Apparently it wasn't a life threatening ailment, but the car needed some sort of minor operation to restore it to full health. Daniel was always muttering about cylinder heads and piston rods, so it looked like we would not be able to get the car for at least two more weeks.

That evening my cousins decided to go off to the nearby town and take in a movie. I had seen it before so stayed at home with my parents and Wilhelm and Queen. The two sisters were filling in the time playing a few hands of cards, and we were having a drink; all together, one of the most pleasant nights that we had had on the farm. Wilhelm was even relaxing a little. He was asking me about my recent visit to England, when suddenly the atmosphere froze.

"The police whistle!" Yes, there it was again, three piercing blasts from the farm policeman! Wilhelm had a startled expression, and then something like fear came over his face. I did not know what was happening, but as the boys were not here it was up to me to go out with Wilhelm to find out what the problem was. At the front door, Wilhelm picked up a heavy stick.

It was dark besides the rose garden and even darker inside the compound where the natives lived. I was hoping there was nobody waiting for us, but in my anxious state I imagined a dark body crouching behind each rose bush. It was quiet in the compound now, just a few native men and women standing around in the poor light. In response to Wilhelm's rapid flow of Zulu, they nodded their heads towards one of the doors.

One small electric light emphasised the darkness of the long room. Beds, if you could call these concrete block platforms beds, were arranged along one wall and a fire flickered in an open fireplace at the far end. Standing in the half-light of the fire were two men. They stood quietly now, and at their feet were two cane knives. One man had a tourniquet twisted around his wrist but it didn't seem to be doing much good at stemming the flow of blood from his hand, as there was a large pool of blood at his feet. He also had a cut about three-inches long on his chest, but it had almost stopped bleeding. I told them to take off the tourniquet, as it was not tight enough and was only making the bleeding worse.

"Just leave it alone and the bleeding will stop by itself soon."

I was on my own ground now and felt good to be able to help around the place at last.

"Bring the other man over to the fire and let's have a look at him." It was easy to see that he had a scalp cut, as there was plenty of clotted blood mixed up with the short curly hairs of his scalp. When I pulled the wound apart I saw that the cane knife had cut through to the bone. It looked as if it might have gone through the bone but I remembered that I'd been told at medical school that the bone of a Negro's skull was thicker than that of a European. Nowadays that's known to be untrue, but it was an urban myth at the time. It could be that the cane knife had actually penetrated to the brain. Wilhelm had recovered himself enough to resume control of the situation. After all, it was his farm and these were HIS boys.

"These damn boys drinking and fighting again! They annoy me. I have a good mind to leave them until the morning!"

I could see that Wilhelm was excited, and annoyed, but didn't say anything, hoping he would cool down. But no, he repeated himself

"I have a good mind to leave them until the morning."

I realised that he meant it, and had to intercede. "Well, Wilhelm, I certainly don't mind staying up for a couple of hours to stitch them up."

"Yes, but these damn boys have done this before. I have a good mind to leave them until morning,"

"Look, if this boy with the cut hand is left it could well get infected and he won't be back at work for months. Even with the best of care it looks as if he will be off for weeks."

That rang a bell somewhere in Wilhelm's mind and he said. "Lets take them into the house, or rather, the policeman will bring them along. We can go on ahead." He said stomping off towards the big house.

As soon as we returned a whirr of activity ensued. Queen shot off to get the water boiling and look after the needles, nylon and bandages. Dais joined in the womanly services of tending the sick and Arch decided that it was time that he went off to bed. He said that he had had a long day, and the African sun made him tired – more likely that he realised there was nothing he could do and he had had enough.

When everything was ready the first boy was called in. His finger was really in a mess, with all the soft tissue on one side removed, and the chest laceration went down to the rib cartilages. It was routine work for me, and when it was underway Wilhelm joined in and was very helpful.

When I showed just how deep the chest wound was, Wilhelm turned pale and Queen helped him out of the kitchen. Well, I didn't really need any help anyway and the patient was sitting quietly. True, he winced a little each time the thick needle bit into his chest but it should not have hurt too much as the wound was fresh and he was still partly anaesthetised from the Kaffir beer that they had been drinking.

Just as the first boy had been cleaned up, my cousins came bounding in.

"We saw a light in the office. What is the matter?" Daniel asked.

Now the second boy with the head wound had taken his seat and both cousins came to examine the wound with me. While I went on with the washing and cleaning, they fired a barrage of questions in Zulu at the poor man. When he moved a little they told him to sit still. I made the mistake of showing the lads just how deep the cane knife had cut onto the bone. David excused himself and went off to join his father in the dining room, and Daniel followed after another peek at the wound.

The patient was still obviously nervous, but relaxed a little once my uncle and cousins had left the scene. When it was all over, he managed a small grin in response to my smile.

When the wounded men had been sent back to their quarters, Queen made a cup of tea for the family and we sat around drinking it. It was almost midnight by then, and I was feeling some fatigue and strain myself. Wilhelm was not as authoritative as he usually was, as he had almost passed out in the kitchen. I thought this would be a good time to talk about the after-treatment for the two injured workmen.

"Wilhelm, both of those boys will need some penicillin to guard against infection. If either of them get infected it could be serious."

"I will run down myself in the morning to see the district surgeon. His office opens at 9.00 in the morning," he replied.

"If you give me one of the trucks I could do it. It would be a good opportunity to meet him anyhow," I suggested, hoping for an independent trip to town. Unfortunately Wilhelm was adamant,

"No, I will do it myself. Just penicillin you think?"

"Well, see what the district surgeon says, as I think they could do with some anti-tetanus serum too."

I got up for breakfast at 8.30 the next morning, but Wilhelm had loaded the two boys aboard one of the light trucks and had taken them off to town. I was disappointed to miss meeting the district surgeon after staying up stitching for two hours the previous evening, but after all it was Wilhelm's farm and there would possibly be other occasions to meet the doctor.

While the family was having breakfast, Wilhelm arrived back from town, full of good humour.

"The surgeon thought that you'd done a good job."

"Did he take off the bandages?"

"No, but he had a look at the outside and gave them the penicillin."

"I'll have a look at the wounds in four days. Try and persuade them to leave the bandages on until then. It is better if they're not opened as it only allows infection to get in if they're uncovered" was my follow up advice, and he seemed satisfied with that.

I still wondered why Wilhelm didn't take me with the injured workers, but I soon forgot this, as I was soon to go to town with David in the truck, to pick up money to pay the workers their wages. We set off for town on the narrow road in a cloud of dust with the speedometer touching seventy. I asked David to slow down. Fortunately he took this with the greatest good humour, and we dropped back to a more moderate fifty miles an hour.

"Don't worry, John, wait till we get you up in the air. Then we'll show you something" he said laughing.

At the next bend a heavy cane truck had swung out wide and bore down on us. It looked as if we were going to crash but at the last minute the driver of the truck saw us and swerved back to his own side of the road. David and I took a second to recover our breath and then he started, "Did you see that bloody Indian? He was asleep! I feel like going back after the bastard and showing him how to drive."

There was no suggestion of David taking any responsibility for our near miss. He said that the local trucking firm was owned by Halliburton. David said, "Halliburton wouldn't like us to touch one of his drivers, so I'll ring him up as soon as we get home and he can deal with the driver himself."

David went on, "The Indians have beaten all the European traders in the smaller towns around here, and now they are trying to push us off the roads! If they see that you are likely to be in the wrong, they will go ahead and have an accident even if they could have avoided it. Never trust an Indian."

Once we arrived in town, David let me take the truck to inspect the new hospital that was being built for the district. It was a magnificent new concrete structure, and one of the foremen showed me over the site. There would be wards for the Europeans and separate accommodation for the Indians and the natives. When I had finished and pulled up outside the bank, David was waiting. There was something wrong.

"Oh John, I forgot the cheque. It's lying on the desk at home."

"Well, can't you write another one?"

"No, it takes three signatures on each of the cheques from the common account."

"Well, write a cheque on your personal account."

"I have tried that but my account is with a bank in Durban. They won't cash them here. The men expect to get their wages today, but now they will just have to wait."

It seemed to me that there must be some way to get the cash. "Couldn't you go back and get the cheque?"

"Well, we could, but Dad will be rip-roaring mad about doing the long trip to town twice. He will be mad enough as it is that I've forgotten it." The discussion went on and on, but David seemed unable to handle the situation and could not to solve this problem without his father to tell him what to do. It was obvious that he didn't want to upset Wilhelm. I tried to get him to go in and see the Bank Manager again. There must have been some way to get the money out. After all, there was plenty of money in the account. It seemed that it was easier to put money into a bank than to withdraw it. But it appeared that we could do nothing more, so we decided to go off to the local tearooms for a cup of tea before returning to the estate.

We met another young European man in the tearoom and settled into conversation. It seemed that once the young white people who lived on the estates had got the boys started on the cane cutting in the morning, they had only to do a few administrative jobs and had the rest of the day free. We took our time getting home, and I never did find out the solution they found for the problem of paying the workers.

When we returned to the farm we found that the man with the cane knife cut to his hand had returned to have his bandage changed. He said that it was pulling on the raw area and was painful. I felt that it would be better left, but also was concerned that if I didn't change it the man would take it off himself. It would be better for me to take it off in the relative cleanliness of the kitchen, than him removing it in the compound dormitory.

Both the wound on the hand and the chest cut were still as clean as they could possibly be, so that was good to see. In two more days the stitches could come out. The patient was no trouble at all and managed a little smile now. Wilhelm was pleased when I reported the progress, "That's good. The other one with the head injury wanted to do some work this morning. The lads didn't let him go back to work cutting cane, but he's out with the weeders."

"Does he have to go back to work so soon?" I asked.

"He has to pay for the penicillin. That will cost them one pound each."

"That seems a bit high for penicillin," I said.

"That's what the doctor charges them. We pay him of course but we take it off the men's wages at the end of the month."

"But one pound is as much as they earn in a week."

I was upset about this, but also aware of the usual response from the European South Africans when I questioned their attitudes or ways: "People from overseas shouldn't come here and tell us how to run our country. They shouldn't comment unless they have been here ten years and can speak Afrikaans." That stock-standard reply always put me on my back foot, as I was not ambitious to learn Afrikaans and I doubted that I could tolerate being there for ten years

Wilhelm was being instructive now. "You have to be firm with them. If you aren't they will be at this kind of thing all the time."

It didn't look as if these two boys would have much to send home to their families that pay day. A week's wage for a single shot of penicillin, and they had to pay for the cotton gauze and bandages. They would have no wages for a month. I never did find out if they were saving for labola, or if they were supporting a wife and children on a reservation, but this incident would put their savings plan back. As soon as I had taken their stitches out and found the wounds clean they disappeared from my care. I thought I would have seen them again, but one morning Wilhelm reported that they were both doing well, adding that he had done their dressings himself. He had taken over their medical care. They were his boys and it was up to him to decide if they needed further medical attention.

Usually I had nothing to do all day, and this left me feeling a little ornamental. I had been asked to take one of the light trucks and get a load of gravel for the new hangar, but two boys had come along to do the work and it had been all over in half an hour. As my cousins were up at 4.30 each morning they disappeared for an hour's sleep at lunchtime. Dais was happy to be able to spend time with Queen, but Arch was bored and hoped that we could move on soon. I was able to swim during the day and play tennis with my cousins in the evenings, so I did have some activities to fill my day and life wasn't all bad.

I was looking to take a break from the Bohler family, when I saw a trip advertised by Jeep transport into the highlands of Basutoland. It ascended over a partly formed road into the remote heart of this British colony set in the middle of the Union of South Africa.

I rang to enquire about the Basutoland trip and the phone was answered by a pleasant sounding European woman. She told me that her husband Edwin James, owned and drove a Jeep service which ascended a partially built road into the mountains of Basutoland. I would be the only European passenger but I must be prepared for an adventure. She would meet me at the bus stop and deliver me onto the Jeep for a perilous ascent into Basutoland.

Daniels's car was still not ready and this would be a fine opportunity to do something while waiting for it. In the meantime, my father was occupying himself with the local lawn bowling club, and Dais had a thousand things to do with Queen in the kitchen and sewing room. Their latest project was to make a windsock for Wilhelm's flying field. It was going to be ten feet long and when I suggested that they embellish it with the Bohler Baronial Crest Wilhelm was decidedly not amused.

It seemed they were barons and lived like barons, but they did not have a crest. I thought that could be easily remedied. Perhaps they could get one from the College of Heralds in London, if the Berlin office was closed after the WWII bombings.

As each Sunday came along Dais was distressed to know that Queen went off, with her family, to the local Anglican Church. She had explained to Dais that for the sake of family unity she had abandoned her Catholic faith and went with Wilhelm and the boys to the Church of England. After all, Wilhelm had been brought up a Lutheran and they had compromised on Anglicanism.

The Catholic priests were obligated to tell Dais that Queen, by abandoning Catholicism, was destined for Hell. As Hell is eternal, Queen could not get time off for the hell that Wilhelm was giving her in the here and now. This was just awful for Dais; her mother had died young, her brother Jack had suicided, and Pampa Joe had also died and now she knew that her sister was damned. While Arch was as sympathetic as he could be he wasn't a Catholic, so could not fully understand Dais's conflict and depth of despair surrounding this issue. While I had not told Dais that I was a bit loose in my Catholic socket, as I was aware that this would be extremely upsetting for her, she must have suspected it.

Wilhelm was a member of the governing body of the Anglican Church and had donated most of the money needed for the church organ. Just two months before, he and the other Church Elders decided that they would not take communion at the altar rails if there were Indians there. The priest had been a missionary and he wanted to let the Indians converts come to church with the Europeans. Wilhelm and the others had put their foot down on this idea. The Indians probably had some right to come to church, but not at the same time as the masters. If you let them come to the church with you they would want to come into your house next! One had to maintain certain standards in this life, if the whole thing wasn't going to rack and ruin. The elders had asked each other, "Would you shake hands with an Indian?" When the answer came back, "No", they elected to keep the status quo and the Indians had to be kept in their designated place.

I was not too displeased that David's car was still not repaired because although it consigned Arch and Dais to be restricted on the Bohler estate, I was free to go on my Basutoland trip.

CHAPTER 13

Swaziland and Basuto Land
December 1955 - 8 January 1956

INTRODUCED CHARACTERS

EDWIN JAMES, the owner and driver of the Jeep service to Mokhotlong in Basutoland.
MRS. BETTY JAMES, Edwin's European wife.
OLD NANNY, who looked after the James' child.
RESIDENT COMMISSIONER AND HIS WIFE, residing in Mokhotlong.
THE SECRETARY OF THE LOCAL COOPERATIVE in Mokhotlong.
A LOCAL CHIEF from Basutoland.
DOCTOR VAN DYCK, A doctor in Germania who employed me as a locum
MRS. VAN DYCK, his wife.
TWO YOUNG ZULU MAIDS, working in the van Dyck household.
DR. EYCK, an Afrikaner doctor who was Dr. van Dyck's partner.
JESS and GEORGE, two native medical assistants working with Dr. Eyck.

IT TOOK TWO DAYS OF INTERRUPTED TRAVEL FOR me to get to Hiemieville on the Natal-Basutoland border. This tiny town could have been the setting for a Western movie. All was quiet on the main street which was lined with false fronted buildings with dozens of small horses tied to hitching rails. The only movement was the occasional flick of a horse's tail as it sent a fly on its way. As I stepped down from the bus, a pleasant, mid-thirties European woman was waiting for me.

"Well, I presume that you're Dr. Valentine. I'm Mrs. James, but please call me Betty. As Edwin is still up the mountain, I'm going to take you to the first depot in our car." She noticed me looking at the little run down French vehicle. "I hope you don't mind riding in this. It doesn't look very good but it'll get us there; I use it all the time." Betty started loading supplies into the car and I helped her with a small sack of potatoes and her three year old son.

"You stay at a rest house up there and have to do most of your own cooking. I hope that you like canned sausages." she ventured, as we loaded the supplies.

"I eat anything when I'm hungry." I assured her.

"Well that's good, because you'll be hungry by the time you end the day's travel. It's an eight and a half hour trip over the worst road in the world. Edwin and the native driver have been taking a little longer over the last few days because the road is very slippery from the recent rains."

"I have ridden on rough roads before."

"Not as rough as this one you haven't. One of the three Jeeps always seems to be broken down from the continuous jolting. Now, we'll have to hurry as Edwin told me that he'd be back at the depot at 1.30 and it's 12.30 now." The baby, potatoes and Betty James were now installed in the car, so I jumped into the front seat and slammed the door. The handle fell off.

"Don't worry about that. Edwin's going to fix it when he has time. Just stick the handle back into position and it'll stay there. Next time, don't use the handle to slam the door". After this reassuring introduction I wondered if the engine would start, but it did and we were soon underway, bouncing along merrily. The car emitted squeaks from every corner, but the engine kept firing consistently enough to get along at a good 30 miles per hour.

"Don't be frightened," she assured me "I drive this road often and haven't had an accident yet. It's nothing compared to what awaits you on the mountain though!"

Soon after we had left the village I saw a large native woman waiting at the side of the road. Betty jerked the car to a halt and off-loaded the potatoes and her son. She helped the native woman put the child into a sling on her back and lift the potatoes onto her head. As the Nanny walked away, the child seemed happy, the potatoes stable and her deportment was 'stately'. "He just loves his fat old nanny. They're really very good with children you know." Betty told me as we got underway to the depot, where we were meeting Edwin.

A Basuto muleteer tightening the girth on one of the pack animals.

At the depot there were two large wooden sheds, and outside one was a man with a blanket thrown over his shoulders. "That man is a Basuto. They all wear the blanket over their shoulders. In fact, their blankets are their proudest possessions. Even the smallest child is taught to wear it".

We had to wait for Edwin now. He had gone up the mountain that morning with a delegation from the Natal Roads Board. There had been complaints that the Jeeps were frightening the pack horses coming down the pass, so the delegation had come to check it out personally.

"You see virtually everything that comes in or goes out of this part of Basutoland is transported over the pass by pack animals" Betty explained.

"What about the Jeep service?"

"Well, the whole of the commerce of this region is controlled by two European traders who have been in the business for years. They have both made fortunes and it suits them that things should continue the way that they are."

"Don't they make use of the Jeep service then?"

"Far from that, they are putting every hindrance they can in our way. You see, they have stores in Mokhotlong as well as here at the bottom of the pass. In general they transport their sales items up the mountain on pack animals. They bring back the wool they've received in trade on the return trip."

"Is it a big business?"

"Just big enough to keep two hundred pack animals hard at it all the time. They have a virtual monopoly on the trade. Not only do they make a very good profit on their trade goods but they buy the wool from the Basutos at a very low price."

"So they get it coming and going?"

"They certainly do. They've both got big houses and one is reported to be a millionaire."

There were lots of ponies moving up and down the road. All the men were wearing the typical blanket and most also wore the unique conical straw hat with a knob on top. They sat on their horses in a relaxed manner. These people were quite different from the oppressed natives on the Bohler estate. They looked calm and happy with their lot. I thought it was probably because they were the masters of their own destiny, rather than being poorly treated employees on a European farm.

I said to Betty "Is that one of the stores over there?"

"Yes, but we seldom go there."

"Well, it's a public store isn't it? I've been thrown out of better places. If that's where your husband's Jeep is stopping off, let's go over there and wait."

Gathered around in front of a rather run down concrete building were thirty native Basutos with their blankets over their shoulders. There seemed to be equal numbers of horses, ponies and mules. The men glanced at the car when we drove up but soon went back to their tasks of loading animals or keeping the flies off themselves. There was no forced hurry or stress here and they were contentedly

307

A family in Basutoland. The colourful blankets and alert and happy demeanor of these people was typical. Note the lack of grass cover.

going about their business. Most of the men were loading animals in preparation for the trip over the pass. The loads looked large but as they mainly took corn and blankets up to Mokhotlong they were not as heavy as they appeared to be. There was no elaborate system of saddles and pack boxes. The loads were put directly on to the animal's back and tied on with raw hide ropes. Most of the animals looked well cared for but an occasional animal had sores where the ropes had cut into its flesh. Most of the animals looked contented enough but while we were watching, one of them decided that this drudge work was not for him. When the last cinch had been tied around his belly one of the men had put his foot on the load and heaved it up tight. The mule broke away, put his head down and his heels up. He then reversed the process and kept doing this until there was a trail of corn for a hundred yards along the road. When last seen he was still bucking with the rawhide ropes dragging from his hind legs. The men who had loaded this mule joined in the general laughter and then borrowed horses to set off after the reluctant beast of burden. "They sometimes have to go six or seven miles before catching up with the runaway animals. It doesn't bother them. They have plenty of time." Betty explained. They were employed to take the corn up the mountain and the store owner took the loss for any spilled corn.

I decided to press on into the store, as no one had told us to go away. There were ten or fifteen men and women standing inside the large single roomed building. Around the walls were counters, and native salesmen were handing out the stock that was arranged on the walls behind them. Here were all the things required for the simple life that the Basutos led in the mountains. Near the door there were saddles and bridles for their horses and mules. The shelves were stacked high with canned goods and there were sacks and sacks of the dried corn that formed their staple diet. They also fermented some of the corn to make Kaffir beer.

I was more interested in the hundreds and hundreds of wool blankets that occupied one whole wall of the building. Most of the blankets were of bright colours, which had been manufactured for this market by mills in Manchester. Some were fully displayed with the maker's name showing. These were of thick wool and of the best quality; they were priced as high as fifteen dollars each. This was a lot of money for the ordinary Basuto, but the blanket is their most precious possession and they were prepared to sacrifice a lot to be well dressed and warm. The men and women in the shop all had blankets draped across their shoulders like a poncho. It gave them a characteristic appearance and was a relief after the drab sameness of the dress of the natives and Indians in Durban.

Across the way there was a lot of activity in one of the big warehouses, so I strolled over there. The whole of the floor was covered with piles of raw wool. Some was being sorted into different classes while next to the door a Basuto boy was tramping some down into a large bale. I had just given a bale a kick to see how tight it was filled and when I looked up I was staring straight at a European who had a note book in his hand. Perhaps I'd got myself in trouble.

"Do you mind if I look around? I'm interested in the wool business."

"Help yourself" was the curt reply that didn't seem to invite conversation, and I soon retreated to the car where Betty was waiting.

"It's time we got back to the depot. I think that I heard Edwin's Jeep coming down a few minutes ago." Betty was mistaken, as it was not Edwin, who would not arrive for another hour yet. She was becoming a little worried by this delay, but it was not unusual for the Jeeps to be three or four hours late. There was nothing to do but wait.

When Edwin came bouncing in he had good news. "I think that I impressed the Road Board with our service. None of the animals that we passed were frightened off the road and I pointed out the places where erosion had started on the mountain side. Two hundred pack animals travelling up here all the time have been taking their toll on it." Betty introduced me to Edwin but after a nod in my general direction he busied himself loading the Jeep for the mountain journey. He was six feet tall, thirtyish and with his army beret on the back of his uncut hair looked like a British Officer under active duty conditions. "We have to get back up the pass before the sun sets. That only gives us two hours from now." he explained, as he hurried through his preparations. Finally, Betty, as pretty and petite as ever, waved us goodbye and we were off, bumping up the rough track.

The first mile was not too bad, but then the road reduced in width and became more of a horse track than a recognisable road. There had been some attempt at formation but it had been designed for horses and mules. Every few hundred yards we passed a group of loaded animals that were moving down to the store with the bulky loads of wool. Most were driven by Basuto boys mounted on small hardy ponies. Some of the drivers simply walked behind the string of pack animals.

"It takes the pack animals two whole days to come from Mokhotlong, but by Jeep we'll be there in seven hours. They carry most of their own food and the animals are hobbled and eat on the sides of the mountain when they camp in the evenings. Just have a look at the erosion that they are starting from here on." Edwin pointed out the margins of the road which had been washed away, and I became a ready convert to his idea that the horses' hooves were wrecking the track.

The road was really getting to be steep now. The surface in most places was made up of stones as big as a man's fist. The Jeep had to be driven in low gear to grind its way up the steeper slopes. We were in the bare foot hills and I could see the mountain looming ahead. At the Basutoland border there were a few huts and in response to Edwin's tooting a native policeman came out of an office and had him sign a book. There were no passports required and no other formalities but every European going through had to sign the book.

Edwin's demeanour became more serious as he explained "After this, the climb really begins. At places the grade is one in five. It just zig-zags right up the mountain and up onto the pass. When we are up over the pass the worst is over". The Jeep simply could not cope with the grades in low now and Edwin had to put the vehicle into compound low and four wheel drive. The Jeep ranted and roared under the strain but never really looked like failing. On some of the hair pin turns I was able to look out over the side of the track onto rocks 300 feet below.

"I usually ask the passengers to get out and walk around the next corner but you can stay in if you like" said Edwin as we approached the worst corner on the road. The slope was one in five and the angle was so sharp that the Jeep had to be driven half way round, then backed up, and if all was well it got around on the next try. The traction was not good because the great rocks that had been used to build the road slipped under the tyres and the road surface sloped towards the outer edge that simply dropped off into space. After successfully navigating that bend it took another twenty minutes to reach the top of the pass. At that point the road flattened out and we found ourselves on a bare, windswept plateau. A few miles over to the right, in the distance, were a few low hills

"If I could get a merchant's licence to sell and buy I could help them a lot." At this point, due to Edwin's cigarette flicking, I was more sensitive to the danger of the Jeep being blown up than the very real threat of slipping off into the wet gorge.

"If one of those sparks sets off this gasoline in the back you won't be helping anybody." I said, seeing the opportunity to voice my concern.

"Oh, don't worry about that. I smoke all the time and there is always gasoline in the back. There is no danger unless it is out in the open."

"But say there is a leak in one of the tins?"

"Well, there's plenty of breeze blowing through the Jeep, so there won't be a build up of gas to explode." Edwin seemed to have the answers.

In a short time he asked "Would you mind jumping out and pushing the side of the Jeep to stop it falling off the road over this next patch?" It was not difficult to walk beside the Jeep which was down into compound low gear again. As it was much safer outside than inside the Jeep I was happy to do this. If it did go over the cliff I'd have a better chance of survival walking beside it, rather than sitting in the passenger seat.

When the last red of the sunset had gone from the mountain tops and darkness was settling in, twinkling lights began to appear on the hill sides. There had been no houses on the pass but now that we were in farming land, small villages were appearing around us. When the lights of Mokhotlong appeared it was a relief to both of us. We wasted no time in getting along to the guest house and Edwin began preparations for a meal.

The guest house was a small round house built in the native style and even if the doors did creak badly the roof was made of corrugated iron and so was water proof. The stove had a fit of temperament and Edwin retreated with a black face when the thing blew up. It did work eventually and we were able to heat up some of the food that Betty had sent up for us. We decided that I should be up bright and early in the morning so that I could see as much as possible before the Jeep left at midday.

The morning broke fair and fresh and I could see that Mokhotlong was a completely different place by day. The first impression was of limitless space. The town's collection of buildings sat in the middle of a flat surrounded by bare hills and mountains. Few trees grew at this height and the sparse grass had been cropped low by the mountain ponies. Through the clear air I could see the tiny villages and their cultivated terraces, that produced modest amounts of grain, rising into the sky. From each village a tiny trail wound down the mountain side to disappear into the intervening valleys. Even at 8.30 in the morning there were plenty of people about, all with bright blankets over their shoulders. At the trader's store there were thirty horses standing tied to hitching rails in front of the building.

One of the main tracks passed right besides the guest house and a continual stream of mounted men and pedestrians passed by. They skirted the tiny grass airfield but nobody bothered glancing at the mono-plane which had come to grief at the end of the runway three weeks previously.

They were getting a little worried about whether the air service would continue, as there had been four crashes in three months and one of the best pilots had been killed. Edwin told me about the mishaps with just a hint of satisfaction. If the air service went out his Jeep service would be much better patronised.

"They have had four accidents. It seems that the height here and thin atmosphere gives the plane very little leeway for taking off on these rough, sloping fields. Even so, the modern pilots don't seem to be as good as the older more experienced ones. You don't hear of many of the old bush pilots having serious crashes."

"If they have had serious crashes they're not here to tell the story" I said, and Edwin replied "True enough. Come on over and I'll introduce you to the resident Commissioner and his wife. We would have gone over last night but we were too late in."

The Commissioner's house was set in a pleasant garden and the front door looked out onto the airfield, and the mountains to the east. While Edwin went off with the Commissioner to the office to discuss the business side of the Jeep service, I was invited to stay for tea by the Commissioner's wife. She was an attractive brunette in her early thirties, showing signs of her fourth pregnancy. I asked "How do you get on in this isolated post of Empire?"

"We like it here. My husband likes the fact that he is left pretty much to himself. We have lots of servants and a good house provided by the British Commission. It gets lonely at times and we need a trip out every six months. However, we feel that we're really doing something for the people." This struck me as being quite different from what was happening in other parts of South Africa, where the whites seemed more focused on their own welfare.

"Have the people any say in the administration then?" I asked

"Why certainly, they're being prepared for self-government. My husband's first assistant is a Basuto. There are only four Europeans on the staff here, you'll meet the doctor later."

"How do the Basutos respond to your assistance?"

"Well, Rome wasn't built in a day. There are still a lot of dark practices in this land."

"You mean witchcraft?"

"That's just what I mean. Haven't you read in the papers about the local chief being involved in a ritual murder?"

"I don't really know much about the place, only that this area's an isolated part of the British Empire in the middle of South Africa"

"Well, the Witch Doctors still have a tremendous hold on the people. There is a large Catholic French Canadian Mission within five miles of Mokhotlong, but there is still a strong belief in the power of medicine that the Witch Doctors make from the bodies of people sacrificed for the purpose."

"They actually kill people for this purpose?"

"They do just that. Some of the bodies which have been found show unmistakable evidence that body parts have been removed, while the victim was still alive."

"You are not just pulling my leg?" I asked, in case she was teasing me.

"I wish that I were. Tomorrow we're expecting a European officer in, to try some of the principals in the latest case of witchcraft. Just last month the local Chief escaped the death penalty because of a legal flaw."

"They are difficult to convict then?"

"A full conviction is very difficult to obtain. The people are afraid to speak. A mother knows where her missing child has gone, but she dare not accuse anyone if she wishes to avoid death herself. The witch doctors are virtually invulnerable. They hold the people in a terrible power."

"Do they need special people for their purpose when practising their witchcraft?"

"It appears that any one will do. Thank goodness that it's been many years since a white person has gone missing. They find the dismembered bodies of children and old men and women as well as young men. However they seem to consider that the body of an unborn child holds special virtue, and pregnant women have been slaughtered for the child in their body."

"The people look cheerful enough though" I ventured, as despite this practice I hadn't detected any fear in their faces.

"They are a fine race of people. They are forced into these dreadful things by the Chiefs and Witch Doctors. The Chiefs want the medicine to increase their own power or to make the fields more fertile."

"Is everything under the power of the Witch Doctors?"

"Well, obviously they have enough power to cause the death of innocent people."

"I suppose these dreadful rites are effective in consolidating the power of the Chiefs also?"

"This whole subject is a thorn in the side of the administration. Just when we think that we have the people coming around to our idea of democracy there's another outbreak of these terrible crimes." I found this all very fascinating, but it was almost time for Edwin to start off back down the mountain and I had to be ready.

"I have to go off to the post office and send some cards. I believe that the Basutoland post mark is really worth having." I said, preparing for my exit.

"Don't hurry too much, you would realise by now that Edwin's

Jeep service operates on an approximate time table" she replied smiling.

When I got to the Post Office the man behind the counter was a Basuto. Here of course there was no segregation of the customers into Europeans and non-Europeans. Not only was I the only European, I was the only customer. When I was at the Durban Post Office even though we were served at the same counter, the Europeans had to stand in a different queue to the natives and Indians. There, the European girl behind the counter had served the Europeans one after another, and had only started on the Natives when the last European had been served. Only Europeans were employed in the Durban Post Office, so that when the Christmas mail rush came, it was sometimes ten days late because of lack of skilled labour to handle the mail. Clearly, the apartheid system didn't always make for efficiency.

It was now already 1 o'clock, but there was no sign of the Jeep at the starting point outside the police station. A few intending passengers were standing around waiting, but Edwin had disappeared. It was 2 o'clock before he re-appeared and by this time there were a large number of people waiting. Eight men had signed up to go out to work in the mines in Johannesburg and they had preferential seats in the Jeep. It would comfortably hold six men and the intending passengers were all hopeful of a seat. On top of this the native secretary of the local cooperative had turned up and announced that he had been promised a seat two weeks previously. He wanted one of the front seats too. Another fellow, who was one of the minor Chiefs, said that this was the last Jeep that he could catch to get to a conference of Bantu chiefs in Johannesburg, so he needed to travel that day. It looked as if life was going to be complicated. Edwin was unwilling to leave any of the mining labourers behind, because the recruiting organisation would pay their fare and he would be relying on them for a lot of his future business. The secretary of the local cooperative could put a lot of business his way too, and the local Chief was re-asserting his claim. The Chief became fed up with arguing and went off to appeal to the District Commissioner to help him get a seat. He had been gone 15 minutes and came back to announce that the Commissioner's Jeep would take him half way, then he could meet Edwin on the pass and go the rest of the way with him. This still left eight men and the Secretary to fit on board. Perhaps the men could walk? They all had to walk out previously, but as their fare was paid on the Jeep service all felt that they should ride. At last Edwin shook his head and told them all to get on board. They did just that. There were bits and pieces of human bodies bulging out of every corner of the Jeep. The Secretary spoke fairly good English and was better dressed than the men; he claimed the middle front seat for himself. I had paid well for the trip and was allowed the other front seat. Edwin could not speak the Basuto language so used the Secretary as an interpreter

"Look, tell that fellow breathing down the doctor's neck that if he feels sick he must be sick out of the window." This was reassuring indeed.

We set off in reasonable comfort and the Secretary told Edwin and me about the local situation. He explained that the whole country was owned by the Basuto people. Any adult man could run as many sheep as he liked on the mountains. Some people had as many as two hundred sheep, so the administration and Chiefs were worried about over-stocking and were trying to persuade them to limit their animal numbers. The Government was bringing in good quality rams to upgrade the quality of the animals, but I failed to see the quality of the sheep improving if they did not have good quality pasture. Uncharacteristically, I kept my counsel to myself, and we bounced along in inter-racial harmony.

At the moment the cooperative society was not doing well as they had to send the wool out to Durban and it took several weeks before they were paid, and could pass on payment to the farmers. When the men brought the wool into Mokhotlong they brought their wives with them and, being women, they wanted to spend some money in the stores. The men were pressured to accept a lower price from the store keepers to get paid immediately, which allowed the women to do their thing. The Secretary was hoping to arrange their finances so that a portion of the payment could be given to the seller straight away. In time they would start their own cooperative store, where they would sell blankets and food supplies at a reasonable rate to their own people, and avoid exploitation by the European store owners.

The trip down the mountain did not seem as arduous as the upward journey but it was still slow and bumpy. It was dark when the Jeep finally bumped into the compound of the store in Heimieville, at the foot of the pass. Men were lying asleep peacefully on the concrete verandah, tightly wrapped in their blankets. The men who had travelled on our Jeep went off to the recruiting mining company's quarters, while Edwin, the Secretary and I bumped off down the road to Edwin's house. The Secretary went off happily to the servant's quarters while Edwin and I went inside the house for a hot meal.

Edwin lived in an old farmhouse which had been grand in its day, but was now in dissolution and disarray. Everything was in a terrible mess, but Betty made up for any discomfort with her cheerful presence. She was pleased to see her husband back as she didn't like the risks involved, but she knew that he wouldn't be happy doing anything else. Ever since he had visualised the possibility of a Jeep service some ten years previously his routine job in Durban had become a means to this end. He wanted to run a regular service up to Mokhotlong. Perhaps once it was established he could extend other rough routes up through Basutoland. After that who knows? There must have been plenty of other areas in Africa where such a service was needed, but financing it would always be difficult, as few Africans had money to either set one up or use it.

When all the goodbyes had been said the next morning I found myself at the railway station with the Secretary. He was also going to Durban but now seemed lost and out of place. When I went to get the Secretary's ticket for Durban I saw that the ticket window was for Europeans only. Could I buy a ticket for the non-European section of the train or would I have to go to the non-European ticket window? I was told that the Basuto Secretary would have to travel on a different train, which did not leave for four hours. The Afrikaner man behind the glass did not exactly approve of this improper association with a native, and I was happy to get my own ticket and move on. Life in South Africa seemed a little complicated now. Just a few hours ago I'd been riding in the same Jeep as this man, and one of his friends had been breathing down my neck. Now he was not allowed to travel on the same train or even to buy a ticket at the same window. While the difference was striking to me it must have been more so for the Secretary. He was somebody to reckon with in Mokhotlong, and even the minor Chief had not been able to deprive him of his seat. It was obviously different in South Africa.

When I returned to the Bohler homestead I could see that Daniel's car was standing outside the gate; it had been fixed at last. Now there was the chance of some real freedom for myself and my parents. With this little car we would be able to range freely over South Africa. The Kruger Park and Hluhluwe Park in the north of Zululand would all open up to us. We would be able to escape the farm for weeks at a time. Providing we could be on our own most of the time, life would be tolerable.

Everybody in the house seemed pleased to see me again, and the best china appeared for the afternoon tea. The lads were anxious to know what it was like in the mountains of Basutoland. They had heard a lot about it but had never taken the trouble to go and have a look. As soon as the Bohlers were out of the room Dais looked across at me and said

"It's been Hell here since you went away."

"What's been the trouble?"

"Well first of all there was still that trouble about David not getting the money from the bank to pay the natives. Wilhelm still holds that in his mind. Then Daniel told the Indian driver to take a tractor into a wet field. The tractor and it's trailer got bogged down and it is still there."

"Didn't they use the oxen to try and pull it out?"

"The lads were going to get the oxen when Wilhelm came along and insisted that they leave everything until the ground is drier. He said that the digging necessary to get it out would cut up the fields too much."

"Where is the tractor now?"

"It's sitting down by the lower gate. Whenever a visitor passes they notice it and come into the house and ask Wilhelm if he knows it's there."

"And every time it's mentioned Wilhelm loses his temper again?"

"That's true enough. The lads use every excuse to go out and leave us with him. The only reason we have not followed the boys is because we have no car."

"How has Aunty Queen been taking it?"

"She has been as nervous as a kitten about the whole thing. Every time Wilhelm appears she gets up from her chair and starts running around the house pretending that she's busy. He has her really scared."

"What about her headaches?"

"Well, she took to her bed with them for two days. That was the only time we got any peace. The lads were always running up to her room to see how she was and Wilhelm was very good." I felt quite exasperated and stated the obvious.

"If he gave her a little love and more attention, he wouldn't have to buy all those expensive drugs for her headaches."

"The food has been terrible too," Dais continued "When Queen was in bed Wilhelm used to go into the kitchen and growl at the staff for wasting things. We have been eating the same piece of corn beef for three days now. Wilhelm carved it in such thin slices that we had it for two days and now we are eating it in minced pie."

"I hope that we don't get it tonight then."

"No, you seem to be an honoured guest. When they heard that you were coming back they had the garden boy kill a chicken. There are plenty of birds and I wonder why they don't kill one more often."

"Well, we'll be eating in good style this evening. Then we'll see just how soon we can get David's car and take off for the wide open spaces."

"David has shown no signs of offering the car yet." Now this was concerning news to me, as it was our intended means of escape.

"Perhaps Wilhelm is influencing him not to give it?" I asked.

"Well, Arch just refuses to go on a long trip with Wilhelm driving, so what can we do about that?"

I thought I heard someone coming in the front door, and warned Dais to be quiet. She was not surprised by this and replied quietly "This house has so many doors that we we're never sure there isn't somebody listening. Even Queen admits that Wilhelm listens to what they are saying about him."

"Ah well" I said "Those who listen never hear anything good about themselves." As it turned out, it was David. Since I'd been told about the tractor, I asked him.

"Have you pulled the tractor out of the mud?" Maybe a bit tactless, and the annoyed reply was "No, it can stay there forever as far as I'm concerned. Dad wouldn't let us use the bullocks to get it out. It is so obvious sitting there by the gate and every time anyone mentions it Dad just about throws another heart attack." This was the first time I'd heard anything about Wilhelm's heart so I enquired about it.

"Has your father got a bad heart then?"

"Well yes, hasn't he told you about that? He should be taking things very easily. He's has been attending a heart specialist for years."

"He seems to be pretty active now though?"

"Yes, we were all very worried about him until mother went off to see the specialist. He said that Dad didn't have a thing the matter with his heart. It was all in his head."

"So he's been pretending all this time?"

"Well, I suppose he thinks there is something the matter with his heart." The conversation was getting a little out of David's depth. He wisely withdrew, as he knew from past experience that there was trouble coming if he came anywhere close to criticising his father. He had tried to stand up to Wilhelm and given his own opinion in the past, but his father always seemed to win. Better to pull out now before he was too deeply committed and said something he would later regret. As soon as Wilhelm entered the room David made an excuse to find something to do outside. There had been enough trouble about the tractor without him standing around to hear more.

"Welcome home John, I hope you had a good time up the mountain with the Basutos. Pity David had to go out. He could have told you about when he was attacked with a cane knife by a Basuto boy. Since then David has been frightened to go out to the compound at night without a sjambok and a revolver."

"Perhaps that's wise?"

"Well, he's frightened anyhow. Wisdom and fear may go together in this case."

"What happened to the boys who cut each other up before I went away?"

"They're both healing well as far as I can see, however it will teach them not to give us trouble in the middle of the night. I have taken the cost of your services off their wages." Surely he couldn't be serious! Those boys would be weeks or months paying off this debt. It was on the tip of my tongue to refuse any payment for my work, when I remembered that I had not been offered any! He was charging them for something that hadn't cost him a cent. If Wilhelm had not been such a humourless little man, I would have thought he was joking. There was no trace of a smile on his face as he entered into his instructive mode.

"It's the only way. If I am easy with them they won't respect me and there will be trouble every Saturday night." I wondered if this would be the time to protest against his treatment of those boys. Nobody deserved to work for a month just to pay for the comparatively crude stitching I did in the kitchen a few weeks ago. Wilhelm hadn't offered to pay me for my work, so whatever charge he made to the native workers could go towards the cost of our food and lodgings.

I kept remembering that warning given to every visitor to South African soil "…..people should be here for ten years etc. etc." I was a guest in Wilhelm's house and if I had a row with him now Arch and Dais would be embarrassed. All of our luggage was stored in the Bohler's house and there was no way of transporting it unless we got a car, but David had still not offered to let us have free use of his vehicle. All in all it seemed we had to wait, and while hoping for the best, expect the worst.

This was not the only problem that had occurred on the estate while I was away. The wife of one of the coloured tractor drivers had been having trouble feeding her new baby. She had asked Queen for a bottle of milk each day so that she could drink it and improve her own supply. Each day one of the little Indian maids had taken the milk to her. One day Wilhelm had seen this and asked what was happening; then the trouble started. "Giving milk to these people! This stuff cost money to produce. They can damn well pay for it." And pay for it she did. Now that the mother had to pay six pennies for the bottle of milk she could not afford a bottle each day so compromised and bought a bottle every second day. Now that the economy drive was in full swing Wilhelm hit upon the idea for a few more economies. After all he had to be sure that there was enough in the bank to get the two lads away for a trip to Europe at the beginning of the next year.

The two little Indian girls came to work each morning at 4.30 and cleaned and brushed and polished all day. They had a couple of hours off in the middle of the day, but they were there to wash the dishes and clean up after dinner each night. One of them was always there, even on Sundays, and they seldom got a holiday. At the end of the month they were paid three dollars.

Previously on laundry mornings they had been given an egg, even at the risk of this treat spoiling them and subverting Wilhelm's authority. Here Wilhelm identified another chance of saving money. Up until now they had been able to take some food down into a house at the bottom of the garden and have lunch. This was to stop. They were to be sent home to their father's hut at midday and he could provide their lunch. They were sweet little things with long black oiled braids. Now that they knew that I didn't bite they even gave me a little smile when the Bohlers weren't looking. The youngest didn't look a day over ten and the eldest looked about thirteen. Instead of stepping shyly around the house in ridiculous white caps they should have been running about some school playground.

No one could deny that Wilhelm was a man of means. He had an income of 30,000 dollars a year, which was a fortune in those times. He had the best American car in the district and had just added his second aeroplane to the hangar. And another side of his being a 'Man of means' was that he WAS mean; he wouldn't let his sons touch his expensive aeroplane although they both had their pilot's licences. When he brought Queen a present in Durban he would ask for a 'shop keeper's discount' because he thought owning the store on his property entitled him to one. Now that his economy drive had attended to the servant's food costs he put pressure on Queen to save on food in the house. The bread was coming from his end of the table in ever thinner slices and the meat in ever smaller portions. I felt that life was not worth living under these stringent conditions. What is the good of money if it brings no joy or fun and causes continual stress? Each night the grand piano stood unused in the sitting room, and just one hundred yards away the natives, despite their poverty, were enjoying their beer and singing and dancing. They had very little in material possessions but they made the most of what they did have. Perhaps their singing disturbed Wilhelm when he realised that they were having a good time. Whenever he heard them he kept saying "When they have alcohol they fight with knives." I think he thought that if they were ready to turn against each other, they might turn against those in the 'Big House' and everything it stood for. I understood Wilhelm's apprehension and wondered when a violent revolt would erupt.

Only a few years ago natives had attacked the Indians in Durban, and three hundred had been killed before the police and soldiers stopped the slaughter. The lads realised that violence might come at any time. They thought that it would be fifty years before the natives took back their land, but in the meantime they were taking precautions. David was keen on carrying his revolver when he was the only one on the farm. The two great boxer dogs kept at the front gate had been trained from puppies to threaten strange natives. If even a little of the income from the cane crop had been used to improve the lot of the natives it would have helped the situation. A few cheap houses would mean that the men could bring their families to live with them. A few reasonable toilets and washing facilities wouldn't have gone astray either. Perhaps even free milk for the children. Neighbouring farms had improved the lot of their workers and been able to get all the labour that they needed. Whilhelm hadn't seemed to make that connection and his farm was chronically short of labour. Rather than spend money on improving workers' conditions, his money was soundly invested in saving bonds or he shifted his funds offshore to safe funding havens.

Wilhelm was unwilling to improve his workers' conditions. I wondered how long it would be before the black people would rise up against their poverty and discrimination. This revolt has not happened in the last 60 years, so perhaps it will never eventuate in our lifetimes. Despite the apartheid system having been dismantled, there are still very many blacks living on a dollar a day so perhaps revolution may still happen.

I had been tossing these problems over in my mind for a week now; what was I to do? What was my duty towards Queen? After all, she was Dais's sister and she was sick. Could I tolerate this continual atmosphere of tension and greed and continue to stay and try to help her? To be helped she would have to be willing to be assisted and make changes. Queen had not mentioned her medical conditions to me directly, but only in general conversation with other people. She must have realised that her headaches and asthma attacks became worse when her husband had been especially unkind to her. When ever there was a chance to talk to her about her situation she found refuge in the world of drugs. She knew the name of every analgesic preparation on the market. She wanted something from a bottle to cure her. There would be no discussion about the tense state into which she had been driven, she just wanted another drug to dull the anxiety and unhappiness in her life.

Finally I was overwhelmed by the tension, and when we were alone I announced to my parents;

"I am on my way the hell out of here!" Arch and Dais were not used to hearing their oldest unmarried son talking like this. I did not allow myself the luxury of this type of outburst very often. I was fed up with the Bohlers and hated every minute that I had to remain in their company - they were not 'my kind of people'.

Dais said "Queen is my sister and although I hate the whole set up I feel that I am needed here."

"She had her chance to get out thirty years ago. She has lived with Bohler all these years and continually criticises him. If she has lived with him all this time she should be loyal to him." I'd thought about it, and was relieved to finally be saying what I thought.

"I couldn't agree with you more, but she is my sister and blood is thicker than water."

"I am sorry Dais but I cannot stand the atmosphere here for another day. Wilhelm is so damn pious about the whole thing. Prayers before meat but the native children still get three dollars a month."

Arch was smiling now and said "Well, I'm telling you that I don't intend to put up with this situation much longer. I'm coming with you."

At this Dais joined in "I guess you are both right and I'm certainly not staying here by myself. We have all of our luggage here though and there is nowhere else to go. What can we do?" It seemed that we had to hatch a family escape plan.

There followed a whirl of activity in the Valentine family camp. After the decision had been taken to escape from the Bohlers, we needed to get a second hand car and arrange for somewhere to go. I had been playing with the idea of doing a locum while a doctor went on holiday and I had found a position vacant where I could bring my parents. This would give them three weeks breathing space in rural Natal and time for us to sort out the future. They would also be able to experience the workings of another household in South Africa.

I was able to arrange the locum over the phone with Dr. van

Dyck as his English was good and his Afrikaans accent wasn't thick enough to present a difficulty.

"We're glad that you're able to bring your parents Doctor Valentine. It means that you will be able to stay at the house, instead of the hotel."

"They were very pleased to come."

"Do you think that your mother will be able to look after the servants?"

"Just get your wife to give her the briefest of instructions and we will get along. It is only for three weeks anyway."

When I told Wilhelm about our plans, he still did not offer me a car so I bought a small Ford second hand. Arch and Dais and I travelled off to my locum, which was in 'the Valley of a Thousand Hills', inland from Durban. It was in a tiny town which serviced rural Natal. Most of the Europeans were of Dutch stock and spoke Afrikaans most of the time. The van Dycks lived in a comfortable old wooden house with their two infant children.

Mrs. van Dyck was a good looking woman in her late twenties but from the beginning she seemed to take a mildly aggressive disapproval towards us. When Arch, Dais and I were seated in the sitting room she asked "What do you drink?"

I was a little taken back, but I could certainly do with one! Arch and Dais were tired after the drive and something at this time of the day would be just what the doctor ordered. "Well what have you got?" I replied, thinking a drink was on offer. Doctor van Dyck intervened; "Dear! If you ask that question at this time of day in South Africa they think that you mean alcohol!" Mrs. van Dyck was clearly scandalised at the thought and added "Certainly not! I mean, we have coffee, tea and cocoa." My parents looked around expectantly but I gave them a warning glance to tell them there was no scotch or anything else coming and to leave it at that.

We had had a snack at midday and were looking forward to the evening meal. Dr. van Dyck described the local milling industry while the native maids put the few utensils on the snowy white table cloth. Everybody was invited to take their place at the table.

Hell-Bent for Life

The hot steaming soup was brought in in a large bowl and was placed in front of Mrs. van Dyck.

"You all like soup." It was not an invitation but a statement and the full plates of soup were passed around the table.

"There is plenty of fresh bread. My neighbour brought me two home made loaves today. Please don't stint yourselves". The butter was home made but fresh and wholesome. It looked as if Mrs. van Dyck had a good table. They kept their own cow and the garden boy milked it. He made butter from the excess cream. Now everyone had finished their soup and Mrs. van Dyck rang the bell for the Zulu maid.

"Bring in another bowl of soup Madena" ordered our hostess, and turning to her guests asked "You will have another helping of soup or a little more bread perhaps?" Our hostess seemed to be pushing the soup and bread a little, but perhaps the roast wasn't quite ready and she was playing for time. I caught my mother's eye and the thought flashed between us; "Perhaps this was all there was for the evening meal?" We both smiled at the thought. This was a doctor's household in this fabulously rich country, so we put these thoughts out of our mind. Dr. van Dyck interrupted our thoughts with the statement "We do not eat much in the evenings. You sleep much better if you go to bed without a full stomach." Dais and I could not help sharing another smile at this, as we we were both thinking that we were not going to be given the opportunity to refute his theory. We would be going to bed to sleep well. The van Dycks were to be on their way to the Belgian Congo the next day. We could then have free play with all the rich jersey milk and fresh vegetables in the garden. When the meal was over and we had been sent off to our bedrooms I went quietly along to Arch and Dais's room. Arch was in good form despite his empty stomach.

"Doctor van Dyck has told me that the cow produces a lot of milk when it rains, and I just love cream. Do you think that this overcast sky means that it will rain tonight?" he asked hopefully.

"Well," I said "they told me the garden boy makes butter out of the extra cream so there won't be any extra cream for a couple of days."

Arch didn't seem too dispirited by this "Did you bring along that half bottle of scotch?"

"Just let me go through our bag" I said, and as I went off I heard Arch add "Did you see a glass in the bathroom? – better fill it up with water and bring it in".

The Valentine family had escaped the Bohlers and now resorted to covert consumption of contraband from the highlands of Scotland, the 'Land of the brave' and homeland of the Haig & Haig whisky dynasty.

Mrs. van Dyck was really putting her family through hoops the next morning. The two young Zulu maids were running back and forth helping to get the many things needed for the trip. The van Dycks were to fly and their baby had to have pasteurised milk taken along in a bottle. Dais and I were sitting in the main lounge trying to keep out of the way and be inconspicuous, while we watched the baby play on the carpet. Mrs. van Dyck dragged in one of the maids and fired her instructions at the young girl;

"The boss is in the bathroom now but in ten minutes he will be out and you are to take the baby in and give him his bath. Alright? Hurry!" The girl smiled and picked up the struggling child and went out. Dais smiled and looked across at me and said,

"I wonder, does she bath the boss too?" This slightly indecent suggestion was followed by a respectful pause. The silence was rudely shattered by Mrs. van Dyck's voice - she was extremely agitated.

"Haven't I told you never, and I mean NEVER, to go through a closed door without knocking first?"

It was obvious that the maid had gone into the bathroom while 'The Master' was drying himself after his bath. As she was born on a reservation the girl would have been used to seeing much more impressive physiques than that possessed by the good doctor.

When the van Dyck family was getting into the car, which was to take them to the airport, I could not help but notice that the two Zulu girls looked very relieved. They would have three weeks with the new 'Missus' to have a rest. No more getting up at 6.30 a.m. to get the doctor's breakfast. There would be no baby to attend to and

Hell-Bent for Life

there would be little pressure. The Mistress wound down the car window to give some last advice to the two girls;

"You two girls be good now. Do everything that the Missus tells you to, she will be telling me everything about you when I come back." was Mrs. van Dyck's parting shot.

When the family had departed in a cloud of dust, we were just as relieved as the two girls were, but now it was time for me to get down to the office, start work and earn my pay. Hooray, hooray! I was a working man at last.

I had been introduced to the doctor's practice partner the day before, but had not seen the consulting rooms. It was ten past nine when I arrived to find the building open and a middle aged European woman in a white uniform already at work on the accounts. This was Mrs. van Niekerk, who turned out to be friendly and efficient. While I did not think her overweight, I couldn't help but notice she was nicely rounded. "You must be Dr. Valentine," she said "Just go into the office and Dr. Eyck will be over in a few minutes. The native assistants are getting things ready out the back. I think you are to go out into the reservation today."

I had been warned that it was my turn to take the Jeep and go to the native reserves with one of the native assistants. I had been told not to worry and was assured that the boy would be able to give me all the information I needed. The assistant would know the prices to charge for services, and how to handle the drugs and syringes for injections. I was instructed to be especially careful to take the money box myself and to handle the money at all times. The doctor had been suspicious that one of the boys had been stealing.

I was concerned that sooner or later I would be expected to start pulling teeth. There were two sets of instruments for this job. One was old and rusty and served for the native molars and incisors. A newer and polished outfit was kept in the front office for the Europeans.

I was reading the morning paper when the other doctor walked into the room. As I rose to greet him he said "Doctor Valentine, please be seated. Welcome to Germania. I suppose Dr. van Dyck told you most of the things necessary for doing this job?" I was trying to keep up with the short, sharp sentences and get an estimate of Dr. Eyck's personality. He was a short, rather nervous man in his late thirties and he spoke with a heavy Afrikaner accent. He seemed friendly enough.

"If there is anything I can do to assist you, just let me know." I told him that I was not sure of the procedure for pulling teeth. I admitted to being afraid that I would be out in the bush, with a native screaming in pain from a tooth that I had broken off, and I would not know what to do about it.

"Don't worry about that, I will show you how to do a couple in the office here and you won't have the least trouble." he assured me.

"I'm glad that you think so."

"Now, has Dr. van Dyck told you anything about the psychological side of the native practice here?"

"Well no, he hasn't."

"A native has almost always been to the Witch Doctor before he comes to us. The Witch Doctors practice in the reservations and charge a dollar and a half per consultation, so don't feel sorry for the natives having to pay us a dollar a visit."

"What drugs do the Witch Doctors use then?"

"They have effective native herbs and use a few European remedies but more about that later. This is what affects you in a consultation; the relatives take the patient to the Witch Doctor and form a circle around the patient and the doctor. The Inyanga, as he is properly called, then tries to guess the patient's complaint. If he hits on it right away the relatives call out loudly and the Inyanga's medicine will be good. He has proved himself by guessing correctly right off. If he takes a long time before he gets the complaint then his medicine is not likely to be as strong, and the relatives may take the patient away to another Inyanga."

"How does this affect us? Do they come to this clinic if the witch doctor is not guessing correctly this week?"

"They come to this clinic but they expect the guessing game to continue here. They do not expect to tell you what is the matter. They will expect you to tell them what is the matter."

"Oh no, oh no. I'm just a beginner here. I won't know what's the matter with them. Perhaps you had better get yourself another locum."

"No, no. It's easy. I will give you a few hints and the native assistants will help you with the rest. First of all the native comes in and the boys get him or her to lie on that old hair couch you see in the back, and you examine them. Just do a quick routine examination."

"What do I look for then?"

"Well, take a look at the exposed skin areas. If there are scratch marks then you can safely guess that they have had pain in that area and the Inyangas have been scratching them and rubbing in counter-irritants."

"Well, let's hope that there are plenty of scratch marks then."

"No, there won't be too many but you can watch when you are examining their abdomens to see if they wince. There is a lot of stomach trouble. Be especially careful to press down on the bladder and watch; lots of them have bladder pain. It is probably due to the bilharzia in most cases, but these people do not know how to drink adequate water and they are always getting cystitis."

"What about gonorrhea then?" I asked, thinking of other things this symptom could indicate.

"Yes, that can give them bladder trouble too. Don't think that you will get a history of contact. All diseases are sent by some evil agent. There is no such thing as germs in their minds. If they get sick it is due to someone having put a curse on them and not due to an infection."

"Well, I'll do my best but I think I will be lost in a couple of hours." I said, feeling somewhat discouraged.

"Don't you believe a word of it, it's simple and I'll let you have George. He has been with us for twelve years and he knows all the tricks of the trade as well as the native mind. Just let him guide you for a start and all will be well."

"Well, let him in. It looks like he's going to be a necessity for me."

"Come out the back and I'll show you over the set up." Dr. Eyck said, seemingly satisfied that he had assured me enough.

The back rooms were reserved for the treatment of native patients. The walls of one large room were lined with bottles of medicine. Here the mixtures were being made up and at the moment a native boy was pouring coloured liquids into a graduated measuring cylinder. "This is Jess. He's making up some cough mixtures for you to take out with you today." Jess smiled and nodded to me. He was a pleasing looking lad of indeterminate age. Perhaps he was in his late thirties, with a good head of hair and a lean, fit body. We went through that larger room and into the little room at the back where the natives were examined. There was a dilapidated old couch, whose horse hair stuffing was exploding out of the holes in the leather. A native boy was lying on it and the other assistant was beside him to uncover his abdomen for examination.

"This is our other assistant. His name is George and has been with us for four years." George was alert and in his early twenties. "I have this man ready doctor. Temperature normal and there are six more waiting."

Dr. Eyck decided that this was as good a time as any to begin the morning's work and he went ahead with practised deliberation. His orders to the patient were spoken to George who translated rapidly into Zulu;

"Lie down. Sit up. Open your mouth. Take a deep breath." There hardly seemed to be time for the native man to translate all these requests before the examination was over. Dr. Eyck turned to George

"He has bladder pains?" A few rapidly spoken words and the answer came back;

"Yes doctor, and he has pains in the back."

"Bottle of 'Mist. Pot.Cit' (a mixture of Potassium Citrate) and sulphathiazole" was Dr. Eyck's direction, and turning to me he said "That is a pretty safe bet. We just give them the sulphathiazole and alkalizing mixture. It will clear up in a couple of days."

"But isn't the sulphathiazole likely to give real trouble if it precipitates out in the acid urine?"

"Yes, but I've given him the alkalizing mixture and the sulphathiazole is our cheapest drug."

Later that morning I set out with George the medical assistant to do the rounds in the reservations. The Jeep was, quite likely, the roughest vehicle in the world. It had survived many summers and now rattled along happily and helpfully, conveying its jiggled contents to the reserve. The springs were an illusion and the sound effects were so loud that it was only with the utmost difficulty that you could hold a conversation. Despite these difficulties I wanted to ask George about his life.

"When you go to get married George, how much do you have to pay for the bride price?"

"The labola is six cattle but now we often give it as money. That would be 170 dollars but I want to be generous and please the father. I will give two hundred and call it all square."

"But you only get seventeen dollars a month. It must be quite a struggle for you to save that much money."

"It is, you see I have to support my mother and little brother too."

"Surely you can't do that on this salary."

"Doctor, I have to. My father is in a mental hospital and there is no one else to look after them. You see, we have no rights on the reservation now, and we have to rent our house from a European. We can grow a few vegetables to help, but that is all."

"What do you eat then?"

"Mostly mealy flour. That is about all we can afford. It fills your stomach but after a while you have a craving for meat."

"Why not ask for a raise?"

"No, I have been here for four years and they should have offered me an increase but they never think that we need money. Life can be hard for the African here."

"Perhaps I can ask for you later, when I know the doctor better. But tell me, what does the bride's father do with the labola?"

"In the old days he kept the cattle as part of his own herd. If the wife ran away and left her husband and would not go back to him, her father would be obliged to return the labola to the husband. Of course, her father would try and make her return."

"What if the daughter was left a widow?"

"Well, then she would return to live with her father. He would support her and when the male grandchildren wanted to marry, he would pay the labola from his own herd of cattle."

"You know that sounds like our system of Social Security, no wonder the Government Commission wanted the labola system to continue. But what happens when the wife does not have any children?"

"Divorce."

"Just like that if they don't become pregnant?"

"Yes, my uncle was married and his wife didn't have children. He just sent her back to her father."

"Divorce if the wife doesn't become pregnant?" I asked, thinking this sounded very severe.

"Yes, it is easily done."

"Are you in favour of this then?"

"There is something good in all the old traditions. The great danger to family life is separation of families when the men go off to the cities to earn their living."

"Can't they take their wives?"

"No, almost never. The white bosses do not want to build houses for the families. The men are put into compounds in Johannesburg where they sleep in long dormitories, but there are no women allowed there."

"Can't they take a house for themselves outside the compound?"

"They can if they can afford it, and if they can find a place in the native section of the town. In fact, they seldom get paid enough to do this."

"I've heard and seen in the papers that the men will go off for six months and then return to their families for six months."

"Some of them may do that but just look at the people we are passing now doctor; they are almost always women and children. There are a few old men and one or two young men who have been injured at work and are home for a rest."

"Why don't they farm the land?"

"This is a good season, but there is not much grass about even now. There are so many people to get a living from the land that we would starve if we all tried to live by farming alone." What he had told me was consistent with what I had learned before, about labola and the soil degradation caused by overstocking.

"Are we coming to the clinic?" I asked, as we'd been bumping around in the noisy Jeep for a long time.

"Pull in under that tree doctor, there are some people waiting for us there. You just sit here and I will go ahead and give the free injections. I will call you when I am ready." After this stop we made our way to our next clinic.

There was a crowd of women and children waiting outside the door of a plain concrete building. The women were poorly dressed but all seemed to be smiling. George nodded to some of his friends and carried a box past them into the room. After a few minutes he emerged with a large syringe in his hand and walked over to the nearest mother. She turned her child over her knee and showed his bare bottom to George. With dexterity due to long practice George injected the child in the buttock. He had given one c.c. of sterile water and a minute dose of B vitamins. The child responded by lifting his head to the clear blue African sky giving forth the mating call of a hippopotamus. The other children were now alerted to the incipient danger awaiting them and began taking defensive measures by clinging to their mothers' chests. The children's struggles were in vain and George's relentless needle kept on finding his targets.

The native women had become enarmoured with the healing power of injections. They would walk miles with their children to get those few c.c.s of sterile water - the small traces of vitamin B could have had little effect on these babies. A full dose of vitamin B can have a very good effect on a person who is doing hard physical work while eating a poor, carbohydrate based diet. A labourer would frequently come and ask for the vitamin B preparation and happily pay three days' wages for it. After the injection they would often ask if they could continue lying on the couch and wait to feel the good effect. Medically it is doubtful that it could work so fast, but they assured us it did.

Some doctors in the area had used the native's love of injections to give the triple vaccine to the children. They were in need of this protection against Diphtheria, Tetanus and Whooping cough, because at that time over a third of the children were dying before they reached five years of age.

Now George had returned to the Jeep "Everything is ready for you now doctor. We should freeze a tooth first and then we can pull it out." "Oh no," I thought, "not on the very first visit, at the very beginning. A bloody tooth." There was my patient, waiting fearfully with a scarf around her swollen jaw. It would be possible to tell her to come back in a week, but I wasn't callous enough to have her go on suffering with the pain for all that time. We could take her back in the Jeep with us and get Dr. Eyck to do the job, but there were two more clinics to be done after this one and after the extraction she would still have to get back to the reservation. It seemed that I had to go ahead and do it here and now. My reputation and self respect would depend on the job that I made of this tooth. I wished that I had gone to the dental school more frequently for tuition in my student days, and developed a good technique for doing extractions.

It was all in a day's work for George. He handed me the syringe and gave a few sharp words to the girl, who opened her mouth wide. When she moved, as the needle pricked into the mucosa at the back of her jaw, another few words from George were enough to make her still again. George told me which forceps to use and I forced the leaves of the forceps to the tooth's roots; after a moderate struggle I was mightily relieved to hold up the entire tooth in the forceps. The lady seemed none too happy, but I gave her my biggest smile and she cheered up a little. I'd been warned that the patients would want to see the tooth to make sure all the roots were there. I proudly insisted that she have a close inspection of her lately offending molar.

The other cases at the clinic were relatively simple. Most of the children had swollen hands and faces from malnutrition. Many did not have all of the symptoms of Kwashiorkor (a protein, mineral and vitamin deficiency disease) because they had not developed the typical reddening of the hair. When the children on the reservations are taken off the breast they are put on a porridge of strained mealy flour which has virtually no food value. In most cases the baby's abdomen becomes swollen, they have diarrhoea and are brought to the clinic in a listless condition. The strained porridge is called 'Inumbe' and one of the milk companies has been bright enough to put out a dried skimmed milk powder and call it by the same name. It does not contain the expensive but relatively unimportant fats, but it has the essential proteins, vitamins and minerals. The advice to the mother is always the same "Tell her that the Inumbe she has given the child is no good. She should go to the store and buy some Inumbe in tins. She can make this up with water and give it to the child." I always had my own reservation that the mother was unlikely to have enough money to buy the store bought Inumbe. She would have to pay seven and sixpence for this consultation and its accompanying bottle of medicine and would probably give the baby the medicine she had already paid for, and let the store Inumbe go by the board. Perhaps I should not let this get me down. I had better forget about the husbands in Johannesburg, and the whoring and the hash smoking that men went in for in the city of gold. Better to let George take the mother's seven and sixpence and get on with the next patient.

George was a good lad and helped me through lots of difficulties. I'd have been happier if I had known more about dentistry, basic tropical medicine or Bantu psychology, but George was willing to help his new colleague and did not mind teaching a little basic medicine to me; "That's all right Sir, that premolar should only have two roots" or "I think we should give this child a bottle of medicine, as the mother will not be satisfied to just be told to go to the store and buy the modified milk." I kept thinking "this boy knows more about this job than I do. He gets seventeen dollars a month and I am to get two hundred for three weeks work." The unfairness of this disparity bothered me then, and it bothers me now.

The next clinic was in a distant part of the reservation and was held in the back room of the local store. The owners were native people and they continued their commerce in the front while George and I brought modern medicine to our patients in the back. We were separated from the 'store proper' by a cloth curtain. Sometimes the native owner found it necessary to pull the curtain aside when he needed something from the back area. He was always most polite; "Excuse me again Doctor, I will not be long."

This was really medicine in the raw. No chance to do x-rays, nothing in the way of lab. equipment and no chance of a consultation with a colleague. There was, however, a chance to benefit these people, if I was alert and knowledgeable enough.

The great majority of the people really did have something wrong with them. It was difficult to make a diagnosis in these circumstances, and even more difficult to expect the patient to accept the advice. In one case I said to George "Tell them that this child must go to hospital." After a few minutes of rapid conversation the reply came back "They say that if the child goes to hospital, they are afraid it will die. Couldn't you just give them something?" "The other doctor gave them something but the child is still badly nourished. Now it has pneumonia as well, so tell them that if they do not take it to hospital it will die." I tried to explain that if the patients always waited until the illness was very advanced before they went to the local mission hospital, there would always be a high death rate. It was a vicious circle. This philosophy did not help the patients right now. They stood with the infant coughing in his mother's arms. They loved him because they had carried him five miles in the mid-morning sun to the clinic. I knew that a shot of penicillin would carry him over for a couple of days, but after that he would probably die without further treatment. After a few minutes conversation through George, we were able to persuade them to come with us in the Jeep, so that their child could be admitted to the local hospital.

It had been a long day and George had got me through it with minimum trauma to myself and only moderate injuries to the patients. God is great and protects all, Christians, Agnostics, Atheists and men of good faith, no faith and those who think science is sufficient for salvation in this life.

If I thought my day of anxiety and stress was over, I was mistaken; there was a terrific row going on at the house when I returned. The whole establishment was under tension. The garden boy was working vigorously cleaning up the leaves and the girls were hard at work gathering fruit and vegetables from the garden. Dais was upset and almost crying.

"This morning I went out into the kitchen and thought that I would cook something for lunch. I went to the pot cupboard to get a pot but what do you think was in it?"

"A centipede?"

"Now don't be funny, I'm upset too."

"I'm sorry, you tell me what was in the pot?"

"There were passionfruit and a bottle of cream."

"Well, that doesn't seem to be a very startling find. They're a food aren't they?"

"Yes, but one of the girls must have been hiding them there. She was obviously going to steal them when she went away to her room this afternoon."

"Well what happened then?"

"I called the two girls in and asked them about it. Marie confessed that she had done it and I gave her a good talking to. I said they were the best fed native servants that I had seen. They are too. They get three times as much as the little Indian girls at your Aunt's place."

"Your sister's place,"

"She might be my sister, but she's your Aunt."

"I admit that then, but it doesn't seem enough to cause all this activity going on in the garden."

"Well Marie went away and sulked for a while and then Grace came back crying. She is the nicer of the two. Marie had accused her of telling me that she had stolen the fruit and cream. Marie was going to give the food to her mother when she came to visit her today."

"Well, that doesn't seem to be such a bad thing."

"Well, I had to go and tell her that Grace had not told me, and I'd come upon the food myself while looking for a pot."

"What did you do with the fruit Dais?"

"I left it there, let's go and look if it's still there." When we got to the cupboard, the pot was empty. "What do you think has happened to the fruit and cream?"

"I suppose that Marie has given them to her mother." Well, that seemed to be the end of that little saga so we pressed on with the evening meal.

The next day Doctor Eyck was in good form in the morning. He had had a good night and it seemed that his wife still loved him. It was as good a time as any to approach the subject of George's wages. "You know that George is getting married next month?"

"Yes, he did say something about it."

"Look, you think that he has been stealing money from the cash box? He only gets seventeen dollars a month and he has to keep his mother and small brother on it. Now that he is getting married don't you think he should get a raise?" I thought it would clinch the argument for George, so I added "You know he hasn't had a raise since he came here four years ago."

"Well, he's getting more here than he would earn elsewhere. Don't let it worry you, a native family can live quite easily on three dollars a month."

"But I have just been reading books by the South African Institute of Race Relations, and they think it should be nearer to fifty five dollars a month."

"Oh! That's with a European style house, clothing and good food. A native does not need those things. He can have a hut in the reservation for nothing and can grow some kaffir corn and raise oxen. That's about all they need." Doctor Eyck was not being consciously a hypocrite, as he really believed in what he was saying. I decided to press on;

"But George's family do not live on the reserve and have to rent their little house from a European."

"Oh yes, if they move off the reserve for long enough they lose their rights. Still they are an improvident lot. I have asked some of the reserve natives what they are going to do when their trees

343

come to maturity. They have good stands of wattle on their land you know."

"They actually own these trees?"

"Yes, but they get into faction fights over ownership and the police haul them into court where they employ lawyers. As they have no money to pay legal costs their lawyers send out agents to measure off an area of their wattle, as payment for their fees. Now most of the wattle belongs to the lawyers."

"Well I suppose the natives are not the only people who run into trouble with paying their bills and legal fees." Dr. Eyck had the scientific training for medicine but he did not have the slightest idea how much it cost a native family to buy their food and clothes. He was quite sincere in his belief that they could live easily on a few dollars a month.

The next afternoon was moving on, but Dr. Eyck couldn't escape from the large, fat European man in his office. They were talking about the patient's obesity, but Dr. Eyck wanted to get away to the village where an Indian woman had called for him to see an infant who was sick and close to death.

The Europeans paid twelve and six for a consultation, the natives seven and sixpence. As the Europeans were seen in special rooms at the front and used up much more time, they were not nearly as profitable as the Indians, Natives and Coloureds. Dr. Eyck soon saw a way out of his immediate problem; "Dr. Valentine, please come in and meet Mr. Watt. He is a little overweight and wants to ask you about it." A great walrus of a man heaved his great mass out of the chair which gave a relieved groan, and he extended a fish like hand towards me.

"Pleased to meet you 'doc. I've been telling Dr. Eyck how I had to go off my last diet."

"Well, yes, I don't suppose you've been sticking to it lately?" This mild sarcasm slid right off his broad back and on he went with his explanation.

"Tried every diet that they know and can't stick to any of them. I go on a thousand calories for a few days and then I get so weak that

I can't do my work," (there was a reservation coming up) "Don't get me wrong 'doc, it isn't as if I have to go outside and lift things and such like. We have plenty of coons to do that kind of thing."

"What do you mean that you can't do your work then?"

"Well, I feel so weak that I can't even stand up. When I do some walking the whole world spins and I just have to eat something."

"What exercise do you take then?"

"Oh, I don't take any. We have plenty of coons to do any physical work. All mine is mental work." I had to pretend that I had pressing problems else where and so move off into the distance. I wasn't around long enough to find what happened to Mr. Watt but he was just a coronary or diabetic accident waiting to happen. He would need some strong men to carry him to the grave, but if they faltered there would be plenty of 'coons' around to lend a hand and then help fill in the earth.

The rest of the three week period went off uneventfully and we handed back the van Dyck's house and their two African maids without telling any tales.

Arch and Dais and I went to Durban in our second hand car, as we had arranged to meet up with the Bohlers there. We were keen to pick up our luggage from the farm and to be on our way.

We pulled into a garage to get some petrol and their car flew past us at high speed, leaving us in a cloud of dust. They were waiting for us at the farm and we went in to collect our things. Queen came out and looked at our little vehicle and said "Oh, this is a good little car." Arch was 'cock-a-hoop' to be leaving the strained atmosphere of the farm, but the emotional feelings between Dais and Queen was very stressful, as both knew it was unlikely that they would see each other again. I was especially indignant, as we had been as generous as we could be when they were in New Zealand, and in spite of promising us a vehicle when we visited, they had not offered one. They had all that wealth but were mean enough to stint on food for their domestic employees and wouldn't lend us a car. We only needed a small car and though the Bohlers had other

Hell-Bent for Life

Dais getting out of our little car to meet a Zulu woman. The child is dressed in a European style school tunic, while the mother is in traditional dress.

transport they could offer, they didn't. Even a small aeroplane wouldn't help as Kiwis can't fly (or at least this one couldn't) and a bullock team would be very slow. The latter would need a driver and we had not picked up enough Zulu during our short stay to be able to tell him where we wanted to go. I didn't know if they had an enclosed area for bullocks in Kruger Park. If they didn't the lions would have a midnight feast and how would we explain that to Wilhelm when he came to pick up the gnawed bones of his bullocks? The offer of a car would have been practical and helpful, but it was not forthcoming and we were on our own.

So off we went, sailing around in our little car, on our way into Northern Zululand and Swaziland. The country was very dry and the roads were very rough with no bridges across the streams. Concrete had been laid on the bed of the streams and this allowed you to drive your vehicle through the water and not get stuck on the rocks in the stream bed. As our car was quite small and low I decided it would be useful for me to let Arch drive, then we would stop at a stream and I would walk through it to see if the crossing was suitable for our car. I would then signal Arch and he would drive across the ford. We crossed several streams and eventually came to a small country hotel where we obtained beds for the night. I explained to the proprietress what I had done to safely cross the fords and she said "That wasn't very wise because that's where the crocodiles wait for their lunch." Just as I'd swum through the atoll channel in the Islands, I'd avoided feeding another creature while ignorant of the risk.

We eventually ended up in Durban where we rented an apartment for ten days. We spent lots of time on the beach which was segregated into parts for the Europeans and another section for the non-Europeans.

Dais went off to the hairdresser where she was attended by a charming Coloured girl in her twenties. When she knew that Dais

Arch and Dais Valentine

was from New Zealand she told her that she knew one of the All Blacks very well, and she told Dais that she called her son by the All Black's Christian name. Now wasn't that a coincidence? I know that New Zealand readers will read on in the hope of learning the All Black's surname. He can rest assured that his name is locked in my cerebral hemisphere and the memory will die with me.

Our apartment was on the third floor and our landlord advised us to keep the door locked at all times. We were told that even the louvre windows should be kept closed because the black robbers were said to poke fishing rods through the windows to hook up small ornaments or other things of value. I thought that was amusing but my landlord didn't share the joke. I think he thought that I was a little odd and I'm sure he wasn't alone in holding that opinion.

One day I went down to the Durban waterfront, where a massive French passenger ship was berthed. Hundreds of soldiers were lining the rails. Most were French Foreign Legion service men returning from their defeat in Vietnam. It was obvious that these healthy and vigorous men had not been allowed to leave the ship while they were in Durban. A loud buzzing came from the line of men on the deck as a rickshaw came onto the wharf. A French Army Officer stepped out and an attractive young European woman could be seen seated inside the vehicle. The buzzing turned into a long rumble as the soldiers saw her. I could feel the tension but I left before a riot erupted on the ship.

After advertising it, we sold our little Ford car and Arch and Dais were on their way back to New Zealand. It was sad to be saying goodbye to my parents, but we knew we would see each other again.

I was now a third of the way through my life and ten years into my medical career. You will have formed an impression of my character as the story has unfolded. Also, my values are reflected in my attitude to the things I saw and was confronted by during my travels - you will have gained your own ideas about them.

I still had a great desire to travel and see more of the big wide world, so started planning my next step.

I hope you, dear reader, have enjoyed my story so far – if you wish to accompany me further, on the second third of my life I'd best hurry on and write it before my journey comes to its final ending….this being only an intermediary

END

Epilogue

AFTER I PARTED FROM MY PARENTS IN SOUTH Africa, I went to Germany and purchased a new Mercedes Benz to drive to London. The opportunity to undertake a 'road trip' through Europe, in such a magnificent car, was something I wasn't going to pass up!

I felt totally spoiled! In no time I was driving my new car through the mountains in Liechtenstein. My only grey cloud was that I was miserably lonely; South Africa had been depressing and friends made in Austria and other places were far away or pre-occupied with their own affairs. There was nothing the matter with the car though; ever since I'd taken delivery of it she behaved like a lady and purred along perfectly.

Most people would have envied me. I had the best car in the world for the money, the open road and plenty of time, but there was something missing "Perhaps I should get married?" I thought, but then considered that the cure might be worse than the disease. At this point, I now realised, the seed of longing for an enduring female partnership had been sown.

I set off through France and eventually ended up again in London and put the Mercedes into storage, awaiting my return. I was able to get suitable lodgings near the centre of the city and took a week to discover what this great city had to offer.

The Old Bailey was worth visiting, providing well priced viewing entertainment (free), with a broad variety of cases and plots and drama of the highest standard.

I also went to the building where all the wills are kept. When I first walked in I had gone to the desk and asked to see Charles Dickens' will. All sorts of people were looking at wills, having paid the search fee of two shillings. The man behind the counter said "I've just had Dickens's will here, now let me see where it is. If I've lost it I'll have to stay here until I find it." I paid my two shillings and was guided down through several stories of records. It all seemed to be dry and clean. Sitting in a corner were two men who appeared to be as desiccated as some of the documents, and looked all the world like mortuary attendants. They produced Shakespeare's will from a locked safe, and a translation of the will. Amongst other bits and pieces there was an insertion where the Baird directed that his second best bed and furniture be left to his wife.

By the time I had come up from the sub-basement, having spent my time with Mr. Shakespeare's will, the attendant had found Dickens' will. I was shown into a side room where I was able to sit at a table and, unbelievably, I HAD DICKENS' WILL IN MY HANDS! I was able to read this myself and needed no help deciphering the contents. Dickens said that he had lived apart from his wife and had given her six hundred pounds per year while she had done everything for the children. He sounded a thoughtful and caring person.

Despite the continued stimulation of travel and fascinating experiences, my feelings of loneliness persisted. I wrote to my long time childhood friend Adair McCone, with whom I had been in irregular contact throughout my life. She had always impressed me as a kind and good person, and I felt there was a good chance we could make a life partnership work. Adair eventually came to London where we were married in 1956. My love of travel continued but now I was no longer a solitary journeyman and there was a different quality to the experience. With Adair as my companion I continued travelling, and also practised medicine in Fort Erie (Canada), Westport (N.Z) and then New Plymouth (N.Z). This is where I established a General Practice and Adair and I settled and raised our family.

My life long interest in the environment and how it is affected by natural and man made phenomena has also continued. I am keenly aware of ecological issues challenging the environment and a second book recording my further travels and the historic environmental pollution I have knowledge of awaits my attention. I feel compelled to 'bear witness' to the environmental pollution associated with the DowElanco Chemical Complex in New Plymouth, Taranaki. This is the factory infamous for producing 'Agent Orange'; a defoliant that contains dioxin that was used widely by the Americans during the Vietnam War.

Some of the other places I visited, and would like to write about are; France, Holland, Austria, Denmark, Panama, Costa Rica, Spain, Italy, Hong Kong, The Philippines, Malaysia, Indonesia, Australia, Thailand, Singapore, India, America and Nepal, and most recently Samoa, in 2008, after Adair's passing.

These and other projects are being considered……..time, mind and body willing they may happen!

John Valentine
January 2009

Glossary

ABSOLUTION. Ecclesiastical declaration of formal forgiveness of a person's sins.

AFRIKANER. Afrikaans-speaking white person in South Africa.

AFRIKAANS. A language of Southern Africa developed from Dutch.

ALZHEIMER – TYPE DEMENTIA. A condition due to degeneration and loss of cells in the cerebral cortex and other brain areas. The brain shows atrophy and memory loss is the most prominent early symptom.

'ALL BLACKS'. New Zealand's National Rugby Team. Also referred to as the 'top fifteen'.

AMNIOTIC FLUID. The watery medium that surrounds the foetus in the pregnant uterus. The baby floats in the fluid while being nourished through the umbilical cord.

ANTI-OXIDANT. When our body cells use oxygen, free radicals are produced, and these can cause damage to the body. Anti-oxidants act as free radical scavengers and prevent damage. Common anti-oxidants are Vitamins A, C and E. I did not study this area at medical school, and remain sceptical of their efficacy in free radical elimination.

ANOXIA. The reduction of oxygen in blood tissue, to the point of physiological impairment.

ANOXIC. The state of the body and its organs when starved of oxygen.

ASSISTED IMMIGRANTS. Between 1871 – 1880, 100,000 people had their fares from Europe partially paid for by the New

Zealand Government. Half of the immigrants came from England, a quarter from Ireland and lesser numbers from Scotland and the rest of Europe.

B-52's. An American bomber class aircraft. This model was used to carry the nuclear bombs dropped on both Nagasaki and Hiroshima.

BI-POLAR MOOD DISORDER. A psychiatric illness where mood states move between the extremes of over active mania and deep depression.

BUGGER. An unpleasant, contemptible or difficult person.

CHAMORROS. The native people of Guam and the Northern Mariana Island group. Their blood line includes Spanish and Filipino ancestry. They are mostly Roman Catholic.

CHAULMOOGRA OIL (HYNDOCARPUS OIL). This yellow-brown liquid is made by extracting the oil from the seeds of the (genus) Hyndocarpus (family) Flacourtinaceae tree. The oil and its purified derivatives were formerly used as a treatment for leprosy, until being replaced by antibiotics.

CHINOOK. A warm dry wind from the Pacific Ocean that blows down the east side of the Rocky Montains, in Canada during winter. By the time it reaches the east, the air has undergone progressive heating and drying, and has dropped most of its moisture on the western side of the mountains. It may seem odd to have a warm winter wind, but lots of peculiar things occur on this planet. People in Alberta welcome the warm winter Chinooks.

CHIP (as in 'Dry as chips'). Desiccated, containing no moisture.

CRUSH. An area in a cattle yard where animals have their movement restricted. This is usually done by the sides of the fenced passage being adjustable so it can close on the animal's sides. It also incorporates a vertical pole which closes against their neck to limit the beast's head and neck movements.

DEFENESTRATION. The act of throwing a person or thing out of a window.

DIVIDENDS. The sum of money paid in return for a winning wager on a horse race. It is usually the total value of bets divided amongst the winning bettors.

ETON. One of England's top Public (private) schools, founded by King Henry VI (1421 – 71).

EX CATHEDRA. Papal pronouncement which is infallable so cannot be wrong.

FETLOCK. The area on a horse's leg above the hoof.

FIBRILLATION. Spontaneous and uncoordinated rapid contraction of individual muscle fibres, (especially in the heart).

GUMMATOUS. Describes a tumour found in tertiary syphilis that is 'soft' rather than hard. The tumour resembles 'gum' in texture and is called a GUMMY.

HEADING EVENT. This is an event in the Huntaway dog trials competitions, where the dog is required to 'head' (or herd) 3 sheep through a course and get them into a yard. The dog is directed by his handler who must stand far away from the yard and use only voice commands and whistles to control the dog. The event is timed from the start of the dog's directed work, until the gate is shut behind the sheep.

HOCK. The middle joint of an animal's back leg.

HUNTAWAY DOG. A term to describe the bigger working dogs used by musterers to guide and control animals. The dogs are trained to bark ("speak up!") to aid in their control of the sheep or cattle.

HUNTAWAY (DOG) COMPETITION. A Huntaway competition is a specific competition category at dog trials. It tests the handler's and working dogs' skills and ability to work effectively together. The handler commands the dog to direct sheep through a zig-zag course, with the fastest team winning the competition.

HYPOTHERMIA. A condition where the body's temperature is abnormally (and typically dangerously) low. It can lead to a state of shock and, in severe cases, death.

IN THE RED. Having spent more than is in your bank account and being in debt.

INFALLIBLE. Incapable of making mistakes, or of being wrong. When referring to the Pope, it is acknowledgement that he is not able to err when proclaiming, ex cathedra, a doctrine of faith or morals.

INTERNATIONAL LEPROSY ASSOCIATION. Founded in January 1931 in Manila. The objectives/aims/principles of the Association are:
- To facilitate the dissemination of knowledge of leprosy and it's control.
- To help in any other practicable manner, the anti-leprosy campaign throughout the world.
- To co-operate with any other institution or organisation concerned with leprosy.

INTUBATION. The insertion of a tube down the throat and past the larynx (or voice-box). This creates an unrestricted air passage to the lungs.

KAIK. A Maori village

KRAAL. A traditional South African village.

KUMERA. A relative of the sweet potato and yam family. The staple carbohydrate of the New Zealand Maori in the North Island.

KUSAIE ISLAND (Latitude is 5° 21' N. Longitude is 162° 57') An island in Micronesia, now renamed KOSRAE ISLAND.

KWASHIORKOR. A diet adequate in non-protein calories from starch, sugar and fat but deficient in total protein, results in protein deficiency. This type of malnutrition is known as Kwashiorkor. When Kwashiorkor is severe enough to reduce body weight to less than 80% of normal body weight, the sufferers have impairment of immune function and typically develop huge, swollen abdomens. The word Kwashiorkor originates from Ghana.

KUROW (possibly a derivative of the Maori name Te Kohurau). A small town established in the 1870s to service the surrounding rural sheep farming properties. By the 1920s its population had grown to 300 people, and it was the second largest 'city' centre in the North Otago Region.

LABOLA. The payment or 'Bride price' that must be paid by a prospective husband to the intended bride's parents.

LAST RITES. A religious ceremony of the Catholic Church administered to those about to die.

LINE OUT (in RUGBY). When the ball is thrown-in to restart the game, parallel lines of opposing forwards compete for it by jumping to gain possession of it.

MATAGOURI. A hardy, resilient native shrub able to survive in marginal conditions and often found in the South Island tussock country.

MANIC DEPRESSIVE (Bi-polar) DISORDER. A psychiatric illness where mood states move between the extremes of morbid sadness and intense elation.

MAORI. The indigenous people of New Zealand. Today Maori language and culture has regenerated to the point where there are total immersion language kindergartens, schools and a University and a dedicated TV channel.

MAU MAU. The Mau Mau Uprising was an insurgency by Kenyan rebels against British rule. It lasted from 1952 to 1960. The core of the resistance was formed by members of the Kikuyu ethnic group, along with smaller numbers of Embu and Meru.

MEALIE(S). A coarse, ground African maize grain which is a food staple for poor South Africans.

MEKE. A Fijian dance.

MICRONESIA. An island group in the Pacific Ocean comprising the Eastern and Western Caroline, Marianas and Marshall Island groups (see map). The area covered by Micronesia is approximately equal to that of the entire U.S. mainland.

MORIBUND. In a dying state.

MR. / MISTER. The English medical profession traditionally call doctors who are specialist surgeons 'Mister'.

MUSTERER. A person who musters (or herds and moves) livestock. They collect livestock and bring them into yards for inspection. There they are counted, treated for parasites and (in the case of sheep), shorn of their woollen fleece.

NAVY PBY. Usually Catalinas but can be any number of aircraft capable of landing and taking off from the water or land.

NITROGLYCERINE. (Also known as the explosive Trinitrin or T.N.T.) Small amounts are administered and absorbed from the oral mucosa under the tongue. This lessens cardiac vessel spasm and therefore relieves the pain of angina pectoris.

PERDITION. A state of eternal damnation into which a sinful and unrepentant person passes after death.

PHANTOM LIMBS. This is a sensation where the patient feels pain and other sensations, from an amputated limb, as if it were still present and attached.

PRIMARY SCHOOLS. The N.Z. Government-funded lower schools, where children usually begin their education between 5 and 6 years of age. They attend for six years, gaining a basic initial education.

PUBS. Shortened name for public houses, where beer and spirits are served and sold.

QUONSET HUT. A prefabricated building with a semi-circular, corrugated tin roof. It was easily erected and common in WWII. The name originated from Quonset in Rhode Island (U.S.A.), where the huts were first made.

RUN-HOLDER. The owner of a high country farm (or 'run').

SCROTUM. The pouch of skin containing the testicles.

SEABEES. The Construction Battalions of the United States Navy (C.B's = Seabees).

SECONDARY SCHOOL. The N.Z. Government-funded and run school education for children from 11-12 years. The five years spent in secondary school took them to UNIVERSITY ENTRANCE level, the qualification for further tertiary learning.

SJAMBOK. A South African word describing a short, heavy whip, cut from rhinoceros or other thick hide.

SLIPPED FEMORAL HEAD. The upper end of the femur (thigh bone) is displaced, most usually in adolescent boys. If untreated, it goes on to cause shortening of the leg and painful arthritis of the hip joint.

STATION (WAITANGI). 'Station' is the term used for large farming properties, usually remote and carrying sheep and cattle. In 1873, Waitangi Station (of which Joe Condon, the author's grandfather became foreman) was 57,000 acres. It was previously 72,000 acres, but in the early 1860's had 30,000 acres split from it to form the Akatawara Station.

SYPHILIS. A contagious disease caused by the Treponema Pallidum spirochete . It is characterised by sequential clinical phases and by years of symptomless latency. It can infect any body tissue and is usually sexually transmitted, but can be passed from mother to foetus and cause congenital defects. Some doctors were taught that Columbus' crew brought it from the West Indies when they 'discovered' America. Even in those days. "All work and no play made Jack a dull boy" it seemed, so it spread wherever they went. Many doctors feel that syphilis had been in Europe for generations and there was a 'flare up' after "1492, when Columbus sailed the ocean blue".

TAMBU. A whales tooth, held in high regard by the Fijian people.

TOXAEMIA (during pregnancy). A pathological condition found in pregnant women that includes hyper tension, and convulsions.

TOWER OF LONDON. A castle in London situated on the Thames river. Building of it started in 1078 and for centuries it functioned as the main state prison, where inmates were held before eventual execution.

TRUK ISLAND. (Latitude: 5° 30' 17 N, Longitude: 153° 42' 48 E) An island in Micronesia, now renamed CHUUK ISLAND.

U.S. TRUST TERRITORIES of the PACIFIC ISLANDS. A group of Islands in the West Pacific situated to the north, south and east of Guam (see map). It was administered by the U.S. before being granted Independent status by the United Nations.

TUSSOCK. One of the New Zealand coarse grasses that grow in clumps in sub-alpine habitats.

VOCATION. A Divine call to a career in the church.

WAITAKI RIVER. The main river that meets the ocean north of Otago, on the East coast of the New Zealand South Island. It extends almost three quarters of the way across the island, in an easterly direction.